AAT
INTERACTIVE TEXT

Technician Unit 19

Preparing personal taxation computations

(FA 2001)

In this August 2001 edition

- Layout designed to be easy on the eye – and easy to use

- Icons to guide you through a 'Fast track' approach if you wish

- The Text fully reflects the Finance Act 2001.

- The Text is focused and takes account of information received from the AAT and the Chief Assessor

- **FOR DEVOLVED ASSESSMENTS UNDER THE FINANCE ACT 2001 TAX LEGISLATION.**

BPP Publishing
August 2001

Fifth edition August 2001

ISBN 0 7517 0747 3 *(Previous edition 0 7517 6225 3)*

British Library Cataloguing-in-Publication Data
A catalogue record for this book
is available from the British Library

Published by

BPP Publishing Limited
Aldine House, Aldine Place
London W12 8AW

www.bpp.com

Printed in Great Britain by W M Print
Frederick Street
Walsall
West Midlands, WS2 9NE

All our rights reserved. No part of this publication may be reproduced, stored in a retrieval system or transmitted, in any form or by any means, electronic, mechanical, photocopying, recording or otherwise, without the prior written permission of BPP Publishing Limited.

We are grateful to the Lead Body for Accounting for permission to reproduce extracts from the Standards of Competence for Accounting, and to the AAT for permission to reproduce extracts from the mapping and Guidance Notes.

©
BPP Publishing Limited
2001

TAX RATES AND ALLOWANCES

A INCOME TAX

1 Rates

	2000/01 £	%	2001/02 £	%
Starting rate	0 - 1,520	10	1 - 1,880	10
Basic rate	1,521 - 28,400	22	1,881 - 29,400	22
Higher rate	28,401 and above	40	29,401 and above	40

Savings (excl. Dividend) income is taxed at 20% if it falls in the basic rate band. Dividend income in both the starting rate and the basic rate bands is taxed at 10%. Dividend income within the higher rate band is taxed at 32.5%.

2 Allowances and tax reducers

	2000/01 £	2001/02 £
Personal allowance	4,385	4,535
Personal allowance (65 - 74)	5,790	5,990
Personal allowance (75 and over)	6,050	6,260
Married couple's allowance – minimum amount	2,000	2,070
Married couple's allowance for people born before 6 April 1935	5,185	5,365
Married couple's allowance (75 and over)	5,255	5,435
Income limit for age-related allowances	17,000	17,600
Blind person's allowance	1,400	1,450
Children's tax credit	-	5,200

3 Car fuel scale charges

	2001/02 Petrol £	2001/02 Diesel £
Cars having a cylinder capacity		
1,400 cc or less	1,930	2,460
1,401 cc to 2,000 cc	2,460	2,460
More than 2,000 cc	3,620	3,620
Cars not having a cylinder capacity	3,620	3,620

4 Authorised mileage rates (AMR) - 2001/02 rates

Car mileage rates

	On first 4,000 miles	On each mile over 4,000
Size of car engine		
Up to 1,500 cc	40p	25p
1,501 cc - 2,000 cc	45p	25p
Over 2,000 cc	63p	36p

Bicycle mileage rate

12p per mile

Motor cycle mileage rate

24p per mile

Tax rates and allowances

5 *Personal pension contribution limits*

Age	Maximum percentage %
Up to 35	17.5
36 – 45	20.0
46 – 50	25.0
51 – 55	30.0
56 – 60	35.0
61 or more	40.0

Subject to earnings cap of £91,800 for 2000/01 and £95,400 for 2001/02.

Contributions threshold for those with no net relevant earnings or with concurrent membership of an occupational scheme. £3,600

b RATES OF INTEREST

Official rate of interest: 6.25% (assumed)

Rate of interest on underpaid tax: 8.5% (assumed)

Rate of interest on overpaid tax: 4% (assumed)

c CAPITAL GAINS TAX

1 *Lease percentage table*

Years	Percentage	Years	Percentage	Years	Percentage
50 or more	100.000	33	90.280	16	64.116
49	99.657	32	89.354	15	61.617
48	99.289	31	88.371	14	58.971
47	98.902	30	87.330	13	56.167
46	98.490	29	86.226	12	53.191
45	98.059	28	85.053	11	50.038
44	97.595	27	83.816	10	46.695
43	97.107	26	82.496	9	43.154
42	96.593	25	81.100	8	39.399
41	96.041	24	79.622	7	35.414
40	95.457	23	78.055	6	31.195
39	94.842	22	76.399	5	26.722
38	94.189	21	74.635	4	21.983
37	93.497	20	72.770	3	16.959
36	92.761	19	70.791	2	11.629
35	91.981	18	68.697	1	5.983
34	91.156	17	66.470	0	0.000

2 Retail prices index (January 1987 = 100.0)

	1982	1983	1984	1985	1986	1987	1988	1989	1990
Jan		82.6	86.8	91.2	96.2	100.0	103.3	111.0	119.5
Feb		83.0	87.2	91.9	96.6	100.4	103.7	111.8	120.2
Mar	79.4	83.1	87.5	92.8	96.7	100.6	104.1	112.3	121.4
Apr	81.0	84.3	88.6	94.8	97.7	101.8	105.8	114.3	125.1
May	81.6	84.6	89.0	95.2	97.8	101.9	106.2	115.0	126.2
Jun	81.9	84.8	89.2	95.4	97.8	101.9	106.6	115.4	126.7
Jul	81.9	85.3	89.1	95.2	97.5	101.8	106.7	115.5	126.8
Aug	81.9	85.7	89.9	95.5	97.8	102.1	107.9	115.8	128.1
Sept	81.9	86.1	90.1	95.4	98.3	102.4	108.4	116.6	129.3
Oct	82.3	86.4	90.7	95.6	98.5	102.9	109.5	117.5	130.3
Nov	82.7	86.7	91.0	95.9	99.3	103.4	110.0	118.5	130.0
Dec	82.5	86.9	90.9	96.0	99.6	103.3	110.3	118.8	129.9

	1991	1992	1993	1994	1995	1996	1997	1998	1999	2000	2001*	2002*
Jan	130.2	135.6	137.9	141.3	146.0	150.2	154.4	159.5	163.4	166.6	172.5	178.5
Feb	130.9	136.3	138.8	142.1	146.9	150.9	155.0	160.3	163.7	167.5	173.0	179.0
Mar	131.4	136.7	139.3	142.5	147.5	151.5	154.4	160.8	164.1	168.4	173.5	179.5
Apr	133.1	138.8	140.6	144.2	149.0	152.6	156.3	162.6	165.2	170.1	174.0	180.0
May	133.5	139.3	141.1	144.7	149.6	152.9	156.9	163.5	165.6	170.7	174.5	180.5
Jun	134.1	139.3	141.0	144.7	149.8	153.0	157.5	163.4	165.6	171.1	175.0	181.0
Jul	133.8	138.8	140.7	144.0	149.1	152.4	157.5	163.0	165.1	170.5	175.5	181.5
Aug	134.1	138.9	141.3	144.7	149.9	153.1	158.5	163.7	165.5	170.5	176.0	182.0
Sept	134.6	139.4	141.9	145.0	150.6	153.8	159.3	164.4	166.2	171.7	176.5	182.5
Oct	135.1	139.9	141.8	145.2	149.8	153.8	159.6	164.5	166.5	171.6	177.0	183.0
Nov	135.6	139.7	141.6	145.3	149.8	153.9	159.6	164.4	166.7	172.1	177.5	183.5
Dec	135.7	139.2	141.9	146.0	150.7	154.4	160.0	164.4	167.3	172.2	178.0	185.0

* Estimated figures.

3 Annual exemption (individuals)

	£
1998/99	6,800
1999/00	7,100
2000/01	7,200
2001/02	7,500

4 Taper relief: Disposals after 6 April 2000

Number of complete years after 5.4.98 for which asset held	Business assets % of gain chargeable	Non business assets % of gain chargeable
0	100	100
1	87.5	100
2	75	100
3	50	95
4	25	90
5	25	85
6	25	80
7	25	75
8	25	70
9	25	65
10 or more	25	60

	Page
TAX RATES AND ALLOWANCES	(iii)
INTRODUCTION How to use this Interactive Text – Technician Qualification Structure – Unit 19 Standards of Competence – Assessment Strategy	(ix)

PART A: INCOME TAX

1	An outline of income tax	3
2	Administration	27
3	The taxation of employment	43
4	Investments and land	75

PART B: CAPITAL GAINS TAX

5	An outline of capital gains tax	93
6	The computation of gains and losses	105
7	Shares and securities	117
8	Chattels, wasting assets, leases and private residences	129
9	CGT reliefs	143

PART C: RELIEF FOR LOSSES

10	Relief for losses	153

APPENDIX: TAX FORMS	161
KEY TERMS AND INDEX	193
ORDER FORM	
REVIEW FORM & FREE PRIZE DRAW	

HOW TO USE THIS INTERACTIVE TEXT

Aims of this Interactive Text

> To provide the knowledge and practice to help you succeed in the devolved assessments for Technician Unit 19 *Preparing Personal Taxation Computations.*

To pass the devolved assessments you need a thorough understanding in all areas covered by the standards of competence.

> To tie in with the other components of the BPP Effective Study Package to ensure you have the best possible chance of success.

Interactive Text

This covers all you need to know for devolved assessment for Unit 19 *Preparing Personal Taxation Computations.* Icons clearly mark key areas of the text. Numerous activities and quizzes throughout the text help you practise what you have just learnt.

Devolved Assessment Kit

When you have understood and practised the material in the Interactive Text, you will have the knowledge and experience to tackle the Devolved Assessment Kit for Unit 19. This aims to get you through the devolved assessment, whether in the form of the AAT simulation or in the workplace. It contains the AAT's sample simulation for Unit 19 plus other simulations.

Recommended approach to this Interactive Text

- To achieve competence in Unit 19 (and all the other units), you need to be able to do **everything** specified by the standards. Study the text very carefully and do not skip any of it.

- Learning is an **active** process. Do **all** the activities and quizzes as you work through the text so you can be sure you really understand what you have read.

- After you have covered the material in the Interactive Text, work through the **Devolved Assessment Kit**.

- Before you take the devolved assessment, check that you still remember the material using the following quick revision plan for each chapter.

    (i) Read through the **chapter contents**. Are there any gaps in your knowledge? If so, study the section again.

    (ii) Read and learn the key terms

    (iii) Do the activities for the chapter again.

    (iv) Read and learn the key learning points which are a summary of the chapter

    (v) Do the quick quiz again. If you know what you're doing, it shouldn't take long.

    This approach is only a suggestion. Your college may well adapt it to suit your needs.

Remember this is a **practical** course.

(a) Try to relate the material to your experience in the workplace or any other work experience you may have had.

(b) Try to make as many links as you can to your study of the other Units at the Technician level.

(c) Keep this text, hopefully you will find it invaluable in your every day work too!

How to use this Interactive Text

Inland Revenue forms

In your Devolved Assessment you are likely to have to either complete or take information from Inland Revenue Forms. We have included the applicable forms within an appendix to this text for illustrative purposes. You will practice using these forms when you try the Devolved Assessments in BPP's Unit 19 Devolved Assessment Kit.

Please note that at the time this Text was printed 2001/02 versions of the Inland Revenue forms were not available. We have therefore updated the 2000/01 versions of the forms and amended them where necessary to fit in with Finance Act 2001 tax legislation. This necessarily involves us in making 'guesses' about how the 2001/02 forms will change. Although, it is unlikely that the 2001/02 versions of the forms will differ significantly from what we have included here, it is important that you contact the Inland Revenue for updated copies before you take your assessment.

If you have internet access you should be able to find the 2001/02 forms on the Inland Revenue's website (www.inlandrevenue.gov.UK).

TECHNICIAN QUALIFICATION STRUCTURE

The competence-based Education and Training Scheme of the Association of Accounting Technicians is based on an analysis of the work of accounting staff in a wide range of industries and types of organisation. The Standards of Competence for Accounting which students are expected to meet are based on this analysis.

The Standards identify the **key purpose** of the accounting occupation, which is **to operate, maintain and improve systems to record, plan, monitor and report on the financial activities of an organisation,** and a number of **key roles** of the occupation. Each key role is subdivided into **units of competence,** which are further divided into **elements of competences.** By successfully completing assessments in specified units of competence, students can gain qualifications at NVQ/SVQ levels 2, 3 and 4, which correspond to the AAT Foundation, Intermediate and Technician stages of competence respectively.

Whether you are competent in a Unit is demonstrated by means of:

- *either* a Central Assessment (set and marked by AAT assessors)

- *or* a Devolved Assessment (where competence is judged by an Approved Assessment Centre to whom responsibility for this is devolved)

- or *both* a Central *and* Devolved Assessment.

Below we set out the overall structure of the Technician (NVQ/SVQ Level 4) stage, indicating how competence in each Unit is assessed. In the next section there is more detail about the Devolved Assessments for Unit 19.

Note that Units 8, 9 and 10 are compulsory. You can choose one of Units 11 to 14, and then three out of Units 15 to 19.

Technician Qualification Structure

NVQ/SVQ Level 4 - Technician

Unit of competence	Elements of competence
Unit 8 Contributing to the management of costs and the enhancement of value *(Central Assessment only)* [TO DO]	8.1 Collect, analyse and disseminate information about costs 8.2 Make recommendations to reduce costs and enhance value
Unit 9 Contributing to the planning and allocation of resources *(Central Assessment only)* [DONE]	9.1 Prepare forecasts of income and expenditure 9.2 Produce draft budget proposals 9.3 Monitor the performance of responsiblity centres against budgets
Unit 10 Managing accounting systems *(Devolved Assessment only)*	10.1 Co-ordinate work activities within the accounting environment 10.2 Identify opportunities to improve the effectiveness of an accounting system 10.3 Prevent fraud in an accounting system
Unit 22 Monitor and maintain a healthy, safe and secure workplace (ASC) *(Devolved Assessment only)* [TO DO]	22.1 Monitor and maintain health and safety within the workplace 22.2 Monitor and maintain the security of the workplace
Unit 11 Drafting financial statements (Accounting Practice, Industry and Commerce) *(Central Assessment only)* [DONE]	11.1 Interpret financial statements 11.2 Draft limited company, sole trader and partnership year end financial statements
Unit 12 Drafting financial statements (Central Government) *(Central Assessment only)*	12.1 Interpret financial statements 12.2 Draft central government financial statements
Unit 13 Drafting financial statements (Local Government) *(Central Assessment only)*	13.1 Interpret financial statements 13.2 Draft local authority financial statements

Technician Qualification Structure

Unit of competence | **Elements of competence**

Unit 14 Drafting financial statements (National Health Service)
Central Assessment *only*

14.1	Interpret financial statements
14.2	Draft NHS accounting statements and returns

Unit 15 Operating a cash management and credit control system
Devolved Assessment *only*

15.1	Monitor and control cash receipts and payments
15.2	Manage cash balances
15.3	Grant credit
15.4	Monitor and control the collection of debts

TO DO

Unit 16 Evaluating current and proposed activities
Devolved Assessment *only*

16.1	Prepare cost estimates
16.2	Recommend ways to improve cost ratios and revenue generation

TO DO?

Unit 17 Implementing auditing procedures
Devolved Assessment *only*

17.1	Contribute to the planning of an audit assignment
17.2	Contribute to the conduct of an audit assignment
17.3	Prepare related draft reports

Unit 18 Preparing business taxation computations
Devolved Assessment *only*

18.1	Adjust accounting profits and losses for trades and professions
18.2	Prepare capital allowances computations
18.3	Prepare Capital Gains Tax computations
18.4	Account for Income Tax payable or recoverable by a company
18.5	Prepare Corporation Tax computations and returns

?

Unit 19 Preparing personal taxation computations
Devolved Assessment *only*

19.1	Calculate income from employment
19.2	Prepare computations of property and investment income
19.3	Prepare Capital Gains Tax computations
19.4	Prepare personal tax returns

DOING

UNIT 19 STANDARDS OF COMPETENCE

The structure of the Standards for Unit 19

The Unit commences with a statement of the **knowledge and understanding** which underpin competence in the Unit's elements.

The Unit is then divided into **elements of competence** describing activities which the individual should be able to perform.

Each element includes:

(a) A set of **performance criteria** which define what constitutes competent performance

(b) A **range statement** which defines the situations, contexts, methods etc in which competence should be displayed

(c) **Evidence requirements,** which state that competence must be demonstrated consistently, over an appropriate time scale with evidence of performance being provided from the appropriate sources

(e) **Sources of evidence**, being suggestions of ways in which you can find evidence to demonstrate that competence. These fall under the headings: 'observed performance; work produced by the candidate; authenticated testimonies from relevant witnesses; personal account of competence; other sources of evidence.' They are reproduced in full in our Devolved Assessment Kit for Unit 19.

The elements of competence for Unit 19 *Preparing Personal Taxation Computations* are set out below. Knowledge and understanding required for the unit as a whole are listed first, followed by the performance criteria and range statements for each element. Performance criteria are cross-referenced below to chapters in this Unit 19 *Preparing Personal Taxation Computations* Interactive Text.

Unit 19 Preparing Personal Taxation Computations

This unit relates to preparing tax computations and returns for individuals. The candidate is required to undertake tax computations and be responsible for taking account of current tax law and revenue practice. The submission of tax returns is part of the unit, as is the provision of advice to clients. The candidate would also be responsible for consulting with the Inland Revenue when necessary.

Elements contained within this unit are:

ELEMENT 19.1   CALCULATE INCOME FROM EMPLOYMENT

ELEMENT 19.2   PREPARE COMPUTATIONS OF PROPERTY AND INVESTMENT INCOME

ELEMENT 19.3   PREPARE CAPITAL GAINS TAX COMPUTATIONS

ELEMENT 19.4   PREPARE PERSONAL TAX RETURNS

This unit is assessed by **devolved assessment only**.

Knowledge and understanding

The business environment

- A general understanding of the duties and responsibilities of the taxation practitioner (Elements 19.1, 19.2, 19.3 & 19.4)

- A general understanding of the issues of taxation liability (Elements 19.1, 19.2, 19.3 & 19.4)

- Relevant legislation and guidance from Inland Revenue (Elements 19.1, 19.2, 19.3 & 19.4)

Taxation principles and theory

- The basic law and practice relating to all issues covered in the range and referred to in the performance criteria (Elements 19.1, 19.2, 19.3 & 19.4)

- The implications of the distinction between 'employment' and 'self employment' (Element 19.1)

- Allowable expenses: contributions to pension schemes; contributions to charities under the payroll deduction scheme; basic pension contributions; charitable givings; charges on income (Element 19.1)

- Factors effecting investments: tax exempt investments; ISAs; PEPs; TESSAs (Element 19.1)

- Allowable expenditure on property (Element 19.2)

- Loss relief (Element 19.2)

- Rates of CGT for individuals (Element 19.3)

- Exemptions and reliefs from CGT (Element 19.3)

- Methods of calculation: the rollover principle; reinvestment relief; holdover relief (Element 19.3)

- The taxation of married couples: independent taxation of married women (Element 19.4)

The client

- Understanding that the taxation liabilities of the individual are affected by their legal status and the nature of their business transactions (Elements 19.1, 19.2, 19.3 & 19.4)

- An understanding of the individual's employment status and knowledge of their business transactions (Elements 19.1, 19.2, 19.3 & 19.4)

Unit 19 Standards of Competence

Element 19.1 Calculate income from employment

Performance criteria	Chapters in this Text
1 Computations of emoluments, including benefits in kind, allowable expenses and deductions are accurately prepared	3
2 Computations and submissions are made in accordance with current tax law and take account of current revenue practice and factors effecting investments	1, 2, 3
3 Consultations with Inland Revenue staff are conducted openly and constructively	2
4 Returns are completed accurately and legibly and are submitted within the Inland Revenue's timescale	2
5 Timely and constructive advice is given to clients on the maintenance of records relevant to tax returns	2
6 Confidentiality of the client is maintained at all times	2

Range statement

1 Emoluments: received by UK resident employees; duties performed wholly or partly in the UK

2 Allowable expenses: contributions to pension schemes; contributions to charities under the payroll deduction scheme; basic pension contributions; charitable givings; charges on income

3 Benefits in kind: lower paid employees; higher paid employees

4 Returns: P11Ds

5 Factors effecting investments: tax exempt investments, ISAs

Element 19.2 Prepare computations of property and investment income

Performance criteria	Chapters in this Text
1 Schedules of dividends and interest received on all shares and securities are accurately prepared and checked for completeness	1, 4
2 Schedules of property income are accurately prepared, profits and losses properly determined and appropriate reliefs applied	4
3 Computations and submissions are made in accordance with current tax law and take account of current revenue practice	1, 2, 4
4 Consultation with Inland Revenue staff is conducted openly and constructively	2
5 Returns are submitted within the Inland Revenue's timescale	2
6 Timely and constructive advice is given to clients on the maintenance of accounts and the recording of information relevant to tax returns	2
7 Confidentiality of the client is maintained at all times	2

Range statement

1 Computations: sources of investment income from companies, banks, building societies, trusts and settlements; property income assessable under Schedules A and D VI; wear and tear

Unit 19 Standards of Competence

Element 19.3 Prepare Capital Gains Tax computations

Performance criteria		Chapters in this Text
1	Computations and submissions are made in accordance with current tax law and take account of current revenue practice	5, 6, 7, 8, 9, 10
2	Chargeable assets disposed of are correctly identified and valued	5, 9
3	Chargeable gains, allowable losses and annual exemptions are correctly determined	6, 7, 8, 9
4	Reliefs and transactions relating to shares and securities are taken into account	7
5	Claims for deferrals are correctly identified and submitted to the Inland Revenue within statutory time limits	9
6	Relevant details are accurately and legibly recorded in the Income Tax return	5
7	Consultation with Inland Revenue staff is conducted openly and constructively	2
8	Returns are submitted within the Inland Revenue timescale	2
9	Timely and constructive advice is given to clients on the maintenance of records and the recording of information relevant to tax returns	2
10	Confidentiality of the client is maintained at all times	2

Range statement

1. Computations of: capital gains arising from the sale, gift, loss and destruction of chargeable assets for individuals
2. Reliefs: retirement relief; relief for gifts
3. Transactions relating to shares and securities: pooling; short term transactions; bonus and right issues

Element 19.4 Prepare personal tax returns

Performance criteria		Chapters in this Text
1	Computations and schedules of income from all sources, capital gains and losses and allowable deductions are correctly calculated and recorded	1, 10, 5
2	Returns are legibly and accurately completed and submitted within statutory time limits	2
3	Computations and submissions are made in accordance with current tax law and take account of current revenue practice	1, 2, 5, 10
4	Consultation with Inland Revenue staff is conducted openly and constructively	2
5	Timely and constructive advice is given to clients on the maintenance of records and the recording of information relevant to tax returns	2
6	Confidentiality of the client is maintained at all times	2

Range statement

1. Returns relating to: individuals; partners
2. Allowable deductions: personal relief; age allowance; personal pensions; maintenance payments

Assessment strategy

ASSESSMENT STRATEGY

This unit is assessed entirely by means of *devolved* assessment.

Devolved Assessment (*more detail can be found in the Devolved Assessment Kit*)

Devolved assessment is a means of collecting evidence of your ability to carry out **practical activities** and to **operate effectively in the conditions of the workplace** to the standards required. Evidence may be collected at your place of work or at an Approved Assessment Centre by means of simulations of workplace activity, or by a combination of these methods.

If the Approved Assessment Centre is a **workplace**, you may be observed carrying out accounting activities as part of your normal work routine. You should collect documentary evidence of the work you have done, or contributed to, in an **accounting portfolio**. Evidence collected in a portfolio can be assessed in addition to observed performance or where it is not possible to assess by observation.

Where the Approved Assessment Centre is a **college or training organisation**, devolved assessment will be by means of a combination of the following.

(a) Documentary evidence of activities carried out at the workplace, collected by you in an **accounting portfolio**.

(b) Realistic **simulations** of workplace activities. These simulations may take the form of case studies and in-tray exercises and involve the use of primary documents and reference sources.

(c) **Projects and assignments** designed to assess the Standards of Competence.

If you are unable to provide workplace evidence you will be able to complete the assessment requirements by the alternative methods listed above.

Part A
Income tax

Chapter 1   An outline of income tax

Chapter topic list

1 Taxes in the UK
2 The administration of taxation
3 The schedular system, income received gross and income taxed at source
4 The aggregation of income
5 Charges on income
6 Allowances deducted from STI
7 Charitable donations
8 Tax reducers
9 Personal tax computations
10 Families

Learning objectives

On completion of this chapter you will be able to:

	Performance criteria	Range Statement
• calculate the income tax payable by an individual for the tax year	19.4.1	19.4.1
• recognise the different treatment of savings income from other income	19.4.1	19.4.1
• allocate the correct personal allowances to individuals	19.4.1	19.4.2
• identify different sources of income	19.4.1	19.4.1
• identify different annual payments made by an individual which can reduce his overall tax bill for the year	19.4.1	19.4.2

Part A: Income tax

1 TAXES IN THE UK

1.1 Central government raises revenue through a wide range of taxes. Tax law is made by **statute** and as this can be notoriously ambiguous and difficult to understand, the Revenue are currently involved in a project to rewrite it in simpler more user-friendly language. The first Act to result from this rewrite project was the Capital Allowances Act 2001.

Statute is interpreted and amplified by **case law**. The Inland Revenue also issue:

(a) **statements of practice**, setting out how they intend to apply the law;

(b) **extra-statutory concessions**, setting out circumstances in which they will not apply the strict letter of the law;

(c) a wide range of **explanatory leaflets**;

(d) **business economic notes**. These are notes on particular types of business, which are used as background information by the Inland Revenue and are also published;

(e) the **Tax Bulletin**. This is a newsletter giving the Inland Revenue's view on specific points. It is published every two months;

(f) the **Internal Guidance**, a series of manuals used by Inland Revenue staff.

However, none of these Inland Revenue publications has the force of law.

A great deal of information and the Inland Revenue publications can now be found on the Revenue's internet site.

1.2 The main taxes suffered by individuals are income tax and capital gains tax. You will study these taxes in this unit.

1.3 **As a general rule, income tax is charged on receipts which might be expected to recur** (such as weekly wages) **whereas capital gains tax is charged on one-off gains** (for example from selling a painting owned for 20 years). Both taxes are charged for tax years.

> **KEY TERM**
>
> The **tax year**, or **fiscal year**, or **year of assessment** runs from 6 April to 5 April. For example, the tax year 2001/02 runs from 6 April 2001 to 5 April 2002.

1.4 **Finance Acts** are passed each year, incorporating proposals set out in the **Budget**. They make changes which apply mainly to the tax year ahead. This text includes the provisions of the Finance Act 2001.

2 THE ADMINISTRATION OF TAXATION

2.1 The **Treasury** formally imposes and collects taxation. The management of the Treasury is the responsibility of the Chancellor of the Exchequer. The Treasury appoint the **Board of Inland Revenue** (sometimes referred to as the **Commissioners of Inland Revenue (CIR)**), a body of civil servants. The Board administers income tax and capital gains tax.

2.2 For income tax purposes, the UK is divided into a number of **regions** (each under a regional controller). Each region is subdivided into **districts**. There are also a number of business streams such as the Inland Revenue's Savings, Pension and Share Schemes 'business stream'. Each district has a **district inspector** in charge and he is assisted by other

1: An outline of income tax

inspectors and clerical staff. The official title for an inspector is **HM Inspector of Taxes (HMIT)**. The main work of the districts consists of examining tax returns and accounts.

2.3 The collection of tax is not the responsibility of inspectors but of **collectors** of taxes. The collector will pursue the debt through the courts. In extreme circumstances, the collector may seize the assets of the taxpayer.

2.4 Although the functions of 'Collectors' and 'Inspectors' are currently kept separate the Treasury is considering combining them and has enacted legislation which enables 'Collectors' and 'Inspectors' to be interchangeable terms in the legislation. The term '**Officer of the Board**' is now generally used in legislation.

2.5 The structure of offices set out above is also being changed. **Taxpayer service offices** are being set up to do routine checking, computation *and* collection work, while **Taxpayer district offices** investigate selected accounts and enforce the payment of tax. **Taxpayer assistance offices** handle enquiries and arrange specialist help for taxpayers.

2.6 The **General Commissioners** (not to be confused with the CIR) are appointed by the Lord Chancellor to hear **appeals** against Revenue decisions. They are part-time and unpaid. They are appointed for a local area (a **division**). They appoint a clerk who is often a lawyer or accountant and who is paid for his services by the Board of Inland Revenue.

2.7 The **Special Commissioners** are also appointed by the Lord Chancellor. They are full-time paid professionals. They generally hear the more complex appeals.

2.8 **Many taxpayers arrange for their accountants to prepare and submit their tax returns. The taxpayer is still the person responsible for submitting the return and for paying whatever tax becomes due: the accountant is only acting as the taxpayer's agent.**

3 THE SCHEDULAR SYSTEM, INCOME RECEIVED GROSS AND INCOME TAXED AT SOURCE

3.1 **Some income is received in full, with no tax deducted in advance.** An example of such income is gilt interest (interest paid on government securities) which is normally received gross. National Savings Bank interest is also received gross.

3.2 **Other income is received after deduction of tax. This is income taxed at source.** The taxable income for a tax year is the **gross** amount (that is, adding back any tax deducted at source). For example, bank interest is normally received after the deduction of 20% tax at source. This means that if £80 interest is received you must gross it up by multiplying by 100/80. The gross amount of £100 (£80 × 100/80) is included in the individual's income tax computation.

3.3 **Dividends on UK shares are received net of a 10% tax credit.** The taxable income for a tax year is the gross dividend (the dividends received multiplied by 100/90). For example if a dividend of £180 is received, include the gross dividend of £200 (£180 × 100/90) in the income tax computation.

Activity 1.1: Gross dividends and interest

Harriet receives dividends of £2,250 and building society interest (net of 20% tax) of £2,400 in 2001/02. What are the gross amounts of dividends and interest to be included in her income tax computation for 2001/02?

Part A: Income tax

The schedular system

3.4 **Each type of income is taxed under a set of rules known as a schedule.** Schedules D and E are divided into cases.

Schedule A	Income from land and buildings (rents and so on) in the UK
Schedules B and C	Abolished
Schedule D	
Case I	Profits of trades
Case II	Profits of professions or vocations
Case III	Interest
Case VI	Income not falling under any other schedule or case
Schedule E	Income from an office or employment including salaries, bonuses, benefits in kind and pensions. Most tax is collected under the PAYE system. (See Chapter 3)
Schedule F	UK dividends

Foreign income may be taxed under Schedule D Cases IV and V but this is not assessable in Unit 19. In addition you will not be expected to compute Schedule D Case I or II income in Unit 19 although you may be expected to include a given amount of such income in the individual's income tax computation and income tax return.

3.5 **The schedules and cases are important because each has its own set of rules.** Once we have decided that income is taxed under, say, Schedule A, the rules of Schedule A determine the amount of income taxed in any year. Each type of income assessable at Unit 19 is considered in detail later in this text.

4 THE AGGREGATION OF INCOME

4.1 **An individual's income from all sources is brought together in a personal tax computation. We split income into dividend income, savings (excl. dividend) income and non-savings income.**

4.2 Interest and dividends are **'savings income'**. All other income is non-savings income.

Interest received net of 20% tax

4.3 The following interest income is received by individuals net of 20% tax.

(a) Interest paid by UK companies on debentures and loan stocks
(b) Bank and building society interest (but not National Savings Bank interest)

The amount received must be grossed up by multiplying by 100/80 and it must be included gross in the income tax computation.

DEVOLVED ASSESSMENT ALERT

In the devolved assessment you may be given either the net or the gross amount of such income: read the question carefully. If you are given the net amount (the amount received or credited), you should gross up the figure at the rate of 20%. However, if you are given the gross amount include the figure you are given in the income tax computation.

4.4 Although building society and bank deposit interest are generally paid net of 20% tax a recipient who is not liable to tax can recover the tax suffered For example, net building society interest of £160 is equivalent to gross income of £160 × 100/80 = £200 on which tax of £40 (20% of £200) has been suffered and a non-taxpayer can get the £40 tax suffered repaid to him. Alternatively, he can certify in advance that he is a non-taxpayer and get the interest paid gross.

Dividends on UK shares

4.5 Dividends received on UK shares are received net of a 10% tax credit. This means a dividend received of £90 has a £10 tax credit, giving gross income of £100 to be included in the tax computation. The tax credit attached to dividends **cannot be repaid to non-taxpayers but it is offsettable and can be set against a taxpayer's tax liability.**

Exempt income

4.6 **Some income is exempt from income tax.** This income is not included in the income tax computation.

4.7 Several of the exemptions are mentioned at places in this text where the types of income are described in detail, but note the following types of exempt income now.

(a) Scholarships (exempt as income of the scholar. If paid by a parent's employer, a scholarship may be taxable income of the parent)

(b) Betting and gaming winnings, including premium bond prizes

(c) Income on National Savings Certificates

(d) Many social security benefits, although the jobseeker's allowance, the state pension and certain incapacity benefits are taxable

(e) Gifts

(f) Damages for personal injury

(g) Income arising on Individual Savings accounts (ISAs)

(h) Income arising on Tax Exempt Special Savings accounts (TESSAs)

(i) Income and gains arising in Personal Equity Plans (PEPs)

(j) Interest on amounts repaid to borrowers under the income contingent student loans scheme

(k) Payments made under the 'new deal 50 plus' scheme and payments made under the employment zones programme.

PEPs and TESSAs were tax free investments that could be acquired prior to 6.4.99. Since this date it has not been possible to make new investments in PEPs and TESSAs but existing investments retain their tax free status.

DEVOLVED ASSESSMENT ALERT

Learn the different types of exempt income as they are popular items of income in the devolved assessment. Always state on your workings sheets that such income is exempt (do not ignore it) to gain an easy half mark.

Part A: Income tax

4.8 Once income from all sources has been aggregated, charges and personal allowances are deducted to arrive at taxable income. We will look at these items in more detail later in this chapter but now let us see an example of the layout of the computation of taxable income.

RICHARD: INCOME TAX COMPUTATION 2001/02

	Non-savings income £	Savings (excl dividend) income £	Dividend income £	Total £
Income from employment	38,000			
Building society interest		1,000		
National savings bank interest		320		
UK dividends			1,000	
	38,000	1,320	1,000	
Less charges on income	(2,000)			
Statutory total income (STI)	36,000	1,320	1,000	38,320
Less personal allowance	(4,535)			
Taxable income	31,465	1,320	1,000	33,785

4.9 Now follow the above layout to try the next activity for yourself.

Activity 1.2: Taxable income

An individual has the following income in 2001/02.

	£
Schedule E	16,000
Building society interest received	4,800
Dividends received	7,875
Premium bond prize	5,000

His personal allowance is £4,535. What is his taxable income?

4.10 To calculate an individual's tax liability on taxable income **deal with non-savings income first, then savings (excl. dividend) income and then dividend income**. There is one set of income tax bands that applies to all the income.

4.11 For non-savings income, the first £1,880 is taxed at the starting rate (10%), the next £27,520 is taxed at the basic rate (22%) and the rest at the higher rate (40%).

4.12 Any savings (excl. dividend) income that falls within the starting rate band is taxed at 10% **but income in the basic rate band is taxed at 20% (not 22%)**. Such income in excess of the basic rate threshold of £29,400 is taxed at 40%.

4.13 Any dividend income from UK company shares falling within the starting or basic rate bands is taxed at 10%. UK dividend income in excess of the basic rate threshold is taxed at 32.5%.

4.14 Continuing Richard's income tax computation above, the tax liability is:

	£
Non savings income	
£1,880 × 10%	188
£27,520 × 22%	6,054
£2,065 × 40%	826
	7,068
Savings (excl. dividend) income	
£1,320 × 40%	528
Dividend income	
£1,000 × 32.5%	325
Tax liability	7,921

1: An outline of income tax

Savings (excl. dividend) and the dividend income are both above the higher rate threshold of £29,400 so they are taxed at 40% and 32.5% respectively.

Activity 1.3: Income tax calculation

An individual has total taxable income of £50,000 for 2001/02. All of his income is non-savings income. What is the total income tax liability?

4.15 Once the tax liability has been calculated, any tax suffered or deducted at source (for example, PAYE tax) and the tax credit on dividend income are deducted to arrive at tax payable. Tax suffered on savings (excl. dividend) income is repayable if it exceeds the individual's tax liability. The tax credit on UK dividends is never repayable.

Activity 1.4: Income tax payable

Kate, who is single and entitled to a personal allowance of £4,535, has a salary of £10,430 (PAYE tax deducted at source £1,000) and building society interest received of £4,000. Calculate Kate's tax payable for 2001/02.

Activity 1.5: Tax credit on dividends

Doris received dividend income of £30,600 in 2001/02. She has no other income. Her personal allowance to deduct from dividend income is £4,535. Calculate the tax payable.

4.16 We will look at some further examples of the computation of income tax later in this chapter.

5 CHARGES ON INCOME

5.1 **Charges on income are deducted in computing taxable income.**

> **KEY TERM**
>
> A **charge on income** is a payment by the taxpayer which income tax law allows as a deduction.

5.2 Examples of charges on income are:

(a) eligible interest;
(b) patent royalties;
(c) copyright royalties.

5.3 **Charges on income fall into two categories: those from which basic rate (22%) income tax is first deducted by the payer (charges paid net) and those which are paid without any deduction (charges paid gross).**

5.4 Patent royalties are an example of a charge on income which is paid net. Eligible interest and copyright royalties are paid gross.

5.5 **We always deduct the gross figure in the payer's tax computation.** If a charge is paid net you must gross it up by multiplying by 100/78. For example if Sue pays a patent royalty of

9

Part A: Income tax

£1,014 you must gross it up to £1,300 (£1,014 × 100/78) and deduct the gross figure in Sue's income tax computation.

Activity 1.6: Charges on income

In 2001/02 Harriet pays a patent royalty of £3,900 and a copyright royalty of £1,000. What is the total amount that Harriet can deduct as charges on income in her income tax computation for 2001/02?

5.6 If you are preparing the personal tax computation of someone who *receives* a charge, for example the owner of a patent who gets royalties from someone who exploits the patent, do the following.

(a) Include the **gross** amount under non-savings income. If the charge is paid gross, the gross amount is the amount received. If it is paid net, the gross amount is the amount received × 100/78.

(b) If the charge was received net, then under the heading 'less tax suffered' (between tax liability and tax payable) include the tax deducted. This is the gross amount × 22%.

Eligible interest

5.7 Interest on a loan is a charge when the loan is used for one of the following purposes.

(a) **To invest in a partnership.**

(b) **To purchase ordinary shares in a close company.** A close company is broadly a company that is controlled by 5 or fewer shareholders or its directors.

(c) **To invest in a co-operative.**

(d) **To purchase of shares in an employee-controlled company.**

(e) **By a partner to purchase plant or machinery used in the business.**

(f) **By an employee to purchase plant or machinery used by him in the performance of his duties.**

(g) **By personal representatives to pay inheritance tax.**

(h) **To replace other qualifying loans.**

Interest on an overdraft or on a credit card debt does not qualify as a charge on income.

Business interest

5.8 **A taxpayer paying interest wholly and exclusively for business purposes is allowed to deduct such interest in the computation of his profit under Schedule D Case I, instead of as a charge.** The computation of Schedule D Case I profits is assessed in Unit 18 preparing business tax computations rather than in this Unit.

Charges in personal tax computations

5.9 The gross amount of any charge is deducted from the taxpayer's income to arrive at Statutory Total Income (STI).

5.10 Deduct charges from non-savings income then from savings (excl. dividend income) and lastly from dividend income.

1: An outline of income tax

5.11 If a charge has been paid net, the basic rate income tax deducted (22% of the gross amount) is added into the tax liability. The taxpayer gets tax relief by deducting the gross amount of the payment in computing his STI: he cannot keep the basic rate tax withheld from the payment as well, but he must pay it to the Inland Revenue. This means that the final step in computing the tax liability should be to add on any tax withheld on charges paid net. Note that this addition is made **after** the deduction of tax reducers (see below).

5.12 EXAMPLE

Three taxpayers have the following schedule D Case I income and allowances for 2001/02. Taxpayers A and B pay a patent royalty of £176 (net). Taxpayer C pays a patent royalty of £1,248 (net).

	A £	B £	C £
Schedule D Case I Income	5,000	3,000	35,615
Less: charge on income (× 100/78)	(226)	(226)	(1,600)
	4,774	2,774	34,015
Less: personal allowance	(4,535)	(4,535)	(4,535)
Taxable income	239	–	29,480
	£	£	£
Income tax			
10% on £239/–/£1,880	24	–	188
22% on –/–/£27,520			6,054
40% on –/–/£80			32
	24	–	6,274
Add: 22% tax retained on charge	50	50	352
Tax payable	74	50	6,626

Activity 1.7: Charges in personal tax computations

John, who is single and entitled to a personal allowance of £4,535, has schedule D case I profits of £8,000 in 2001/02. He also received building society interest of £14,000 and dividends of £450. He paid a patent royalty of £9,360. Show John's income tax liability for 2001/02.

ALLOWANCES DEDUCTED FROM STI

6.1 Once taxable income from all sources has been aggregated and any charges on income deducted, the remainder is the taxpayer's statutory total income (STI). Two allowances, the personal allowance and the blind person's allowance, are deducted from STI. Like charges, they come off non savings income first, then off savings (excl. dividend) income and lastly off dividend income. The amounts given in the following paragraphs are for 2001/02.

6.2 Other allowances are not deducted from STI, but reduce tax instead. These allowances are explained below.

PA: personal allowance

6.3 **All persons (including children) are entitled to the personal allowance of £4,535.**

6.4 A person aged 65 or over (at any time in the tax year) gets an age allowance of £5,990 instead of the ordinary PA of £4,535.

6.5 Where statutory total income exceeds £17,600, cut the age allowance by £1 for every £2 of income over £17,600 until it comes down to £4,535.

Part A: Income tax

6.6 Individuals aged 75 or over (at any time in the tax year) get a slightly more generous age allowance of £6,260. In all respects, the higher age allowance works in the same way as the basic age allowance, with the same income limit of £17,600.

Someone who dies in the tax year in which they would have had their 65th or 75th birthday gets the age allowance (for 65 year olds or 75 year olds) for that year.

6.7 When a taxpayer has made a donation under the gift aid scheme (see below) the STI that is compared with the income limit must be reduced by the gross amount of the gift aid donation.

BPA: blind person's allowance

6.8 A taxpayer who is registered with a local authority as a blind person gets an allowance of £1,450. The allowance is also given for the year before registration, if the taxpayer had obtained the proof of blindness needed for registration before the end of that earlier year.

Activity 1.8: Calculation of taxable income

Michael, who is single and aged 66, earns £7,500 in 2001/02. He also receives building society interest of £2,000. Calculate Michael's taxable income for 2001/02.

7 CHARITABLE DONATIONS

Gift aid donations

KEY TERM

One-off and regular charitable gifts of money, including donations made under a legally enforceable deed of covenant, qualify for tax relief under the **gift aid scheme** provided the donor gives the charity a gift aid declaration.

7.1 Gift aid declarations can be made in writing, electronically through the internet or orally over the phone. A declaration can cover a one-off gift or any number of gifts for the future or retrospectively.

7.2 **A gift aid donation is treated as though it was paid net of basic rate tax (22%, 2001/02).**

7.3 **Additional tax relief is given in the personal tax computation by increasing the donor's basic rate band by the gross amount of the gift.**

Activity 1.9: Tax relief for gift aid donation

James earns a salary of £58,000 but has no other income. In 2001/02 he paid £7,800 (net) under the gift aid scheme.

Compute James' income tax liability for 2001/02.

7.4 **When comparing statutory total income (STI) with the income limit for age allowance purposes, you must reduce the STI by the gross amount of any gift aid payment. This reduction is made as a working in computing age allowances only: the gift aid payment is not deducted in arriving at taxable income.**

1: An outline of income tax

7.5 An income tax deduction is available if the whole of any beneficial interest in qualifying shares or securities is given, or sold at an undervalue, to a charity. Broadly, an individual can deduct the market value of the share or securities at the date of disposal in calculating his total income.

8 TAX REDUCERS

8.1 **Tax reducers do not affect income; they reduce tax on income.** The tax reducers are:

(a) Investments in venture capital trusts and under the enterprise investment scheme
(b) The married couple's age allowance
(c) Maintenance payments following the breakdown of a marriage
(d) Children's tax credit

8.2 In case (a), the tax reduction is 20% of the investment. In the other cases, the tax reduction is 10% of the allowance or payment.

8.3 We will look at the enterprise investment scheme and venture capital trusts later in this text.

Allowances

MCAA: married couple's age allowance

8.4 **A married man whose wife is living with him gets a married couples age allowance (MCAA) of £5,365 if he or his wife was 65 before 6 April 2000.**

8.5 There is a minimum amount of MCAA of £2,070. The wife can unilaterally elect, by the start of the relevant tax year, to have half of the tax reduction from the minimum amount of MCAA set against her tax instead of her husband's. Alternatively, the couple can jointly elect, by the start of the relevant tax year, to transfer half or all of this tax reduction to the wife.

8.6 Any MCAA which turns out to be wasted (because the husband or wife has insufficient tax to reduce) may be passed to the other spouse.

8.7 A married man, if he **or his wife** is 75 or over (at any time in the tax year), gets an age allowance of £5,435 instead of the ordinary MCAA of £5,365. Half or all of the tax reduction from the minimum amount may be transferred to the wife, exactly as for ordinary MCAA.

8.8 **When statutory total income exceeds £17,600, cut the personal age allowance by half of the excess to a minimum of £4,535. Once £4,535 has been reached, cut the married couple's age allowance by any remaining excess,** but not to below the minimum amount of £2,070. The reduction in the married couple's age allowance always depends on the **husband's STI.** STI for this purpose must be reduced by the gross amount of any gift aid donation (see Section 7).

8.9 If one of the married couple dies in the tax year in which they would have had their 75th birthday the couple is still entitled to the higher age-related MCAA for that year.

8.10 In the year of marriage the MCAA is reduced by 1/12 for each complete tax month (from the 6th of one month to the 5th of the next) which has passed before the wedding.

Part A: Income tax

8.11 Individuals (or their spouses) who are entitled to the MCAA after 6 April 2001, will not be able to claim the children's tax credit (see below) unless they elect not to claim the MCAA.

Activity 1.10: Computation of MCAA

A married man aged 78 has STI of £21,400 for 2001/02. He did not make any gift aid payments. His wife has no income. What personal allowance and MCAA is he entitled to?

Maintenance payments

8.12 **All maintenance payments are made gross (without deduction of tax at source).** Tax relief for qualifying maintenance payments is available if at least one party to the marriage was aged 65 or over on 5 April 2000. **Qualifying payments** are certain legally enforceable payments made under written agreements.

8.13 Provided that the payment is made for the benefit of the former or separated spouse or of a child of the family and is made to the spouse (but not directly to a child or to an agent such as a school), **the payer can claim a tax reduction of 10% of the lower of:**

(a) **The payments due in the tax year,** and
(b) **£2,070** (for 2001/02).

There is no tax reduction for payments made after the recipient remarries.

8.14 The recipient is not liable to income tax on maintenance payments made, however large.

Children's tax credit (CTC)

8.15 The children's tax credit (CTC) was introduced in April 2001. **The allowance of £5,200 for 2001/02 qualifies for 10% tax relief as a tax reducer.** From April 2002 the allowance will be increased to £10,400 in the year of a child's birth.

8.16 **All taxpayers who have one or more 'qualifying' children resident with them during a tax year can claim the CTC but where any part of the claimant's income is chargeable at the higher rate, the amount of credit due is tapered away:** the amount of £5,200 will be reduced by £2.00 for every £3.00 of income in the higher rate tax band. For this purpose the basic rate band limit is increased by gift aid payments (see above) and personal pension contributions (see later in this text).

8.17 People who retain their entitlement to MCAA after 5 April 2001 (see above) will not be able to claim the CTC unless they elect not to claim the MCAA.

8.18 A 'qualifying child' is:

(a) **A child of the claimant who is under 16,** or
(b) **A child under 16, who is maintained by, and at the expense of, the claimant during any part of the tax year.**

Illegitimate children and stepchildren are included in the definition of 'child'.

Child living with more than one adult: married and unmarried couples

8.19 Both cohabiting and married taxpayers (referred to as 'partners') can claim the CTC.

8.20 **The CTC is initially allocated to the partner who has the higher total income for the tax year.** If both partners have the same total income for the year, they should elect for one of them to be treated as the lower-earning partner. If an election is not made, neither party is entitled to the CTC in that tax year.

8.21 If either partner has income chargeable at the higher rate for a tax year, only the higher-earning partner can claim the CTC in that year. **If neither partner has income chargeable at the higher rate, the lower-earning partner can claim half the CTC. Alternatively, if both partners elect, the whole of the CTC may be allocated to the lower-earning partner.**

8.22 Any CTC in excess of the claimant's income tax liability can be passed to their partner.

Child living with more than one adult: other cases

8.23 If a child is resident with two or more taxpayers during a tax year and is a qualifying child in relation to at least two of those people, the taxpayers may agree how to allocate the CTC. A taxpayer may be allotted the whole of a the CTC but cannot be allocated more than one whole tax credit. If the taxpayers do not agree on how to divide the CTC, the general commissioners (or in some cases, the special commissioners) will decide for them.

Changes of circumstance

8.24 If a change in circumstance (eg a marriage or a separation) occurs, the year is divided into the period up to and after the change. The rules for each period apply as appropriate.

8.25 The credit is time-apportioned by reference to the length of the periods before and after the change but any questions as to income levels are settled on the basis of income for the tax year and not for a particular period.

Activity 1.11: Children's tax credit

Janet and John are co-habiting and have a child, Danny, aged 10. Janet expects to earn £38,000 in 2001/02 and John expects to earn £10,000 in 2001/02. Janet also makes a gift aid donation of £1,560 net to Oxfam in 2001/02. Neither Janet nor John have any other income.

Show the amount of the CTC tax reducer available in 2001/02, assuming the relevant claim has been made and Janet and John earn what they expect.

Giving tax reductions

8.26 Tax reducers are deducted in computing an individual's income tax liability. The full tax reduction can only be given if the individual has enough tax to reduce. If, for example, the tax before the reduction is £50 and the reduction is £200, the tax liability is only reduced to zero. The individual **cannot** claim a repayment of £(50 − 200) = £150.

8.27 The tax which can be reduced is the tax on taxable income. It does not include tax retained on charges paid net.

8.28 An individual may be entitled to several different tax reducers. In such cases they must be applied in a set order, and we must stop when the tax is reduced to zero.

Part A: Income tax

8.29 The order is as follows.

(a) Investments in venture capital trusts
(b) Investments under the enterprise investment scheme
(c) Maintenance payments
(d) The children's tax credit
(e) The married couple's age allowance

Activity 1.12: Tax reducers

Peter, a married man aged 69, makes qualifying investments of £2,000 a year under the enterprise investment scheme. His wife has no income. Show his tax position for 2001/02 if his income consists of:

(a) trading profits of £40,000 and building society interest of £2,600 net;
(b) trading profits of £3,405 and building society interest of £2,600 net.

9 PERSONAL TAX COMPUTATIONS

9.1 Now let us work through some complete computations of income tax payable.

9.2 In each of the following examples, the taxpayer is single and aged under 65.

9.3 EXAMPLES: PERSONAL TAX COMPUTATIONS

(a) Kathe has a salary of £10,000 and receives dividends of £4,500. Kathe lives with her 12 year old daughter and her husband Tom. Tom has taxable income of £6,000 in 2001/02. No elections have been made in respect of the children's tax credit.

	Non-savings £	Dividends £	Total £
Schedule E	10,000		
Dividends £4,500 × 100/90		5,000	
STI	10,000	5,000	15,000
Less personal allowance	(4,535)		
Taxable income	5,465	5,000	10,465

	£
Income tax	
Non savings income	
£1,880 × 10%	188
£3,585 × 22%	789
Dividend income	
£5,000 × 10%	500
Less: tax reducers	
Children's tax credit (£5,200 × 10%)	(520)
Tax liability	957
Less tax credit on dividend	(500)
Tax payable	457

Some of the tax payable has probably already been paid on the salary under PAYE.

The dividend income falls within the basic rate band so it is taxed at 10% (*not* 22%).

The children's tax credit will be allocated to Kathe as she has higher total income for the tax year than her husband Tom.

1: An outline of income tax

(b) Jules has a salary of £20,000, business profits of £30,000, net dividends of £6,750 and building society interest of £3,000 net. He pays gross charges of £2,000 and makes a gift aid donation of £780 (net).

	Non-savings £	Savings (excl dividend) £	Dividend £	Total £
Schedule D Case I	30,000			
Schedule E	20,000			
Dividends £6,750 × 100/90			7,500	
Building society interest £3,000 × 100/80	-	3,750	-	
	50,000	3,750	7,500	
Less charges	(2,000)			
STI	48,000	3,750	7,500	59,250
Less personal allowance	(4,535)			
Taxable income	43,465	3,750	7,500	54,715

Income tax £

Non savings income
£1,880 × 10%   188
£27,520 × 22%   6,054
£1,000 (£780 × $\frac{100}{78}$) × 22%   220
£13,065 × 40%   5,226
   11,688

Savings (excl. dividend) income
£3,750 × 40%   1,500

Dividend income
£7,500 × 32.5%   2,438

Less tax credit on dividend income   (750)
Less tax suffered on building society interest   (750)
Tax payable   14,126

Savings (excl. dividend) income and dividend income fall above the basic rate threshold so they are taxed at 40% and 32.5% respectively. The basic rate band is extended by the gross amount of the gift aid donation.

(c) Jim does not work. He receives net bank interest of £38,000. He pays gross charges of £2,000.

	Savings (excl dividend) £	Total £
Bank interest × 100/80	47,500	
Less charges	(2,000)	
STI	45,500	45,500
Less personal allowance	(4,535)	
	40,965	40,965

   £

Savings (excluding dividend) income
£1,880 × 10%   188
£27,520 × 20%   5,504
£11,565 × 40%   4,626
Tax liability   10,318
Less tax suffered   (9,500)
Tax payable   818

Savings (excl. dividend) income within the basic rate band is taxed at 20% (*not* 22%).

Part A: Income tax

The complete proforma

9.4 Here is a complete proforma computation of taxable income. It is probably too much for you to absorb at this stage, but refer back to it as you come to the chapters dealing with the types of income shown.

	Non-savings £	Savings (excl dividend) £	Dividend £	Total £
Business profits	X			
Less losses set against business profits	(X)			
	X			
Wages less occupational pension contributions	X			
Other non-savings (as many lines as necessary)	X			
Building society interest (gross)		X		
Other savings (excl. dividends) (gross) (as many lines as necessary)		X		
Dividends (gross)			X	
	X	X	X	
Less charges (gross)	(X)	(X)	(X)	
	X	X	X	
Less losses set against general income	(X)	(X)	(X)	
STI	X	X	X	X
Less personal allowance	(X)	(X)	(X)	
Taxable income	X	X	X	X

Activity 1.13: Calculation of tax payable

Jackie, a single woman aged 45 has the following income and outgoings for 2001/02.

	£
Salary (tax deducted under PAYE £4,750)	24,200
Building society interest received (net)	1,600
Dividends received (net)	14,625
One-off charitable donation qualifying under the gift aid scheme (gross amount)	800

What is Jackie's tax payable for 2001/02?

10 FAMILIES

10.1 **Husband and wife are taxed as two separate people.** The general position on allowances (PA, MCAA and the CTC) has been set out above.

Joint property

10.2 **Where a husband and wife jointly own income-generating property, it is assumed that they are entitled to equal shares of the income. But if, in fact, they are not entitled to equal shares, they may make a joint declaration to the Revenue, specifying the proportion to which each is entitled. These proportions are used to tax each of them separately, in respect of income arising on or after the date of the declaration.**

10.3 If one spouse's marginal rate of tax (the rate on the highest part of his or her income) is higher than the other spouse's marginal rate, it is sensible to transfer income-yielding assets to the spouse with the lower rate.

The year of marriage

10.4 **The husband may receive part of the married couple's age allowance (MCAA). He receives the full amount less 1/12 for each complete tax month during which the couple were unmarried.** A tax month runs from the 6th of one month to the 5th of the next month.

10.5 In any year, one half or all of the minimum amount of MCAA (£2,070, 2001/02) may be transferred to the wife by election. The maximum amount that may be transferred in the year of marriage is the minimum amount reduced by 1/12 for each complete tax month before the wedding.

10.6 **The periods before and after the marriage are looked at separately for the purpose of calculating the CTC.**

The year of death

10.7 **If a wife dies during a tax year her widower receives the personal allowance (PA) and a full MCAA (if appropriate) for that year. The wife will have a full PA to cover income to the date of death.**

10.8 **When a husband dies, his tax affairs up to the date of his death are dealt with on the basis of his receiving the full PA and MCAA (if appropriate). The widow obtains her PA for the year.**

Divorce and separation

10.9 Divorce is usually preceded by separation. Where a couple become separated under a court order or separation deed, or in circumstances such that the separation is likely to be permanent, they are then taxed as single people from the date of separation.

10.10 In the tax year in which the separation takes place, however, the husband receives the PA plus a full MCAA (if appropriate). As usual, half or all of the £2,070 minimum amount of MCAA may be transferred to the wife.

10.11 The periods before and after the separation are looked at separately for the purpose of calculating the CTC.

Minor children

10.12 There is legislation to prevent the parent of a minor child transferring income to the child in order to use the child's personal allowance and starting and basic rate tax bands. **Income which is directly transferred by the parent, or is derived from capital so transferred, remains income of the parent for tax purposes.** This applies only to parents, however, and tax saving is therefore possible by other relatives. Even where a parent is involved, the child's income is not treated as the parent's if it does not exceed £100 a year.

10.13 **This legislation is concerned with gifts from a parent to a child.** It may therefore be possible to use the child's personal allowance and starting and basic rate bands if the child is employed in the parent's trade.

Part A: Income tax

The working families tax credit and disabled person's tax credit

10.14 **The working families tax credit (WFTC) is a tax credit which is deducted from a taxpayer's tax liability.** Claimants must have one or more children living with them, be working at least 16 hours a week and have savings not exceeding £8,000.

10.15 **The disabled persons tax credit (DPTC) is a tax credit available to certain ill or disabled taxpayers.**

10.16 Employers pay the tax credits to employees through the PAYE system (see Chapter 3), unless a couple choose to have them paid by the Revenue to the self-employed or non-earning partner. The main features of the scheme are as follows:

(a) the Revenue notify employers if and when to start paying a tax credit. The notification informs the employer how much tax credit to pay and when to stop;

(b) once notified when to start payments, the employer must add the tax credit to the employee's net wages for each pay period;

(c) employers can set off the amount of tax credit they pay against their PAYE tax. Employers whose liabilities are too small to cover the credits due can apply to the Revenue for funding.

Activity 1.14: End of chapter activity

John and Helen Pink who are both in their thirties are a married couple. Mr and Mrs Pink currently have no children. Mr and Mrs Pink received the following income in 2001/02.

	Mr Pink £	Mrs Pink £
Salary (gross)	36,000	20,000
PAYE tax deducted	6,000	2,611
Dividends (amount received)	1,090	2,538
Bank deposit interest (amount received)	200	76
Building society interest (amount received)	143	420
Premium bond prizes (amount)	-	500

In 2001/02 Mr Pink paid £200 (gross) under the gift aid scheme. He also paid interest of £6,000 a year gross on a loan of £55,000 to buy his home (in which he and Mrs Pink have lived since their marriage).

Task

Compute the net tax payable by Mr Pink and by Mrs Pink for 2001/02.

Key learning points

- In this chapter we have covered both the legal framework of taxation and the basic rules for working out the income tax an individual must pay.

- In a personal income tax computation, we bring together income from all sources, splitting the sources into non-savings income, savings (excl. dividend) and dividend income. We deduct charges, and then the personal allowance and the blind person's allowance. Finally, we work out income tax on the taxable income; we take account of gift aid donations, tax reducers, tax retained on charges and tax already suffered.

- Husbands, wives and children are all separate taxpayers. There are special rules to prevent parents from exploiting a child's personal allowance.

1: An outline of income tax

Quick quiz

1. At what rates is income tax charged on non-savings income?
2. Under what schedule is UK rental income taxed?
3. List three types of savings income that is received by individuals net of 20% tax.
4. Give an example of a charge on income paid net.
5. How is tax relief given for a gift aid donation?
6. At what rate does the children's tax credit reduce tax?
7. How is dividend income taxed?
8. What is the de-minimis threshold below which a child's income deriving from a parental disposition is not taxed as the parents?

Quick quiz answers

1. 10%, 22% and 40%
2. Schedule A.
3. Interest paid by UK companies on UK debentures and loan stock, bank and building society interest (but not National Savings Bank interest) and the income portion of a purchased annuity.
4. Patent royalties
5. Basic rate tax relief is given by treating a gift aid donation as though it were paid of net of basic rate tax. Additional tax relief is given in the personal tax computation by increasing the donor's basic rate band by the gross amount of the gift.
6. 10%
7. Dividend income in the starting and basic rate band is taxed at 10%. Dividend income in excess of the higher rate threshold is taxed at 32.5%
8. £100

Answer to activities

Activity 1.1

The gross amounts are: Dividends (£2,250 × 100/90)   £2,500
                        Building society interest (£2,400 × 100/80) £3,000

Activity 1.2

	Non-savings Income £	Savings (excl. dividend) income £	Dividend income £	Total £
Schedule E	16,000	0	0	
Building society interest £4,800 × 100/80	0	6,000	0	
Dividends £7,875 × 100/90	0	0	8,750	
Premium bond prize: exempt	0	0	0	
STI	16,000	6,000	8,750	30,750
Less personal allowance	(4,535)			
Taxable income	11,465	6,000	8,750	26,215

Did you remember to gross up dividends by 100/90 and building society interest by 100/80?

Did you remember that premium bond prizes are exempt?

Part A: Income tax

Activity 1.3

	£
£1,880 × 10%	188
£27,520 × 22%	6,054
£20,600 × 40%	8,240
50,000	14,482

Activity 1.4

	Non-savings income £	Savings (excl dividend) income £	Total £
Schedule E	10,430		
Building society interest (× 100/80)		5,000	
	10,430	5,000	15,430
Less personal allowance	(4,535)		
	5,895	5,000	10,895

	£
Tax on non-savings income	
£1,880 × 10%	188
£4,015 × 22%	883
Tax on savings (excl dividend)	
£5,000 × 20%	1,000
Tax Liability	2,071
Less: PAYE	(1,000)
Tax suffered on building society interest	(1,000)
Tax payable	71

The building society interest falls within the basic rate threshold so it is taxed at 20%.

Activity 1.5

	Dividend income £
Dividends (× 100/90)	34,000
Less personal allowance	(4,535)
Taxable income	29,465
Tax on dividend income	

	£
£29,400 × 10%	2,940
£65 × 32.5%	21
	2,961
Less: Tax credit on dividend (max)	(2,961)
Tax payable	-

The dividend income that falls within the starting and basic rate thresholds is taxed at 10%. Dividend income over the threshold of £29,400 is taxed at 32.5%. The tax credit suffered on the dividend income, £3,400, can be offset against the tax liability to reduce it to £nil. However, the excess tax credit, £439 (£3,400 − £2,961) cannot be repaid. The tax credit is offsettable but not repayable.

1: An outline of income tax

Activity 1.6

	£
Patent royalty (£3,900 × 100/78)	5,000
Copyright royalty	1,000
Total to deduct income tax computation	6,000

Copyright royalties are paid gross. The patent royalties are paid net of 22% tax but Harriet will deduct the gross amounts in her income tax computation.

Activity 1.7

	Non-savings Income £	Savings (excl dividend) income £	Dividend income £	
Schedule D Case I	8,000			
Building society interest (× 100/80)		17,500		
Dividends (× 100/90)			500	
Patent royalty (× 100/78)	(8,000)	£(4,000)		
	-	13,500	500	14,000
Less personal allowance	-	(4,535)	-	
	-	8,965	500	9,465

Income tax savings (excl dividend) income	£
£1,880 × 10%	188
£7,085 × 20%	1,417
Dividend income £500 × 10%	50
	1,655
Add: Tax retained on charge	2,640
Income tax liability	4,295

Activity 1.8

	Non-savings £	Savings (excl dividend) £	Total £
Schedule E	7,500		
Building society interest (× 100/80)		2,500	
STI	7,500	2,500	10,000
Less personal allowance	(5,990)		
Taxable income	1,510	2,500	4,010

As Michael is aged 66 and his STI is below £17,600 he gets a personal allowance of £5,990.

Activity 1.9

	Non-savings £	
Salary	58,000	
Less: personal allowance	(4,535)	
Taxable income	53,465	

Income tax	£	£
Starting rate band	1,880 × 10%	188
Basic rate band	27,520 × 22%	6,054
Basic rate band (extended)	10,000 × 22%	2,200
Higher rate band	14,065 × 40%	5,626
	53,465	14,068

The basic rate band is extended by the gross amount of the gift aid donation, £10,000 (£7,800 × $\frac{100}{78}$)

Part A: Income tax

Activity 1.10

As STI exceeds £17,600, the age allowances are reduced.

Reduction: £(21,400 − 17,600) × 0.5 = £1,900
Personal allowance = £(6,260 − 1,665) = £4,535
Married couple's allowance = £(5,435 − 175) = £5,260

Activity 1.11

Janet must have made a claim for the CTC as she has income chargeable at the higher rate.

The basic rate band limit of £29,400 is increased by the grossed up gift aid donation £(1,560 × 100/78 = £2,000) in order to work out the restriction on the CTC. The basic rate band limit is therefore £(29,400 + 2,000) = £31,400.

	£
STI	38,000
Less: PA	(4,535)
Taxable income	33,465
Excess of taxable income over basic rate band £(33,465 − 31,400)	2,065
Restriction £2,065 × 2/3	1,377
CTC allowable £(5,200 − 1,377) = £3,823 @ 10%	£382

Activity 1.12

	(a): High income		(b): Low income	
	Non-savings	Savings	Non-savings	Savings
		(excl dividends)		(excl dividends)
	£	£	£	£
Schedule D Case I	40,000		3,405	
Building society interest (£2,600 × 100/80)		3,250		3,250
Less personal allowance/age allowance	(4,535)		(3,405)	(2,585)
Taxable income	35,465	3,250	0	665

	(a)	(b)
	£	£
Non savings income		
£1,880 × 10%	188	
£27,520 × 22%	6,054	
£6,065 × 40%	2,426	
	8,668	
Savings (excl. dividend) income		
£3,250 × 40%/£665 × 10%	1,300	67
	9,968	67
Tax reducers		
EIS £2,000 × 20%	(400)	(67)
	9,568	0
MCAA £2,070 × 10% (minimum amount)	(207)	−
Tax liability	9,361	0
Tax suffered on building society interest	(650)	(650)
Tax payable/(repayable)	8,711	(650)

The tax reducers cannot lead to repayments of tax, so in (b) the MCAA and some of the EIS relief is wasted. However, tax suffered on building society interest can be repaid.

In (a) Peter is not entitled to the personal age allowance because his STI is too high. The MCAA is reduced to the minimum amount.

1: An outline of income tax

Activity 1.13

	Non-savings £	Savings (excl. dividend) £	Dividend £	Total £
Schedule E	24,200			
Building society interest £1,600 × 100/80		2,000		
Dividends £14,625 × 100/90			16,250	
	24,200	2,000	16,250	42,450
Less personal allowance	(4,535)			
Taxable income	19,665	2,000	16,250	37,915

	£
Non-savings income	
£1,880 × 10%	188
£17,785 × 22%	3,913
Savings (excl. dividend) income	
£2,000 × 20%	400
Dividend income	
£7,735 × 10%	774
£800 × 10% (Note)	80
£7,715 × 32.5%	2,507
Tax liability	7,862
Less tax suffered: Tax credit on dividend income	1,625
Building society interest	400
PAYE	4,750
	(6,775)
Tax payable	1,087

Note. The basic rate band is extended by the gross amount of the gift aid donation.

Activity 1.14

Mr Pink	Non-savings £	Savings (excl. dividends) £	Dividends £	Total £
Schedule E	36,000			
Dividends × 100/90			1,211	
Bank deposit interest × 100/80		250		
Building society interest × 100/80		179		
STI	36,000	429	1,211	37,640
Less personal allowance	(4,535)			
Taxable income	31,465	429	1,211	33,105

	£
Non savings income	
£1,880 × 10%	188
£27,520 × 22%	6,054
£200 (extended band) × 22%	44
£1,865 × 40%	746
Savings (excluding dividend) income	
£429 × 40%	172
Dividend income	
£1,211 × 32.5%	394
	7,598
Less: tax credit on dividend	121
tax suffered on savings income	86
PAYE	6,000
	(6,207)
Tax payable	1,391

Part A: Income tax

No deduction is available for loan interest to buy a home.

	Non-savings £	Savings (excl. dividends) £	Dividends £	Total £
Mrs Pink				
Schedule E	20,000			
Dividends × 100/90			2,820	
Bank deposit interest × 100/80		95		
Building society interest × 100/80	–	525		
STI	20,000	620	2,820	23,440
Less personal allowance	(4,535)			
Taxable income	15,465	620	2,820	18,905

	£	£
Non-savings income		
£1,880 × 10%		188
£13,585 × 22%		2,989
Savings (excluding dividend) income		
£620 × 20%		124
Dividend income		
£2,820 × 10%		282
Tax liability		3,583
Less: tax credit on dividends	282	
tax suffered on savings income	124	
PAYE	2,611	
		(3,017)
Tax payable		566

Premium bond prizes are tax free

Chapter 2 Administration

Chapter topic list

1. Notification of liability to income tax and CGT
2. Tax returns and keeping records
3. Self assessment and claims
4. The payment of tax, interest and penalities
5. Enquiries, determinations and discovery assessments
6. Client confidentiality

Learning objectives

On completion of this chapter you will be able to:

	Performance criteria	Range Statement
• identify the due payment dates for income tax and CGT	19.1, 19.2, 19.3, 19.4	-
• identify the due date of submission of a tax return	19.1, 19.2, 19.3, 19.4	-
• discuss the consequences of not meeting the due submission payment date	19.1, 19.2, 19.3, 19.4	-
• outline the powers of the Inland Revenue	19.1, 19.2, 19.3, 19.4	-
• outline the rights afforded to a taxpayer	19.1, 19.2, 19.3, 19.4	-

Part A: Income tax

1 NOTIFICATION OF LIABILITY TO INCOME TAX AND CGT

1.1 **Individuals who are chargeable to income tax or CGT for any tax year and who have not received a notice to file a return are, in general, required to give notice of chargeability to an officer of the Board within six months from the end of the year** ie by 5 October 2002 for 2001/02.

1.2 The maximum mitigable penalty where notice of chargeability is not given is 100% of the tax assessed which is not paid on or before 31 January following the tax year.

2 TAX RETURNS AND KEEPING RECORDS

Tax returns

2.1 The tax return comprises a Tax Form, together with supplementary pages for particular sources of income. Taxpayers are sent a Tax Form and a number of supplementary pages depending on their known sources of income, together with a Tax Return Guide and various notes relating to the supplementary pages. Taxpayers with new sources of income may have to ask the orderline for further supplementary pages. The onus is on the taxpayer to ensure he has the correct supplementary pages and to request any additional forms needed.

2.2 In the appendix to this text we include a sample blank tax return form and some of the various supplementary pages that a taxpayer may also need to complete and submit together with the form. Please see page (x) of this Text for a note regarding the version of the form we have used.

2.3 In your devolved assessment you may be asked to complete an extract from the income tax form and you should start to refer to the appendix and familiarise yourself with it now. You will see that the return is broken down into 24 question areas.

Question areas

Q1-9 establish whether a taxpayer has various types of income or gains to check whether or not the correct supplementary pages have been completed. In your Devolved Assessment you may come across and have to tick the 'YES' box of the following:

Employment income
Self employment income
Partnership income
Income from land and property in the UK
Capital gains

You may also be required to complete the supplementary pages which are concerned with the above.

Q10-13 require details of income for sources not covered in the supplementary pages. Look at box 10 in particular. You are very likely to have to complete details of interest and dividends in your assessment. Note that, where amounts are received net of tax, you need to insert the amount received, the tax deducted/tax credit and the gross figure.

Q14-16 are claims for reliefs eg for pension contributions, gift aid payments and the married couple's age allowance. Note that as the rules concerning personal pension contributions changed in 2001/02, it is possible that this section of the form will

2: Administration

change when the Inland Revenue issue the 2001/02 version of the form. It is therefore important that you obtain a copy of the updated form before you sit your assessment. Please see page (x) of this text for a note regarding the version of the form we have used.

Q17   concerns student loan repayments.

Q18   asks whether the taxpayer wants to calculate his own tax. In the Devolved Assessment you may need to calculate total tax and enter it in box 18.3. You may also need to deal with payments on account (see below) in boxes 18.6 - 18.7.

Q19-20   concerns repayments of overpaid tax.

Q21-22   require certain administrative information.

Q23   requires certain additional information.

Q24   contains the declaration and must be signed by the taxpayer. It also provides the final check that the correct supplementary pages have been completed.

2.4   Note that a self employed taxpayer, whether trading alone or in partnership, is taxed on business profits under Schedule D Case I. You will not be expected to compute Schedule D Case I profits in Unit 19 because this computation will be assessed if you study Unit 18. However, in Unit 19 you may be expected to take a given Schedule D Case I profit or loss figure and enter it correctly on the supplementary pages to the income tax return. The supplementary pages to be completed are reproduced in the appendix to this Interactive Text. Familiarise yourself with them now and note that there are separate pages for the self employed sole traders and for partners.

2.5   The Inland Revenue also produce a tax calculation guide to accompany the tax return form. The tax calculation working guide is a booklet which taxpayers can use to help them calculate their tax if they wish. However, it is not compulsory to do so. The latest AAT guidance notes for Unit 19 say that, in your assessment you will not **normally** have to complete the Revenue's tax calculation guide.

2.6   It is not possible for us to reproduce the tax calculation guide in this text. Throughout the Text we, therefore, calculate tax payable in our own computation. However, we suggest that you obtain a copy of the guide from the Revenue and use it to check some of our computations.

2.7   If a return for the previous year was filed electronically, or a computer generated substitute form used, the taxpayer may be sent a notice to file a return, rather than the official Revenue form. This is intended to reduce unnecessary waste of paper etc.

Partnerships

2.8   **A partnership may be required to complete a partnership return.** The partnership return is extra to the normal self-assessment tax returns which each individual partner will have to complete for themselves. For a partner, the normal self assessment return includes supplementary partnership pages that detail his share of partnership profits or losses (see below). On the other hand, the partnership return shows the total profits/losses of the partnership and how they are divided between partners.

Part A: Income tax

Time limit for submission of tax returns

> **KEY TERM**
>
> The filing due date for filing a tax return is the later of:
> - 31 January following the end of the tax year which the return covers.
> - three months after the notice to file the return was issued.

2.9 If an individual wishes the Revenue to prepare the self-assessment on his behalf, earlier deadlines apply. The filing date is then the later of:

- 30 September following the tax year; eg for 2001/02, by 30 September 2002.
- two months after notice to file the return was issued.

Since a partnership return does not include a self-assessment these revised deadlines do not apply to partnership returns. This may, of course, create problems if one of the partners wishes the Revenue to complete his personal self-assessment.

Penalties for late filing

Individual returns

2.10 The maximum penalties for delivering a late tax return are:

(a)	Return up to 6 months late:	£100
(b)	Return more than 6 months but not more than 12 months late:	£200
(c)	Return more than 12 months late:	£200 + 100% of the tax liability

2.11 In addition, the General or Special Commissioners can direct that a maximum penalty of £60 per day be imposed where failure to deliver a tax return continues after notice of the direction has been given to the taxpayer. In this case the additional £100 penalty, imposed under (b) if the return is more than six months late, is not charged.

2.12 The fixed penalties of £100/£200 can be set aside by the Commissioners if they are satisfied that the taxpayer had a reasonable excuse for not delivering the return. If the tax liability shown on the return is less than the fixed penalties, the fixed penalty is reduced to the amount of the tax liability. The tax geared penalty is mitigable by the Revenue or the Commissioners.

Partnership returns

2.13 The maximum penalties for late delivery of a partnership tax return are as shown above, save that there is no tax-geared penalty if the return is more than 12 months late. The penalties apply separately to each partner.

Reasonable excuse

2.14 A taxpayer only has a reasonable excuse for a late filing if a default occurred because of a factor outside his control. This might be non-receipt of the return by the taxpayer, an industrial dispute in the post office after the return was posted, serious illness of the taxpayer or a close relative, or destruction of records through fire and flood. Illness etc is

only accepted as a reasonable excuse if the taxpayer was taking timeous steps to complete the return, and if the return is filed as soon as possible after the illness etc.

Returns rejected as incomplete

2.15 If a return, filed before the filing date, is rejected by the Revenue as incomplete later than 14 days before the filing deadline of 31 January, a late filing penalty will not be charged if the return is completed and returned within 14 days of the rejection. This only applies if the omission from the return was a genuine error. It does not apply if a return was deliberately filed as incomplete in the hope of extending the time limit.

Standard accounting information

2.16 'Three line' accounts (ie income less expenses equals profit) only need be included on the tax return of businesses with a turnover (or gross rents from property) of less than £15,000 pa. This is not as helpful as it might appear, as underlying records must still be kept for tax purposes (disallowable items etc) when producing three line accounts.

2.17 Large businesses with a turnover of at least £5 million which have used figures rounded to the nearest £1,000 in producing their published accounts can compute their profits to the nearest £1,000 for tax purposes.

2.18 The tax return requires trading results to be presented in a standard format. Although there is no requirement to submit accounts with the return, accounts may be filed. If accounts accompany the return, the Revenue's power to raise a discovery assessment (see below) is restricted.

Keeping of records

2.19 All taxpayers must keep and retain all records required to enable them to make and deliver a correct tax return.

2.20 **Records must be retained until the later of:**

(a) (i) **5 years after the 31 January following the tax year where the taxpayer is in business** (as a sole trader or partner or letting property); or

(ii) **1 year after the 31 January following the tax year otherwise;** or

(b) provided notice to deliver a return is given before the date in (a):

(i) **the time after which enquiries by the Inland Revenue into the return can no longer be commenced;** or

(ii) **the date any such enquiries have been completed.**

2.21 Where a person receives a notice to deliver a tax return after the normal record keeping period has expired, he must keep all records in his possession at that time until no enquiries can be raised in respect of the return or until such enquiries have been completed.

2.22 The maximum (mitigable) penalty for each failure to keep and retain records is £3,000 per tax year/accounting period.

Part A: Income tax

3 SELF-ASSESSMENT AND CLAIMS

3.1 **Every personal tax return must be accompanied by a self-assessment.**

> **KEY TERM**
>
> A **self-assessment** is a calculation of the amount of taxable income and gains after deducting reliefs and allowances, and a calculation of the income tax and CGT payable after taking into account tax deducted at source and tax credits.

3.2 Although Tax Calculation Working Sheets are provided with the tax return there is no requirement for the taxpayer to use these in computing his self-assessment. It is sufficient to enter the appropriate figures on the tax return.

3.3 **The self-assessment calculation may either be made by the taxpayer or the Revenue.** If a return is filed within certain time limits (normally, 30 September following the tax year to which it relates, see above) an officer of the board must make a self-assessment on the taxpayer's behalf on the basis of the information contained in the return. He must send a copy of the assessment to the taxpayer. These assessments, even though raised by the Revenue, are treated as self-assessments.

3.4 If the taxpayer files a return after the above deadline but without completing the self-assessment, the Revenue will not normally reject the return as incomplete. However the Revenue are not then bound to complete the self-assessment in time to notify the taxpayer of the tax falling due on the normal due date (generally the following 31 January), and it is the taxpayer's responsibility to estimate and pay his tax on time.

3.5 **Within nine months of receiving a tax return, the Revenue can amend a taxpayer's self-assessment to correct any obvious errors or mistakes;** whether errors of principle, arithmetical mistakes or otherwise. The taxpayer does have the right to reject any corrections of obvious errors made by the Revenue.

3.6 **Within 12 months of the due filing date (*not* the actual filing date), the taxpayer can give notice to an officer to amend his tax return and self-assessment.** Such amendments by taxpayers are not confined to the correction of obvious errors. They may not be made whilst the Revenue are making enquiries into the return.

3.7 The same rules apply to corrections and amendments of partnership statements and stand alone claims (see below).

Claims

3.8 **All claims and elections which can be made in a tax return must be made in this manner if a return has been issued. A claim for any relief, allowance or repayment of tax must be quantified at the time it is made.** These rules do not apply to claims involving two or more years or to claims that can be dealt with through the PAYE system (eg. by amending a code number).

3.9 Certain claims have a time limit that is longer than the time limit for filing or amending a tax return. A claim may therefore be made after the time limit for amending the tax return has expired. Claims not made on the tax return are referred to as **'stand alone' claims**.

3.10 Claims made on a tax return are subject to the administrative rules governing returns, for the making of corrections, enquiries etc whilst stand alone claims are governed by provisions which are similar to the rules governing treatment of returns.

3.11 Self-assessment is intended to avoid the need to reopen earlier years, so relief should be given for the year of the claim. This rule can best be explained by considering a claim to carry back a trading loss to an earlier year of assessment:

(a) The claim for relief is treated as made in relation to the year in which the loss was actually incurred

(b) The amount of any tax repayment due is calculated in terms of tax of the earlier year to which the loss is being carried back, and

(c) Any tax repayment etc is treated as relating to the later year in which the loss was actually incurred.

Time limits

3.12 **The time limit for making a claim is 5 years from 31 January following the tax year, unless a different limit is specifically set for the claim.**

Error or mistake claims

3.13 **An error or mistake claim may be made for errors in a return or partnership statement where tax would otherwise be overcharged.** The claim may not be made where the tax liability was computed in accordance with practice prevailing at the time the return or statement was made.

4 THE PAYMENT OF TAX, INTEREST AND PENALTIES

4.1 The self-assessment system may result in the taxpayer making three payments of income tax.

Date	Payment
31 January in the tax year	1st payment on account
31 July after the tax year	2nd payment on account
31 January after the tax year	Final payment to settle the remaining liability

4.2 The Inland Revenue issue payslips/demand notes in a credit card type 'Statement of Account' format, but there is no statutory obligation for them to do so and **the onus is on the taxpayer to pay the correct amount of tax on the due date.**

KEY TERM

Payments on account are usually required where the income tax due in the previous year exceeded the amount of income tax deducted at source; this excess is known as **'the relevant amount'**. Income tax deducted at source includes tax suffered, PAYE deductions and tax credits on dividends.

4.3 **The payments on account are each equal to 50% of the relevant amount for the previous year.**

Part A: Income tax

Activity 2.1: Payments on account

Sue is a self employed writer who paid tax for 2001/02 as follows:

		£
Total amount of income tax charged		9,200
This included:	Tax deducted on savings income	3,200
She also paid:	Capital gains tax	4,800

How much are the payments on account for 2002/03?

4.4 **Payments on account are not required if the relevant amount falls below a de minimis limit of £500. Also, payments on account are not required from taxpayers who paid 80% or more of their tax liability for the previous year through PAYE or other deduction at source arrangements.**

4.5 If the previous year's liability increases following an amendment to a self-assessment, or the raising of a discovery assessment, an adjustment is made to the payments on account due.

4.6 Payments on account are normally fixed by reference to the previous year's tax liability but if a taxpayer expects his liability to be lower than this **he may claim to reduce his payments on account to:**

   (a) **A stated amount**, or
   (b) **Nil**.

The claim must state the reason why he believes his tax liability will be lower, or nil.

4.7 **If the taxpayer's eventual liability is higher than he estimated he will have reduced the payments on account too far. Although the payments on account will not be adjusted, the taxpayer will suffer an interest charge on late payment.**

4.8 A penalty of the difference between the reduced payment on account and the correct payment on account may be levied if the reduction was claimed fraudulently or negligently.

4.9 **The balance of any income tax together with all CGT due for a year, is normally payable on or before the 31 January following the year.**

Activity 2.2: Payments of tax

Giles made payments on account for 2001/02 of £6,500 each on 31 January 2002 and 31 July 2002, based on his 2000/01 liability. He then calculates his total income tax liability for 2001/02 at £18,000 of which £2,750 was deducted at source. In addition he calculated that his CGT liability for disposals in 2001/02 is £5,120.

What is the final payment due for 2001/02?

4.10 In one case the due date for the final payment is later than 31 January following the end of the year. **If a taxpayer has notified chargeability by 5 October but the notice to file a tax return is not issued before 31 October, then the due date for the payment is three months after the issue of the notice.**

4.11 Tax charged in an amended self-assessment is usually payable on the later of:

   (a) The normal due date, generally 31 January following the end of the tax year, and
   (b) The day following 30 days after the making of the revised self-assessment.

4.12 Tax charged on a discovery assessment is due thirty days after the issue of the assessment.

Surcharges

> **KEY TERM**
>
> **Surcharges** are normally imposed in respect of amounts paid late:
>
> | Paid | Surcharge |
> |---|---|
> | (a) Within 28 days of due date: | none |
> | (b) More than 28 days but not more than six months after the due date: | 5% |
> | (c) More than six months after the due date: | 10% |

4.13 Surcharges apply to:

(a) Balancing payments of income tax and any CGT under self-assessment or a determination

(b) Tax due on the amendment of a self-assessment

(c) Tax due on a discovery assessment

4.14 **The surcharge rules do not apply to late payments on account.**

4.15 No surcharge will be applied where the late paid tax liability has attracted a tax-geared penalty on the failure to notify chargeability to tax, or the failure to submit a return, or on the making of an incorrect return (including a partnership return).

Interest

4.16 **Interest is chargeable on late payment of both payments on account and balancing payments. In both cases interest runs from the due date until the day before the actual date of payment.**

4.17 Interest is charged from 31 January following the tax year (or the normal due date for the balancing payment, in the rare event that this is later), even if this is before the due date for payment on:

(a) Tax payable following an amendment to a self-assessment
(b) Tax payable in a discovery assessment, and
(c) Tax postponed under an appeal which becomes payable.

4.18 Since a determination (see below) is treated as if it were a self-assessment, interest runs from 31 January following the tax year.

4.19 If a taxpayer claims to reduce his payments on account and there is still a final payment to be made, interest is normally charged on the payments on account as if each of those payments had been the lower of:

(a) the reduced amount, plus 50% of the final income tax liability; and
(b) the amount which would have been payable had no claim for reduction been made.

Part A: Income tax

Activity 2.3: Interest

Herbert's payments on account for 2001/02 based on his income tax liability for 2000/01 were £4,500 each. However when he submitted his 2000/01 income tax return in January 2002 he made a claim to reduce the payments on account for 2001/02 to £3,500 each. The first payment on account was made on 29 January 2002, and the second on 12 August 2002.

Herbert filed his 2001/02 tax return in December 2002. The return showed that his tax liabilities for 2001/02 (before deducting payments on account) were income tax: £10,000, capital gains tax: £2,500. Herbert paid the balance of tax due of £5,500 on 19 February 2003.

For what periods and in respect of what amounts will Herbert be charged interest?

4.20 Where interest has been charged on late payments on account but the final balancing settlement for the year produces a repayment, all or part of the original interest is remitted.

4.21 If a taxpayer provided the Revenue in good time with the information needed to calculate the payment on account due on 31 January but did not receive a Statement of Account in time to make the correct payment by 31 January, it is Revenue practice to treat the due date for interest purposes as 30 days after the issue of the Statement.

Repayment of tax and repayment supplement

4.22 Tax is repaid when claimed unless a greater payment of tax is due in the following 30 days, in which case it is set-off against that payment.

4.23 Interest is paid on overpayments of:

(a) Payments on account

(b) Final payments of income tax and CGT, including tax deducted at source or tax credits on dividends, and

(c) Penalties and surcharges.

4.24 Repayment supplement runs from the original date of payment (even if this was prior to the due date), until the day before the date the repayment is made. Income tax deducted at source and tax credits are treated as if they were paid on the 31 January following the tax year concerned.

4.25 Tax repaid is identified with tax payments in the following order:

(a) Final balancing payment
(b) Equally to the payments on account
(c) Income tax deducted at source/tax credits
(d) If it is attributable to tax paid in instalments, to a later instalment before an earlier one.

5 ENQUIRIES, DETERMINATIONS AND DISCOVERY ASSESSMENTS

Enquiries into returns

5.1 **An officer of the Board has a limited period within which to commence enquiries into a return or amendment. The officer must give written notice of his intention by:**

(a) **The first anniversary of the due filing date (not the actual filing date), or**

(b) **If the return is filed after the due filing date, the quarter day following the first anniversary of the actual filing date. The quarter days are 31 January, 30 April, 31 July and 31 October.**

5.2 If the taxpayer amended the return after the due filing date, the enquiry 'window' extends to the quarter day following the first anniversary of the date the amendment was filed. Where the enquiry was not raised within the limit which would have applied had no amendment been filed, the enquiry is restricted to matters contained in the amendment.

5.3 Enquiries may be made into partnership returns (or amendments) upon which a partnership statement is based within the same time limits. A notice to enquire into a partnership return is deemed to incorporate a notice, to enquire into each individual partner's return.

5.4 Enquiries may also be made into stand alone claims, provided notice is given by the officer of the Board by the later of:

(a) The quarter day following the first anniversary of the making or amending of the claim

(b) 31 January next but one following the tax year, if the claim relates to a tax year, or

(c) The first anniversary of the end of the period to which a claim relates if it relates to a period other than a tax year.

5.5 The procedures for enquiries into claims mirror those for enquiries into returns.

5.6 **The officer does not have to have, or give, any reason for raising an enquiry. In particular the taxpayer will not be advised whether he has been selected at random for an audit. Enquiries may be full enquiries, or may be limited to 'aspect' enquiries.**

5.7 In the course of his enquiries **the officer may require the taxpayer to produce documents, accounts or any other information required. The taxpayer can appeal to the Commissioners.**

5.8 During the course of his enquiries an officer may amend a self-assessment if it appears that insufficient tax has been charged and an immediate amendment is necessary to prevent a loss to the Crown. This might apply if, for example, there is a possibility that the taxpayer will emigrate.

5.9 If a return is under enquiry the Revenue may postpone any repayment due as shown in the return until the enquiry is complete. The Revenue have discretion to make a provisional repayment but there is no facility to appeal if the repayment is withheld.

5.10 At any time during the course of an enquiry, the taxpayer may apply to the Commissioners to require the officer to notify the taxpayer within a specified period that the enquiries are complete, unless the officer can demonstrate that he has reasonable grounds for continuing the enquiry.

5.11 If both sides agree, disputes concerning a point of law can be resolved through litigation without having to wait until the whole enquiry is complete.

5.12 An officer must issue a notice that the enquiries are complete, and a statement of the amount of tax due, or the amount of the claim. The taxpayer then has thirty days to amend his self-assessment, partnership statement or claim to give effect to the officer's conclusions.

He may also make any other amendments that he could have made had the enquiry not been commenced (amendments may not be made whilst enquiries are in progress).

5.13 If the officer is not satisfied with the taxpayer's amendment he has thirty days in which to amend the self-assessment, partnership statement or claim. Also if a claim has been disallowed, but does not affect the self-assessment, he must advise the taxpayer of the extent to which it has been disallowed.

If the taxpayer is not satisfied with the officer's amendment he may, within 30 days, appeal to the Commissioners.

5.14 Once an enquiry is complete the officer cannot make further enquiries. The Revenue may, in limited circumstances, raise a discovery assessment if they believe that there has been a loss of tax (see below).

Revenue procedures

5.15 The majority of investigation cases are handled by local inspectors, but serious cases are dealt with by the Special Compliance Office.

5.16 **Where an irregularity is detected, unless it appears to be of a very serious nature, the first overture will often be made by the local inspector writing to the taxpayer or his agent suggesting that he has reason to doubt that full and correct returns have been made and inviting the taxpayer's comments. Correspondence will be followed by interviews at which the inspector will try to collect further evidence, and the taxpayer's accountant may be asked to prepare a detailed report showing the estimated tax unpaid.**

5.17 The Revenue use various methods to attempt to calculate undisclosed income. Gross profit margins either for previous periods or for similar businesses are standardly used. As a last resort, some indication can be derived from the taxpayer's personal assets. A growth in these, taken together with an assumed level of personal expenditure, can point to an unexplained source, presumably undisclosed income.

5.18 **A sensible taxpayer will co-operate with the Revenue as any resistance on his part at this stage will count heavily against him in the final assessment of penalties.** If the taxpayer fails to make a full disclosure once enquiries have begun the Revenue will conclude that his transgressions go beyond simple oversight or negligence. Furthermore, where the Revenue might take criminal proceedings, full co-operation will make it more likely that they will accept a cash settlement instead.

The Revenue's powers

5.19 **The Revenue's powers include the following.**

(a) **The power to call for documents of taxpayers and others.** The Revenue may require any person to produce any documents which may contain information relevant to any taxpayer's tax liability. The Revenue may also require the taxpayer to provide written answers about questions of fact. The Inspector must give the person holding the documents reasons for applying for the right to demand documents, unless the commissioner is satisfied that giving reasons would prejudice the assessment or collection of tax.

(b) **The power to call for papers of tax accountants.** The Revenue is not normally empowered to demand documents from the taxpayer's barrister, solicitor or accountant. However, if a tax accountant has either:

(i) been convicted of an offence in relation to tax; or
(ii) been penalised for assisting in making an incorrect return,

the Revenue can, with the consent of a circuit judge, demand documents relating to the taxpayer's affairs. A tax accountant is anyone (including a barrister or solicitor) who helps a taxpayer to prepare or deliver documents for tax purposes.

This power extends only for one year after the date of conviction or penalty and does not apply if an appeal against the conviction or penalty is pending. The power does not extend to documents held by a barrister or solicitor and covered by professional privilege.

(c) **The power of entry with a warrant to obtain documents.** Where there are reasonable grounds for suspecting that an offence involving fraud in connection with tax has been, is being or is about to be committed and that evidence is to be found on certain premises, a warrant can be obtained authorising an officer of the Board to enter the premises and search them. The officer may seize and remove anything which he has reasonable cause to suppose may be required as evidence.

(d) **The power to obtain information about interest and dividends.** The Revenue can require banks and building societies to supply details of interest (and dividends on building society shares) paid to investors.

Determinations and discovery assessments

5.20 The Revenue may only raise enquiries if a return has been submitted.

5.21 If notice has been served on a taxpayer to submit a return but the return is not submitted by the due filing date, an officer of the Board may make a determination of the amounts liable to income tax and CGT and of the tax due. Such a determination must be made to the best of the officer's information and belief, and is then treated as if it were a self-assessment.

5.22 If an officer of the Board discovers that profits have been omitted from assessment, that any assessment has become insufficient, or that any relief given is, or has become excessive, an assessment may be raised to recover the tax lost.

5.23 If the tax lost results from an error in the taxpayer's return but the return was made in accordance with prevailing practice at the time, no discovery assessment may be made.

5.24 A discovery assessment may only be raised where a return has been made if:

(a) There has been fraudulent or negligent conduct by the taxpayer or his agent, or

(b) At the time that enquiries into the return were completed, or could no longer be made, the officer did not have information to make him aware of the loss of tax.

5.25 These rules do not prevent the Revenue from raising assessments in cases of genuine discoveries, but prevent assessments from being raised due to the Revenue's failure to make timely use of information or to a change of opinion on information made available.

Part A: Income tax

Appeals and postponement of payment of tax

5.26 A taxpayer may appeal against an amendment to a self-assessment or partnership statement, or an amendment to or disallowance of a claim, following an enquiry, or against an assessment which is not a self-assessment, such as a discovery assessment.

5.27 **The appeal must normally be made within 30 days of the amendment or self-assessment.**

5.28 The notice of appeal must state the **grounds** of appeal. These may be stated in general terms. At the hearing the Commissioners may allow the appellant to put forward grounds not stated in his notice if they are satisfied that his omission was not wilful or unreasonable.

5.29 In some cases it may be possible to agree the point at issue by negotiation with the Revenue, in which case the appeal may be settled by agreement. If the appeal cannot be agreed, it will be heard by the General or Special Commissioners.

5.30 An appeal does not relieve the taxpayer of liability to pay tax on the normal due date unless he obtains a 'determination' of the Commissioners or agreement of the Inspector that payment of all or some of the tax may be postponed pending determination of the appeal. The amount not postponed is due 30 days after the determination or agreement is issued, if that is later than the normal due date.

5.31 If any part of the postponed tax becomes due a notice of the amount payable is issued and the amount is payable 30 days after the issue of the notice. Interest, however, is still payable from the normal due date.

Income tax fraud

5.32 There is a statutory offence of evading income tax. The penalty may be up to seven years in prison or an unlimited fine, or both.

6 CLIENT CONFIDENTIALITY

6.1 Whenever you prepare accounts or returns on behalf of a client you should remember that you are bound by the ethical guideline of client confidentiality. This means that you should not discuss a client's affairs with third parties without the client's permission. You should also take care not to leave documents relating to a client's affairs in public places such as on trains or in restaurants.

Activity 2.4: End of chapter activity

Tim is a medical consultant. His total tax liability for 2000/01 was £16,800. Of this £7,200 was paid under the PAYE system, £800 was withheld at source from bank interest and £200 was suffered on dividends received during the year.

Tim's total tax liability for 2001/02 was £22,000. £7,100 of this was paid under PAYE system, £900 was withheld at source from bank interest and there was a £250 tax credit on dividends.

Tim did not make any claim in respect of his payments on account for 2001/02. The Revenue issued a 2001/02 tax return to Tim on 5 May 2002.

Task

State what payments Tim was required to make in respect of his 2001/02 tax liability and the due dates for the payment of these amounts.

Key learning points

- A return is due for filing by 31 January following the end of the tax year. However, if the taxpayer wants the Revenue to calculate the amount of tax due in time for him to pay the correct amount by the due date, the return must be submitted by 30 September following the end of the tax year.
- Two payments on account of income tax based on the prior year tax bill are due on 31 January during the tax year and 31 July after the tax year. On 31 January following the tax year the balance of any income tax due is paid.
- CGT is due to be paid by 31 January following the tax year end. There are no payments on account of CGT.
- The Revenue normally obtain the information needed to charge income tax and CGT from tax returns.
- Taxpayers have rights of appeal.
- The Revenue have extensive, but not unlimited, powers to enquire into returns.
- There is an extensive regime of interest, surcharges and penalties.

Quick quiz

1. By when must a taxpayer who has not received a tax return give notice of his chargeability to capital gains tax due in 2001/02?
2. By when must a taxpayer who intends to calculate his own tax file a tax return for 2001/02?
3. What are the normal payment dates for income tax?
4. What surcharges are due in respect of income tax payments on account that are paid two months after the due date?

Quick quiz answers

1. Within six months of the end of the year, ie by 5 October 2002.
2. By 31 January 2003 or, if later, 3 months after a notice to file the return was issued.
3. Two payments on account of income tax are due on 31 January in the tax year and on the 31 July following. A final balancing payment is due on 31 January following the tax year.
4. None. Surcharges do not apply to late payment of payment on account.

Answers to activities

Activity 2.1

	£
Income tax:	
Total income tax charged for 2001/02	9,200
Less: tax deducted for 2001/02	(3,200)
Relevant amount'	6,000
Payments on account for 2002/03:	
31 January 2003 £6,000 × ½	3,000
31 July 2003 As before	3,000

There is no requirement to make payments on account of capital gains tax.

Part A: Income tax

Activity 2.2

Income tax: £18,000 – £2,750 – £6,500 – £6,500 = £2,250. CGT = £5,120.

Final payment due on 31 January 2003 for 2001/2002 £2,250 + £5,120 = £7,370

Activity 2.3

Herbert made an excessive claim to reduce his payments on account, and will therefore be charged interest on the reduction. The payments on account should have been £4,500 each based on the 2000/01 liability (not £5,000 each based on the 2001/02 liability). Interest will be charged as follows:

(a) First payment on account

    (i) On £3,500 - nil - paid on time
    (ii) On £1,000 from due date of 31 January 2002 to day before payment, 18 February 2003

(b) Second payment on account

    (i) On £3,500 from due date of 31 July 2002 to day before payment, 11 August 2002
    (ii) On £1,000 from due date of 31 July 2002 to day before payment, 18 February 2003

(c) Balancing payment

    (i) On £2,500 from due date of 31 January 2003 to day before payment, 18 February 2003

Activity 2.4

Tim's Payments on Account for 2001/02 were based on the excess of his 2000/01 tax liability over amounts deducted under the PAYE system, amounts deducted at source and tax credits on dividends:

	£
2000/01 tax liability	16,800
Less: PAYE	(7,200)
Tax deducted at source	(800)
Tax credit on dividends	(200)
Total payments on account for 2001/02	8,600

Two equal payments on account of £4,300 (£8,600 / 2) were required. The due dates for these payments were 31 January 2002 and 31 July 2002 respectively.

The final payment in respect of Tim's 2001/02 tax liability was due on 31 January 2003 and was calculated as follows:

	£
2001/02 tax liability	22,000
Less: PAYE	(7,100)
Tax deducted at source	(900)
Tax credit on dividends	(250)
	13,750
Less: Payments on account	(8,600)
Final payment due 31.1.03	5,150

Chapter 3 The taxation of employment

Chapter topic list

1. The Schedule E charge
2. Benefits in kind: all employees
3. Benefits in kind: P11D employees
4. Allowable deductions
5. The PAYE system
6. Pensions
7. Inland Revenue forms

Learning objectives

On completion of this chapter you will be able to:

	Performance criteria	Range Statement
discuss whether an individual is an employee or self employed	19.1.1	-
distinguish between a lower paid employee and a higher paid employee	19.1.1	19.1.3
value for income tax purposes a variety of non-cash perks provided for employees	19.1.1	19.1.3
outline the types of expense incurred by an employee that can reduce his taxable income	19.1.1	19.1.2
understand how PAYE operates in general	19.1.2	19.1.4
discuss how the payment of money into a pension scheme can reduce the overall tax bill of an employee	19.1.1	19.1.2

Part A: Income tax

1 THE SCHEDULE E CHARGE

Taxable income

KEY TERM

'Emoluments' from an office or employment are taxed under Schedule E.

1.1 Emoluments include benefits in kind. Benefits in kind are converted into their cash equivalent using the rules set out in this chapter. Employees must pay income tax on this amount.

1.2 **Earnings (or 'emoluments') are taxed in the year of receipt.** There is a general definition of 'receipt' and a wider one for directors (who are in a position to manipulate the timing of payments). **The general rule is that emoluments are treated as received on the earlier of:**

- **the time payment is made;**
- **the time entitlement to payment arises.**

1.3 The time of receipt for directors' earnings is the earliest of:

- the earlier of the two alternatives given in the general rule (above);
- when the amount is credited in the company's accounting records;
- the end of the company's period of account (if the amount was determined by then);
- when the amount is determined (if after the end of the company's period of account).

1.4 The receipts basis does not apply to benefits in kind. Benefits are taxable when they are provided.

1.5 Pensions and taxable state benefits (such as the jobseeker's allowance) are also taxable under Schedule E. Unlike normal salary, however, the taxable amount is the amount accruing during the tax year, irrespective of whether or not it has actually been received in the tax year.

Activity 3.1: Date of receipt

All directors of a company receive bonuses for the year ended 31 January 2002. On what date are they treated as receiving these bonuses if they are determined on:

(a) 15 January 2002;
(b) 30 April 2002,

and paid a month after they are determined? (The directors only become entitled to payment of the bonuses when they are paid.) The bonuses are credited to the company's accounts when paid.

Employment and self employment

1.6 **The distinction between employment (Schedule E) and self employment (Schedule D) is a fine one. It has been held that employment involves a contract of service, whereas self employment involves a contract for services.** Taxpayers tend to prefer self employment, because the rules on deductions for expenses are more generous.

1.7 Factors which may be of importance include:

- the degree of control exercised over the person doing the work;
- whether he must accept further work;

- whether the other party must provide further work;
- whether he provides his own equipment;
- whether he hires his own helpers;
- what degree of financial risk he takes;
- what degree of responsibility for investment and management he has;
- whether he can profit from sound management;
- whether he can work when he chooses;
- the wording used in any agreement between the parties.

1.8 The Revenue look at all the circumstances of the case, including the above factors when deciding if someone is employed or self employed.

2 BENEFITS IN KIND: ALL EMPLOYEES

2.1 **Generally, benefits in kind are taxable at the cost of providing them** (but only the marginal cost, where the benefit is also sold to non-employees).

Activity 3.2: Marginal cost

A private school's average annual cost per pupil is £6,300. Teachers at the school can have their children educated there free of charge. Each extra pupil increases the total annual costs of the school by £2,400. What is the annual taxable benefit for a teacher earning £16,000 a year with two children at the school?

2.2 **The above rule does not apply to employees who are not directors and earn less than £8,500 a year. For them benefits are taxed on their 'cash equivalent', the amount they would fetch if the employee were to dispose of them to a third party.** So if an employer spent £200 on a suit and gave it to an employee earning £9,000 a year, the taxable benefit would be £200. If, on the other hand, the employee earned £7,000 a year, the benefit would be the secondhand value, which might be only £10.

2.3 **Several rules override the cost or secondhand value rule,** as follows:

Vouchers

2.4 If an employee:

(a) receives cash vouchers (vouchers exchangeable for cash);
(b) uses a credit token (such as a credit card) to obtain money, goods or services; or
(c) receives exchangeable vouchers (such as book tokens), also called non-cash vouchers

he is taxed on the cost of providing the benefit, less any amount made good.

2.5 **The first 15p per working day of luncheon vouchers is not taxed.**

Entertainment

2.6 In general no benefit in kind arises on entertainment received by employees from third parties, even if it is provided by giving the employee a voucher.

The exemption also covers gifts of goods (or vouchers exchangeable for goods) if the total cost (including VAT) of all gifts by the same donor to the same employee in the tax year is £150 or less. If the limit is exceeded, the full amount is taxable, not just the excess over £150.

Part A: Income tax

Long service awards

2.7 Awards for long service are in general taxable, but there is an exemption where the period of service is at least 20 years, no similar award has been made to the same employee within the past ten years and the cost is not more than £20 per year of service.

Suggestion schemes

2.8 Awards to employees under suggestion schemes are in general taxable, but there is an exemption for the first £5,000 of awards if all the following conditions are satisfied:

(a) There is a formal scheme, open to all employees on equal terms.

(b) The suggestion rewarded is outside the scope of the employee's normal duties.

(c) Either the award is not more than £25, or the award is only made after a decision is taken to implement the suggestion.

(d) Awards over £25 reflect the financial importance of the suggestion to the business, and either do not exceed 50% of the expected net financial benefit during the first year of implementation or do not exceed 10% of the expected net financial benefit over a period of up to five years.

(e) Awards of over £25 are shared on a reasonable basis between two or more employees putting forward the same suggestion.

Accommodation

2.9 **The taxable value of accommodation provided to any employee or director is** its annual value (taken to be the **rateable value**, despite the abolition of domestic rates). **If the premises are rented** rather than owned by the employer, then **the value to the employee is the higher of the rent actually paid and the annual value**. Where property does not have a rateable value the Revenue estimate a value.

2.10 **Where the cost of any one property exceeds £75,000, an additional benefit in kind is chargeable upon the employee or director.** The additional benefit is

(Cost of providing the living accommodation - £75,000) × the official rate.

Thus with an official rate of 10%, the total benefit for accommodation costing £90,000 and with an annual value of £2,000 would be £2,000 + £(90,000 − 75,000) × 10% = £3,500.

The 'cost of providing' the living accommodation is the aggregate of the cost of purchase and the cost of any improvements made before the start of the tax year for which the benefit is being computed. It is therefore not possible to avoid the charge by buying an inexpensive property requiring substantial repairs and improving it.

Where the property was acquired more than six years before first being provided to the employee, the market value when first so provided plus the cost of subsequent improvements is used as the cost of providing the living accommodation. However, unless the actual cost plus improvements up to the start of the tax year in question exceeds £75,000, the additional charge cannot be imposed, however high the market value.

DEVOLVED ASSESSMENT ALERT

The 'official rate' of interest will be given to you in your assessment.

2.11 Any contribution paid by the employee is deducted from the annual value of the property, and then from the additional benefit.

2.12 **There is no taxable benefit in respect of job related accommodation.** Accommodation is job related if:

(a) residence in the accommodation is necessary for the proper performance of the employee's duties (as with a caretaker); or

(b) the accommodation is provided for the better performance of the employee's duties and the employment is of a kind in which it is customary for accommodation to be provided (as with a policeman); or

(c) the accommodation is provided as part of arrangements in force because of a special threat to the employee's security.

In these cases there is no tax charge in respect of the accommodation. Directors can only claim exemptions (a) or (b) if:

(i) they have no material interest ('material' means over 5%) in the company; and

(ii) either they are full time working directors or the company is non-profit making or is a charity.

2.13 If an employer pays an employee's council tax, the amount paid is always a taxable benefit, unless the tax arises in connection with job related accommodation.

Activity 3.3: Accommodation benefit

A company bought a house in 2000 for £420,000. On 1 January 2001, it was first provided to an employee who has occupied it since then. The rateable value is £1,600. If the official rate of interest was 6.25% on 6 April 2001, what is the taxable benefit for 2001/02?

Removal expenses and benefits

2.14 An employer may pay removal costs for a new employee or for an employee changing his place of work and his family. **There is no taxable benefit in respect of the first £8,000 of such expenses or benefits.** The benefits are valued under the normal benefits rules for the employee concerned. **Payments above the £8,000 limit are taxable,** but PAYE need not be applied to them.

2.15 For the exemption to apply:

(a) The employee must not already live within a reasonable daily travelling distance of his new place of employment, but will do so after moving.

(b) The expenses must be incurred or the benefits provided by the end of the tax year following the tax year of the start of employment at the new location.

Work related benefits

2.16 **If an employer runs a workplace nursery the cost is not a taxable benefit for the employees.** However, cash or vouchers given so that employees can obtain nursery facilities, are taxable.

2.17 **Sporting or recreational facilities available to employees generally and not to the general public do not give rise to taxable benefits,** unless they are provided on domestic

premises, or they consist in an interest in or the use of any mechanically propelled vehicle or any overnight accommodation. Vouchers only exchangeable for such facilities also do not give rise to taxable benefits, but membership fees for sports clubs are taxable benefits.

2.18 Subject to certain exemptions for potentially high value benefits (eg cars and living accommodation), no taxable benefit arises on assets or services used in performing the duties of employment provided any private use of the item concerned is insignificant. This exempts, for example, the benefit arising on the private use of employer-provided tools.

2.19 Welfare counselling and other similar minor benefits are exempt if the benefit concerned is available to employees generally.

Authorised mileage rates

2.20 If an employee uses his own car, pedal cycle or motor cycle on his employer's business, he will normally be paid a mileage allowance. Strictly, this **mileage allowance is taxable. The employee is entitled to make a claim under s 198 ICTA 1988 to deduct any expenses incurred wholly, exclusively and necessarily in the performance of his duties.**

2.21 To facilitate the above employers must return details to tax offices of amounts paid to individual employees. Employees than have to make detailed claims for relief based on their actual expenditure. These reporting and record keeping requirements can be avoided by using **Inland Revenue Authorised Mileage Rates (AMRs)** (previously known as the fixed profit car scheme). If an employer pays amounts at or below the AMRs he may apply to his tax office for a dispensation which will relieve him of the obligation to report expense payments.

2.22 AMRs are the levels of mileage allowances that may be paid free of income tax to employees who use their own cars, pedal cycles and motorcycles for business travel. Any excess allowance received is a taxable benefit. In general, the employee cannot also make a s 198 ICTA 1988 claim in respect of any business expenses actually incurred but exceptionally, a deduction for the business proportion of any interest paid on a loan taken out to buy a car, pedal cycle of motorcycle may be claimed.

2.23 AMRs for 2001/02 are set out in the Rates and Allowances Tables in this text.

Activity 3.4: Authorised mileage rates

Anita travels 9,000 business miles in her own 1800cc car during 2001/02. Her employer pays a mileage allowance of 35p per mile for cars with up to 2000cc engines. What taxable benefit arises on Anita?

2.24 AMRs can be used as a basis for an expense claim if the employee does not receive a mileage allowance or receives less than the tax free amount. So, if Anita in the above example had received total mileage allowances of less than the tax free amount she could also have made a claim to deduct the excess.

Bicycles and motorcycles

2.25 **There is no taxable benefit in respect of bicycles or cycling safety equipment provided to enable employees to get to and from work or to travel between one workplace and**

3: The taxation of employment

another. The equipment must be available to the employer's employees generally. Also, it must be used mainly for the aforementioned journeys.

2.26 There is **no taxable benefit in respect of workplace parking** for bicycles or motorcycles.

Scholarship and apprenticeship schemes

2.27 If an employer allows an employee to go on a full-time course lasting at least a year, with average full-time attendance of at least 20 weeks a year, then the employer may pay the employee up to £7,000 a year tax free. However, if the £7,000 limit is exceeded, the whole amount paid is taxable income of the employee.

Work related training and Individual Learning Accounts

2.28 No taxable benefit arises in respect of work related training or any related cost. Similarly, no taxable benefit arises on:

(a) **Contributions paid directly to an individual learning account (ILA).** The ILA must be eligible for a grant or discount and contributions must be available to all employees on similar terms.

(b) **Any related costs whether paid directly or reimbursed to the employee.**

Air miles and car fuel coupons

2.29 If an employee flies on business, uses a company credit card or buys fuel for business travel, and thereby earns air miles or car fuel coupons which he uses for private purposes, there is no taxable benefit.

Travel

2.30 There is no taxable benefit in respect of work buses and minibuses or subsidies to public bus services provided employees pay the same fare as the public.

A works bus must have a seating capacity of 12 or more and a works minibus a seating capacity of 9 or more but not more than 12 and be available generally to employees of the employer concerned. The bus or minibus must mainly be used by employees for journeys to and from work and for journeys between workplaces.

2.31 The following amounts paid by an employer are exempt benefits.

(a) Transport/overnight costs where public transport is disrupted by industrial action.

(b) Late night taxis.

(c) Travel costs exceptionally incurred where car sharing arrangements unavoidably breakdown.

3 BENEFITS IN KIND: P11D EMPLOYEES

3.1 **The benefit in kind rules discussed in this section apply to directors and employees whose 'emoluments' are at the rate of £8,500 a year or more.** Such individuals are sometimes referred to as 'P11D employees' or as **'higher paid'** employees. A P11D is the form on which the employer must report the benefits available to these individuals to the Inland Revenue.

Part A: Income tax

3.2 **'Emoluments' for this purpose include salary, commissions, fees, reimbursed expenses and also benefits in kind taxable on such employees.** In other words, one must assume that an employee falls into this category in order to determine whether or not he really does. In seeing whether he does, we ignore any deductible expenses.

3.3 An individual is not, however, subject to the special benefit in kind rules solely because he is a director, if he has no material interest in the company ('material' means more than 5%) and either:

(a) He is a full time working director, or
(b) The company is either non-profit making or is established for charitable purposes.

But such a person will be subject to the special rules if he earns £8,500 or more a year.

3.4 A benefit is taxable if it arises 'by reason of the employment' and is provided either to the employee or to a member of his family or household. There is no need for the employer to provide it directly.

General business expenses

3.5 **If business expenses on such items as travel or hotel stays, are reimbursed by an employer, the reimbursed amount is a taxable benefit.** To avoid being taxed on this amount, **an employee must then make a claim to deduct it as an expense** under the rules set out in Section 4 below. **In practice, however, many such expense payments are not reported to the Inland Revenue and can be ignored because it is agreed in advance that a claim to deduct them would be possible (a P11D dispensation).**

3.6 When an individual has to spend one or more nights away from home, his employer may reimburse expenses on items incidental to his absence (for example meals and private telephone calls). Such incidental expenses are not taxable if:

(a) The expenses of travelling to each place where the individual stays overnight, throughout the trip, are incurred necessarily in the performance of the duties of the employment (or would have been, if there had been any expenses), and

(b) The total (for the whole trip) of incidental expenses not deductible under the usual rules is no more than £5 for each night. If this limit is exceeded, all of the expenses are taxable, not just the excess.

3.7 This **incidental expenses exemption** applies to expenses reimbursed, and to benefits obtained using credit tokens and non-cash vouchers.

Expenses connected with living accommodation

3.8 In addition to the benefit of living accommodation itself, which is taxable on all employees, **employees earning £8,500 or more a year and directors are taxed on related expenses paid by the employer,** such as:

(a) **Heating, lighting or cleaning the premises**
(b) **Repairing, maintaining or decorating the premises**
(c) **The provision of furniture** (the annual value is 20% of the cost)

3.9 Unless the accommodation qualifies as 'job related' **the full cost of ancillary services** (excluding structural repairs) **is taxable.** If the accommodation is 'job related', however, **taxable ancillary services are restricted to a maximum of 10% of the employee's 'net** emoluments'. For this purpose, net emoluments are all amounts taxable under Schedule E (excluding the ancillary benefits (a) - (c) above) less any allowable expenses, contributions to approved occupational pension schemes (but not personal pension schemes) and personal pension plans, and capital allowances. If there are ancillary benefits other than those falling within (a) - (c) above (such as a telephone) they are taxable in full.

Activity 3.5: Expenses connected with living accommodation

Mr Quinton has a gross salary in 2001/02 of £28,850. He normally lives and works in London, but he is required to live in a company house in Scotland which cost £70,000 three years ago, so that he can carry out a two year review of his company's operations in Scotland. The annual value of the house is £650. In 2001/02 the company pays an electricity bill of £550, a gas bill of £400, a gardener's bill of £750 and redecoration costs of £1,800. Mr Quinton makes a monthly contribution of £50 for his accommodation. He also pays £1,450 occupational pension contributions.

Calculate the Schedule E income for 2001/02.

Cars

3.10 For employees earning **£8,500 or more a year and directors**, a car provided by reason of the employment gives rise to a taxable benefit.

(a) The benefit chargeable to tax each year is found as follows.

(Price of car – capital contributions) × % × age factor

(b) The price of the car is the sum of the following items.

(i) The list price of the car for a single retail sale at the time of first registration, including charges for delivery and standard accessories. The manufacturer's, importer's or distributor's list price must be used, even if the retailer offered a discount. A notional list price is estimated if no list price was published.

(ii) The price (including fitting) of all optional accessories provided when the car was first provided to the employee, excluding mobile telephones and equipment needed by a disabled employee. The extra cost of adapting or manufacturing a car to run on road fuel gases is not included.

(iii) The price of all optional accessories fitted later and costing at least £100 each. Such accessories affect the taxable benefit from and including the tax year in which they are fitted.

Mobile telephones and amounts needed by disabled employees do not count as accessories.

(c) If a classic car is at least 15 years old (from the time of first registration) at the end of the tax year, and its market value at the end of the year (or, if earlier, when it ceased to be available to the employee) is over £15,000 and greater than the price found under (c), that market value is used instead of the price. The market value takes account of all accessories (except mobile telephones and equipment needed by a disabled employee).

(d) If the price or value found under (c) or (d) exceeds £80,000, then £80,000 is used instead of the price or value.

(e) Capital contributions are payments by the employee in respect of the price of the car or accessories. In any tax year, we take account of capital contributions made in that year and previous years (for the same car). The maximum deductible capital contributions is £5,000: contributions beyond that total are ignored.

Part A: Income tax

(f) If the car is at least four years old (from the date of first registration) at the end of the tax year, then the age factor is ¾. Otherwise it is 1.

(g) The 'percentage' for 2001/02 depends on the **business** mileage in the tax year:

Business mileage	First car	Other cars
Less than 2,500	35%	35%
At least 2,500, less than 18,000	25%	35%
At least 18,000	15%	25%

The 'other cars' percentages apply when two or more cars are provided simultaneously. The car with the greatest business mileage is the first car, and the 'first car' percentages are used for that car only.

(h) The benefit is reduced on a time basis where a car is first made available or ceases to be made available during the tax year or is incapable of being used for a continuous period of not less than 30 days (for example because it is being repaired). The mileage factor limits of 2,500 and 18,000 miles are also reduced on a time basis in such cases. If a car is unavailable for less than 30 days and a replacement car of similar quality is provided, the replacement car is ignored and business mileage in it counts as business mileage in the usual car.

(i) The benefit is reduced by any payment the user must make for the private use of the car (as distinct from a capital contribution to the cost of the car). Payments for insuring the car do not count. The benefit cannot become negative to create a deduction from the employee's income.

(j) Pool cars are exempt. A car is a pool car if **all** the following conditions are satisfied.

- It is used by more than one director or employee and is not ordinarily used by any one of them to the exclusion of the others.

- Any private use is merely incidental to business use.

- It is not normally kept overnight at or near the residence of a director or employee.

Activity 3.6: Car benefit

On 1 July 2001 Sue was provided with a new car by her employer. The list price of the car was £10,000. Sue drove 16,000 business miles in the nine months to 5 April 2002. What is the taxable benefit?

Fuel for cars

3.11 **Where fuel is provided there is a further benefit on a set scale in addition to the car benefit.** The fuel benefits are given in the Rates and Allowances Tables in this text.

No taxable benefit arises where either

(a) All the fuel provided was made available only for business travel, or

(b) The employee is required to make good, and has made good, the whole of the cost of any fuel provided for his private use.

Unlike most benefits, a reimbursement of only part of the cost of the fuel available for private use does not reduce the scale charge.

The benefit is reduced in the same way as the car benefit if the car is not available for 30 days or more, but it is not adjusted for business mileage.

3: The taxation of employment

3.12 There are many ancillary benefits associated with the provision of cars, such as insurance, repairs, vehicle licences and a parking space at or near work. No extra taxable benefit arises as a result of these, with the exception of the cost of providing a driver.

Activity 3.7: Car and Fuel benefit

An employee was provided with a new car (2,500 cc) costing £15,000. During 2001/02 the employer spent £900 on insurance, repairs and a vehicle licence. The employee did 20,000 miles of which 15,000 were on business. The firm paid for all petrol, costing £1,500, without reimbursement. The employee paid the firm £270 for the private use of the car. Calculate the taxable benefit.

Vans and heavier commercial vehicles

3.13 **If a van** (of normal maximum laden weight up to 3,500 kg) **is made available for an employee's private use, there is an annual scale charge of £500, or £350 if the van is at least four years old at the end of the tax year.** The scale charge covers ancillary benefits such as insurance and servicing (but not van telephones). Paragraphs 3.10 (h) and (i) above apply to vans as they do to cars, but there is no adjustment for mileage.

3.14 If a commercial vehicle of normal maximum laden weight over 3,500 kg is made available for an employee's private use, but the employee's use of the vehicle is not wholly or mainly private, no taxable benefit arises except in respect of the provision of a driver.

Mobile telephones

3.15 **No taxable benefit arises in respect of a mobile telephone** made available to an employee or a member of his family **(the employer retaining ownership of the telephone)**.

Activity 3.8: Mobile Telephones

In April 2001, Sarah's employer provided her with a mobile phone on which she made both business and private calls. Her employer paid £100 for the phone and £300 for calls in 2001/02. Sarah estimates that 50% of her calls are private calls. What taxable benefit arises in respect of Sarah's use of the phone in 2001/02?

Other assets made available for private use

3.16 **Assets made available to employees earning £8,500 or more a year and directors are taxable on an annual value of 20% of the market value when first provided as a benefit to any employee, or on the rent paid by the employer if higher.** The 20% charge is time-apportioned when the asset is provided for only part of the year. The charge after any time apportionment is reduced by any contribution made by the employee.

3.17 If an asset made available is subsequently acquired by the employee, **the taxable benefit on the acquisition is the *greater* of:**

- The **current market value minus the price paid by the employee.**

- The **market value when first provided minus any amounts already taxed (ignoring contributions by the employee) minus the price paid by the employee.**

This rule prevents tax free benefits arising on rapidly depreciating items through the employee purchasing them at their low secondhand value.

3.18 EXAMPLE: ASSETS MADE AVAILABLE FOR PRIVATE USE

A suit costing £400 is purchased by an employer for use by an employee on 6 April 2000. On 6 April 2001 the suit is purchased by the employee for £30, its market value then being £50.

The benefit in 2000/01 is £400 × 20% £80

The benefit in 2001/02 is £290, being the *greater* of:

		£
(a)	Market value at acquisition by employee	50
	Less price paid	(30)
		20

		£
(b)	Original market value	400
	Less taxed in respect of use	(80)
		320
	Less price paid	(30)
		290

Computer equipment

3.19 **The first £500 of any benefit which arises under the above rules in respect of computer equipment** made available for the private use of an employee is **exempt**. If the benefit exceeds £500, the excess is taxable.

Activity 3.9: Computer equipment

On 6 March 2001, Tim's employer lent him computer equipment costing £3,800. This equipment, which was situated at Tim's home, was used by Tim for both personal and work purposes. What taxable benefit arises in 2001/02 in respect of Tim's use of the computer?

Assets sold to employers

3.20 If an employee sells an asset to his employer (for example his house when he is being relocated), **there is a taxable benefit of the amount paid minus the market value of the asset**. If the employer pays his own transaction costs (for example solicitors' fees), they do not count as a taxable benefit. However, if the employer pays the employee's transaction costs, there is a taxable benefit unless a specific exemption (for example the removal expenses exemption) applies.

Scholarships

3.21 If scholarships are given to members of a director's or employee's family, the director or **employee is taxable on the cost** unless the scholarship fund's or scheme's payments by reason of people's employments are not more than 25% of its total payments.

PAYE tax liabilities

3.22 **If a company pays any PAYE tax** on behalf of a director (not an employee), **any amount not made good by the director is a taxable benefit**. Directors with no material interest in the company (that is, not more than 5%) who are full time working directors or who work for non profit making or charitable companies are excluded from this rule.

Beneficial loans

3.23 **Loans to employees, directors and their families give rise to a benefit equal to:**

(a) **Any amounts written off** (unless the employee has died), and

(b) **The excess of the interest based on an official rate prescribed by the Treasury, over any interest actually charged.**

3.24 In general, a loan made in the ordinary course of the employer's money lending business is ignored altogether for the purposes of computing taxable income because of low interest (but not for the purposes of the charge on loans written off). A loan made by an individual in the ordinary course of his domestic arrangements is similarly ignored.

Calculating the interest benefit

3.25 There are two alternative methods of calculating the taxable benefit. The simpler **'average' method** automatically applies unless the taxpayer or the Revenue elect for the alternative **'strict' method**. (The Revenue normally only make the election where it appears that the 'average' method is being deliberately exploited.) In both methods, the benefit is the interest at the official rate minus the interest payable.

3.26 The 'average' method averages the balances at the beginning and end of the tax year (or the dates on which the loan was made and discharged if it was not in existence throughout the tax year) and applies the official rate of interest to this average. If the loan was not in existence throughout the tax year only the number of complete tax months (from the 6th of the month) for which it existed are taken into account.

3.27 The 'strict' method is to compute interest at the official rate on the actual amount outstanding on a daily basis.

Activity 3.10: Loan benefit

At 6 April 2001 a low interest loan of £30,000 was outstanding to an employee earning £12,000 a year, who repaid £20,000 on 7 December 2001. The remaining balance of £10,000 was outstanding at 5 April 2002. Interest paid during the year was £250. What was the benefit under both methods for 2001/02, assuming that the official rate of interest was 6.25%?

The de minimis test

3.28 **The benefit is not taxable if:**

(a) The **total of all loans to the employee did not exceed £5,000** at any time in the tax year, or

(b) **The loan is not a qualifying loan and the total of all non-qualifying loans to the employee did not exceed £5,000** at any time in the tax year.

3.29 **A qualifying loan is one on which any interest would qualify as a charge.**

3.30 In applying the £5,000 test, ignore any loans which are to be ignored under the rules above.

3.31 When the £5,000 threshold is exceeded, a benefit arises on interest on the whole loan, not just on the excess of the loan over £5,000.

Part A: Income tax

3.32 When a loan is written off and a benefit arises, there is no £5,000 threshold: writing off a loan of £1 gives rise to a £1 benefit.

Activity 3.11: Loan benefit

An employer lends an employee £4,000 to buy a car, interest-free for six months. The official rate of interest is 6.25%. 65% of the loan is then repaid, and the balance is written off. What is the total taxable benefit?

Qualifying loans

3.33 When an employee is treated as receiving emoluments because the actual rate of interest is below the official rate, he is also treated as paying interest equal to the emoluments. If the loan is used in a business for some other qualifying purpose, this **deemed interest paid may qualify as a business expense or as a charge in addition to any interest actually paid.**

Activity 3.12: Beneficial loans

Anna, who is single, has an annual salary of £30,000, and two loans from her employer.

(a) A season ticket loan of £2,300 at no interest
(b) A loan to buy shares in her employee-controlled company of £54,000 at 3% interest

The official rate of interest is to be taken as 6.25%.

What is Anna's tax liability for 2001/02?

Medical services and insurance

3.34 The cost of medical diagnosis and treatment provided by an employer is a taxable benefit, except for the cost of routine check-ups. **Private medical insurance premiums are also taxable benefits.**

Staff parties

3.35 The **cost of staff parties is taxable, except** when the parties are open to staff generally and the **cost per staff member per year is £75 or less**. The £75 limit may be split between several parties. If it is exceeded, the full amount is taxable, not just the excess over £75.

Uniforms

3.36 No taxable benefit arises in respect of employer provided uniforms which employees must wear as part of their duties.

4 ALLOWABLE DEDUCTIONS

4.1 Certain types of expenditure are specifically deductible against Schedule E income:

(a) **Contributions** (within certain limits) **to approved occupational pension schemes.**

(b) **Subscriptions to professional bodies** on the list of bodies issued by the Inland Revenue (which includes most UK professional bodies), if relevant to the duties of the employment

(c) Payments for certain liabilities and for insurance against them

(d) Payments to charity made under the payroll deduction scheme operated by an employer

4.2 Otherwise, **Schedule E deductions are notoriously hard to obtain. They are limited to:**

(a) **Qualifying travel expenses** (see below)

(b) **Other expenses incurred wholly, exclusively and necessarily in the performance of the duties of the employment**

(c) **Capital allowances on plant and machinery necessarily provided for use in the performance of those duties. Capital allowances may currently be claimed in respect of an employee's car or bicycle used for business purposes without having to satisfy the necessarily test.**

Liabilities and insurance

4.3 If a director or employee incurs a qualifying liability or pays for insurance against such a liability, the cost is a deductible expense. If the employer pays such amounts, there is no taxable benefit in kind.

4.4 A qualifying liability is one which is imposed in respect of the director's or employee's acts or omissions as director or employee. Thus, for example, liability for negligence would be covered. Related costs, for example the costs of legal proceedings, are included.

Travelling expenses

4.5 **Tax relief is not available for an employee's normal commuting costs.** This means relief is not available for any costs an employee incurs in getting from home to his normal place of work. However **employees are entitled to relief for 'qualifying travelling expenses' which basically are the full costs that they are obliged to incur in travelling in the performance of their duties or travelling to or from a place which they have to attend in the performance of their duties (other than the normal place of work).**

4.6 **EXAMPLE: TRAVEL IN THE PERFORMANCE OF DUTIES**

Judi is an accountant. She often travels to meetings at the firm's offices in the North of England returning to her office in Leeds after the meetings. Relief is available for the full cost of these journeys as the travel is undertaken in the performance of her duties.

Activity 3.13: Relief for travelling costs

Zoe lives in Wycombe and normally works in Chiswick. Occasionally she visits a client in Wimbledon and travels direct from home. Distances are shown in the diagram below:

Part A: Income tax

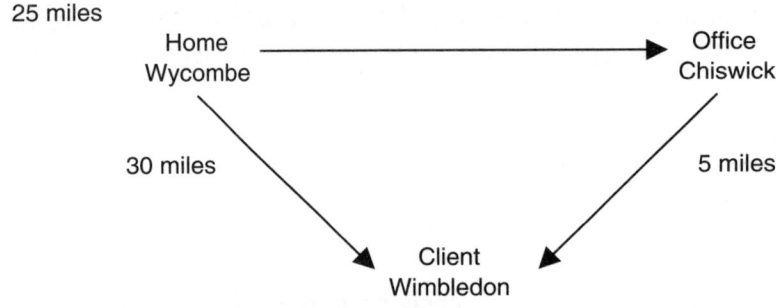

What tax relief is available for Zoe's travel costs?

4.7 To prevent manipulation of the basic rule normal commuting will not become a business journey just because the employee stops en-route to perform a business task (eg make a 'phone call'). Nor will relief be available if the journey is essentially the same as the employee's normal journey to work.

4.8 EXAMPLE: NORMAL COMMUTING

Judi is based at her office in Leeds City Centre. One day she is required to attend a 9.00 am meeting with a client whose premises are around the corner from her Leeds office. Judi travels from home directly to the meeting. As the journey is substantially the same as her ordinary journey to work relief is not available.

4.9 Site based employees (eg construction workers, management consultants etc) who do not have a permanent work place, are entitled to relief for the costs of all journeys made from home to wherever they are working. This is because these employees do not have an ordinary commuting journey or any normal commuting costs. However there is a caveat that the employee does not spend more than 24 months of continuous work at any one site.

4.10 Tax relief is available for travel, accommodation and subsistence expenses incurred by an employee who is working at a temporary location on a secondment expected to last up to 24 months. If a secondment is initially expected not to exceed 24 months, but it is extended, relief ceases to be due from the date the employee becomes aware of the change. When looking at how long a secondment is expected to last, the Revenue will consider not only the terms of the written contract but also any verbal agreement by the employer and other factors such as whether the employee buys a house etc.

Activity 3.14: Temporary workplace

Philip works for Vastbank at its Newcastle City Centre branch. Philip is sent to work full-time at another branch in Morpeth for 20 months at the end of which he will return to the Newcastle branch. Morpeth is about 20 miles north of Newcastle.

What travel costs is Philip entitled to claim as a deduction?

Other expenses

4.11 The word 'exclusively' strictly implies that the expenditure must give no private benefit at all. If it does, none of it is deductible. In practice inspectors may ignore a small element of private benefit or allow an apportionment between business and private use.

4.12 Whether an expense is 'necessary' is not determined by what the employer requires. The test is whether the duties of the employment could not be performed without the outlay.

4.13 The cost of business telephone calls on a private telephone is deductible, but **no part of the line or telephone rental charges is deductible** (*Lucas v Cattell 1972*).

4.14 **The cost of clothes for work is not deductible**, except that for certain trades requiring protective clothing there are annual deductions on a set scale.

4.15 Journalists cannot claim a deduction for the cost of buying newspapers which they read to keep themselves informed, since they are merely preparing themselves to perform their duties.

4.16 **An employee required to work at home may be able to claim a deduction for an appropriate proportion of his or her expenditure on lighting, heating and** (if a room is used exclusively for work purposes) **the council tax.**

5 THE PAYE SYSTEM

5.1 **The objective of the PAYE system is to deduct the correct amount of tax over the year. Its scope is very wide. It applies to most cash payments, other than reimbursed business expenses, and to certain non cash payments.**

5.2 In addition to wages and salaries, PAYE applies to taxable lump sum payments on leaving most lump sum payments on joining, round sum expense allowances and payments instead of benefits in kind. It also applies to any readily convertible asset.

5.3 **It is the employer's duty to deduct income tax from the pay of his employees,** whether or not he has been directed to do so by the Revenue. **If he fails to do this he** (or sometimes the employee) **must pay over the tax which he should have deducted and the employer may be subject to penalties.** Interest will also run from 14 days after the end of the tax year concerned on any underpaid PAYE.

How PAYE works

5.4 To operate PAYE the employer needs:
   (a) deductions working sheets;
   (b) codes for employees that reflect the tax allowances to which the employees are entitled;
   (c) tax tables.

5.5 **The employer works out the amount of PAYE tax to deduct on any particular pay day by using the employees code number (see below) in conjunction with the PAYE tables. The tables are designed so that tax is normally worked out on a cumulative basis.** This means that with each payment of emoluments the running total of tax paid is compared with tax due on total emoluments to that date. The difference between the tax due and the tax paid is the tax to be deducted on that particular payday.

5.6 Although PAYE is normally operated on a cumulative basis, an employee may have a week 1/month 1 code. In this case the figures for pay and tax deducted are not cumulated, and the tax on each payday is worked out on the pay on that payday as if it were the first payday in the tax year.

5.7 **Under PAYE tax is normally paid over to the Inland Revenue monthly, 14 days after the end of each tax month.**

5.8 The PAYE system is also used to collect student loan repayments.

Part A: Income tax

5.9 If an employer's average monthly payments under the PAYE system are less than £1,500, the employer may choose to pay quarterly, within 14 days of the end of each tax quarter. Tax quarters end on 5 July, 5 October, 5 January and 5 April.

PAYE codes

5.10 An employee is normally entitled to various allowances. Under the PAYE system an amount reflecting the effect of a proportion of these allowances is set against his pay each pay day. To determine the amount to set against his pay the allowances are expressed in the form of a code which is used in conjunction with the Pay Adjustment Tables (Tables A).

5.11 An employee's code may be any one of the following:

(a) a code of one, two or three numbers followed by a single suffix letter (a suffix code): for example 453L. The letter allows the Revenue to tell the employer how the code should be adjusted each year to take account of Budget changes. The letter L indicates that an individual is entitled to the personal allowance but other allowance.

(b) the prefix D is usually followed by the number 0; these codes apply on a one-off basis and require the use of higher rate tax tables D.

(c) code BR, which means that tax will be deducted at the basic rate with no tax free allowances;

(d) code NT, which means that no tax is to be deducted;

(e) a code with a K prefix, followed by one to four numbers.

5.12 **Generally, a tax code number is arrived at by deleting the last digit in the sum representing the employee's tax free allowances.** Every individual is entitled to a personal tax free allowance of £4,535. The code number for an individual who is entitled to this but no other allowance is 453L.

The code number may also reflect other items. For example, **it will be restricted to reflect benefits in kind, small amounts of untaxed income** and **unpaid Schedule E tax from earlier years.** If an amount of tax is in point, it is necessary to gross up the tax in the code using the taxpayers estimated marginal rate of income tax.

Activity 3.15: PAYE codes

Adrian is a 40 year old single man (suffix letter L) who earns £15,000 pa. He has benefits in kind of £560 and his unpaid Schedule E tax for 2000/01 was £57.50. As Adrian is single he is entitled to a tax free personal allowance of £4,535 in 2001/02.

Adrian pays income tax at the marginal rate of 22%.

What is Adrian's PAYE code for 2001/02?

5.13 Codes are determined and amended by the Revenue. They are normally notified to the employer on a code list. The employer must act on the code notified to him until amended instructions are received from the Revenue, even if the employee has appealed against the code.

5.14 **By using the code number in conjunction with the tax tables, an employee is generally given $1/52^{nd}$ or $1/12^{th}$ of his tax free allowances against each week's/month's pay.**

However because of the cumulative nature of PAYE, if an employee is first paid in, say, September, that month he will receive six months' allowances against his gross pay.

5.15 **'K' codes increase taxable pay instead of reducing it**. This means benefits exceed allowances. The PAYE deducted under a K code could remove all of an employee's actual remuneration for a pay period. As this could cause hardship, **the PAYE deducted on any payday is not to exceed 50% of the amount of actual remuneration on that pay day.** (This overriding limit does not restrict the tax on non cash payments).

Employer's responsibilities: year end returns and employees leaving or joining

5.16 At the end of each tax year, the employer must provide each employee with a form P60. This shows total taxable emoluments for the year, tax deducted, code number and the employer's name and address. **The P60 must be provided by 31 May following the year of assessment.** In your assessment you may be given a P60 as a source document provided by the client. You would then be expected to obtain information for salary and tax deducted at source from the form. A sample P60 is included in the Appendix to this text. Familiarise yourself with it now.

5.17 Following the end of each tax year, the employer must send the Revenue:

(a) **by 19 May;**

    (i) **End of year Returns P14** (showing the same details as the P60);
    (ii) **Form P35** (summary of tax deducted).

(b) **by 6 July:**

    (i) **Forms P11D** (benefits in kind etc for P11D employees);
    (ii) **Forms P9D** (benefits in kind etc for other employees).

5.18 **A copy of the form P11D (or P9D) must also be provided to the employee by 6 July**. The details shown on the P11D include the full cash equivalent of all benefits, so that the employee may enter the details on his self-assessment tax return. Specific reference numbers for the entries on the P11D are also used on the employment supplementary pages of the self assessment tax return.

5.19 The full value of any assessable benefits must usually be entered on Form P11D. Employees must then make a separate s 198 claim in respect of any expenses incurred wholly, exclusively and necessarily for the purposes of the employment. Alternatively, employers sometimes reach an agreement with the Revenue that certain expenses reimbursed to employees are tax deductible and do not need to be entered on form P11D. The company is then said to have a **'P11D Dispensation'** covering these items.

5.20 A copy of Form P11D is produced in the Appendix to this text. Have a look at it now. Again you may be provided with the form in your assessment. You can practise using the form if you work through the assessments in the Devolved Assessment Kit produced by BPP for Unit 19.

5.21 **When an employee leaves, a certificate on form P45 (particulars of Employee Leaving) must be prepared. This form shows the employee's code and details of his income and tax paid to date and is a four part form. One part is sent to the Revenue, and three parts handed to the employee. One of the parts (part 1A) is the employee's personal copy. If the employee takes up a new employment, he must hand the other two parts of the form P45 to the new employer. The new employer will fill in details of the new employment**

Part A: Income tax

and send one part to the Revenue, retaining the other. The details on the form are used by the new employer to calculate the PAYE due on the next payday.

PAYE settlement agreements

5.22 **PAYE settlement agreements (PSAs) are arrangements under which employers can make single payments to settle their employees' income tax liabilities on expense payments and certain benefits in kind.** Benefits may be included in a PSA if the Inspector considers them to be minor (eg small gifts), irregular (eg, relocation payments of over £8,000) or benefits in respect of which it is impractical to apply PAYE or identify the amount attributable to a particular employee (eg free dental care). Items covered by a PSA do not have to be included on either Forms P9D or P11D or on the employee's tax return.

5.23 PSAs cannot be used to settle tax on:

(a) cash payments of salaries, wages or bonuses

(b) major benefits provided regularly for the sole use of individual employees (for example, company cars)

(c) round sum allowances

Charitable donations under the payroll deduction scheme

5.24 Employees can make tax deductible donations under the payroll deduction scheme to an approved charity of their choice by asking their employer to deduct the donation from their gross earnings prior to calculating PAYE due thereon. The government will pay a 10% supplement on all donations made under the scheme before 6 April 2003.

6 PENSIONS

6.1 The main ways in which individuals can provide for a pension are:

- the state pension scheme;
- occupational pension schemes;
- personal pension schemes.

The state scheme has no impact on income tax during an individual's working career, but the other two systems are discussed below.

Occupational pension schemes

> **KEY TERM**
>
> An employer may set up an **occupational pension scheme** for employees. Such a scheme may either require contributions from employees or be non-contributory.

6.2 Schemes can be of two kinds: Revenue approved and unapproved. **Approved schemes have significant tax advantages** that have made them very popular.

6.3 **The advantages for an employee are:**

- **contributions made by the employee are deductible from his Schedule E income** (up to a limit of 15% of gross emoluments, with gross emoluments limited to the earnings cap (see below));

3: The taxation of employment

- **the employer's contributions are not regarded as benefits in kind for the employee;**
- **the fund of contributions, and the income and gains arising from their investment, are not, in general, liable to tax.** It is this long-term tax-free accumulation of funds that makes approved schemes so beneficial;
- provision can be made for a **lump sum** to be **paid on the employee's death in service.** Provided that it does not exceed four times his final remuneration, it is **tax-free**;
- **a tax-free lump sum may be paid to the employee on retirement.**

6.4 The following limits apply to an approved occupational pension scheme.

- The maximum pension is normally two thirds of the individual's final remuneration, being calculated as one sixtieth for each year of service, with a maximum of 40 years.
- A scheme may provide for part of the pension to be taken as a lump sum. The maximum lump sum is 1.5 times final remuneration, being calculated as 3/80 for each year of service, with a maximum of 40 years.

6.5 The Revenue have discretion to approve schemes which do not comply with these limits. In particular, many schemes provide for a pension of two thirds of final salary after less than 40 years service.

The earnings cap

6.6 An earnings cap applies to tax-approved occupational pension schemes. The cap is £95,400 for 2001/02.

6.7 The earnings cap has two consequences.
   (a) The maximum pension payable from an approved scheme is the cap × 2/3.
   (b) The maximum tax-free lump sum is the cap × 1.5.

Additional voluntary contributions

6.8 **An employee who feels that his employer's scheme is inadequate may make additional voluntary contributions (AVCs), either to the employer's scheme or to a separate scheme (freestanding AVCs). AVCs are deductible from the employee's taxable pay**, but only to the extent that they, plus any contributions by the employee to the employer's scheme, do not exceed 15% of gross emoluments (limited to the earnings cap). The limits on pensions and lump sums which may be taken must be applied to the total sums derived from the employer's scheme and the AVCs.

Freestanding AVCs are paid net of basic rate tax.

6.9 Employers can set up unapproved schemes, to operate alongside approved schemes. Employer's contributions to unapproved schemes are taxed as earnings of the employee. Employee's contributions are not tax-deductible.

Activity 3.16: AVCs

An employee earns £98,000 in 2001/02 and pays £3,500 a year in contributions to his employer's pension scheme. What is the maximum tax-deductible amount he may pay in AVCs?

Part A: Income tax

Personal pension schemes

6.10 The rules relating to personal pensions were substantially revised with effect from 6 April 2001. From this date a new type of personal pension scheme known as a '**Stakeholder' pension** became available.

Eligibility

6.11 **An individual who is below the age of 75** may contribute to a personal pension scheme in a tax year if he satisfies one of the following conditions:

(a) he has **no actual net relevant earnings** (see below) in the year and is not in an occupational pension scheme, or

(b) **he is in an occupational pension scheme** and is entitled to join a personal pension scheme under '**concurrent membership**' (see further below), or

(c) he has **actual net relevant earnings** in the year.

6.12 **It is possible for a personal pension scheme to accept payments from a person other than the scheme member where that member satisfies condition (a).** Thus a parent may make contributions for his child (even under the age of 18) or a working spouse could contribute on behalf of a housewife/husband. **If a scheme member is employed (ie falls under condition (b) or (c)), his employer may make contributions to the personal pension scheme.**

6.13 **Concurrent membership** (ie. membership of both an occupational scheme and a personal pension scheme) is available, broadly, to an individual who:

(a) **is not a controlling director** of a company at any time in the tax year or in any tax year in the last five tax years (counting from 2000/01 onwards only), and

(b) **in at least one out of the last five tax years (counting from 2000/01 onwards only) his earnings were below the remuneration limit.** This is set as £30,000 for 2001/02.

A 'controlling director' is broadly an individual who owns or controls (by himself or with his family or business associates) more than 20% of the company which employs him.

Limits

Time of retirement

6.14 **Normal Retirement Age** can, in general, be at any time between 50 and 75.

Benefits

6.15 There are **no limits** on the amount of the pension allowable. At retirement the fund can be used to buy the highest annuity available.

6.16 It is also possible to take out a **tax-free cash lump sum** on retirement. There is **no restriction** on the **amount** of tax-free cash but it is limited to 25% of the size of the fund at the time. The individual effectively takes a reduced pension in order to obtain the tax free cash simply because only the balance (75%) of the fund remains for an annuity purchase (ie buying an annual pension).

3: The taxation of employment

Contributions

6.17 Although benefits are not limited, there is a restriction placed on **contributions**.

6.18 For individuals within 6.11(a) and (b) above (ie those with no net relevant earnings or with concurrent membership), **annual contributions (by the scheme member and anyone else, eg employer, parent) to the personal pension scheme cannot in total exceed the contributions threshold**. The contributions threshold is fixed at £3,600 for 2001/02. This figure includes tax relief at the basic rate. Therefore, net payments of £2,808 can be made into the scheme. This would be increased by tax relief of £792 (at 22%) given by the Inland Revenue to the pension provider to make up the total of £3,600 (see further below for more details on tax relief).

6.19 For individuals within 6.11(c) (those with net relevant earnings), **annual contributions (by the scheme member and anyone else, eg employer) to the personal pension scheme cannot in total exceed the greater of:**

(a) the **contributions threshold,** and
(b) the **relevant percentage of net relevant earnings** of the **basis year** (see further below).

Again, the amount determined under this test includes tax relief at basic rate. For example, if the permitted contributions were £5,000, a net payment of £3,900 could be made on which tax relief of £1,100 would be given by the Inland Revenue to the pension provider, resulting in a total payment of £5,000 into the personal pension fund.

Net relevant earnings in a tax year cannot exceed the earnings cap (£95,400 for 2001/02).

6.20 Net relevant earnings (NRE) is calculated thus.

	£	£
Earnings under Schedule D Cases I and II		X
Schedule E emoluments not providing occupational pension scheme rights		X
Schedule A income from furnished holiday lettings		X
		X
Less: the excess of trade charges over other income	X	
loss relief*	X	
Schedule E deductions	X	
		(X)
Net relevant earnings		X

* If, in any tax year for which an individual claims relief for a premium payment, a deduction for loss relief is made from income *other* than relevant earnings but that loss relates to activities any income from which *would* be relevant earnings, then the individual's NRE for the *next* tax year are treated as reduced by the loss. Any balance is carried forward to the third year and so on.

6.21 Non-trading charges are not deducted in arriving at NRE even if there is insufficient other income to deduct them from.

6.22 **In any tax year in which he has actual net relevant earnings, an individual may choose a basis year for his deemed net relevant earnings on which contributions are based.** This can be the **current tax year or one of the previous five tax years**. Therefore, for 2001/02 the basis year may be any year from 1996/97 to 2001/02. If a basis year is not chosen, only contributions up to the contributions threshold of £3,600 (gross) can be made.

6.23 The basis year need not be a tax year in which the individual was a member of the personal pension scheme.

Part A: Income tax

6.24 Once a basis year has been chosen, the level of net relevant earnings will be presumed to be the same in the basis year and the next five tax years. Therefore, if 2001/02 is chosen as the basis year, the level of NRE will be deemed to be the same for the years 2001/02 to 2006/07 inclusive and no further evidence of earnings needs to given. However, it is also possible to choose a new basis year with higher earnings within this time if the individual wishes to make increased contributions.

6.25 Having determined the basis year, the next stage is to determine the relevant percentage for the tax year of the contribution. The maximum contributions are:

Age at start *of tax year of contribution*	*% of NRE of the basis year*
Up to 35	17.5
36 - 45	20
46 - 50	25
51 - 55	30
56 - 60	35
61 - 74	40

Activity 3.17: Basis years and relevant percentages

An individual (born 13 January 1956) first has net relevant earnings for 2001/02 and wishes to make maximum personal pension contributions in that year and all following years. He expects to have the following net relevant earnings:

2001/02	£30,000
2002/03	£25,000
2003/04	£20,000
2004/05	£28,000
2005/06	£27,500
2006/07	£24,000
2007/08	£20,000
2008/09	£34,000

Show the maximum amount of pension contributions he can pay for 2001/02 up to 2008/09, assuming the rules in 2001/02 stay the same in later years.

6.26 There are also special rules where an individual ceases to have net relevant earnings which allow contributions to continue to be made above the contributions threshold, in the five years following the cessation.

The first year in which the individual has no net relevant earnings is known as '**the break year**'. The year in which net relevant earnings ceased is known as the '**cessation year**'. The cessation year and the five previous years are known as the '**reference years**'.

6.27 The individual may continue to make contributions based on NRE in the five tax years following the cessation year or, if earlier, until the individual has net relevant earnings again or becomes a member of an occupational pension scheme.

6.28 In determining the basis year for such contributions, **the individual may nominate any one of the reference years to be the basis year.**

Activity 3.18: Cessation

Sharon (born 7 March 1970) gives up work on 7 August 2001, prior to the birth of her first child. She intends to take a career break to stay at home with her small child(ren). Her NRE is:

3: The taxation of employment

1996/97	£40,000
1997/98	£38,000
1998/99	£35,000
1999/00	£37,000
2000/01	£30,000
2001/02	£10,000

What are the maximum contributions that Sharon may make for 2001/02 to 2007/08 inclusive? What would be the effect if Sharon returned to work in January 2004 and earns £8,000 in the tax year to 5 April 2004?

Assume the rules for 2001/02 also apply in later years.

6.29 Some of the premium paid can be used to secure a lump sum or an annuity for a spouse or dependants in the event of death prior to retirement age. The limit (which forms part of the overall limit) for such premiums is 10% of the total contribution (5% of NRE for schemes set up before 6 April 2001).

Carrying back premiums

6.30 It is possible in certain circumstances to treat a contribution as if it had been paid in the previous tax year. This is especially useful to self employed people who wish to maximise their contributions, but cannot determine their net relevant earnings until after the end of the tax year.

6.31 An irrevocable election must be made at or before the time the contribution is made for the carry back to take effect. The contribution must be made by 31 January following the end of the tax year in which the contribution is to be treated has having been paid. So, if a contribution is to be treated as paid in 2001/02 it must be paid by 31 January 2003.

6.32 It is possible to carry back a contribution paid by 31 January 2002 to 2000/01. This means that the contribution is subject to the old rules on carry forward of unused relief (see below).

Unused relief – rules up to 2000/01

6.33 **Unused relief was the amount by which premiums paid were less than the maximum calculated as a percentage of NRE of the year. It could be carried forward for six years.** For example, in 2000/01 unused relief from 1994/95 (six years earlier) to 1999/00 could be taken into account to increase the maximum allowable premium. Any unused relief at 6 April 2001 cannot be carried forward to 2001/02 (although it is possible to carry back a contribution made up to 31 January 2002 to 2000/01).

The relief available for a particular tax year must have been used before unused relief brought forward, and relief brought forward was used on a FIFO basis.

Activity 3.19: Relief for premiums paid

An individual born in 1976 who took out a PPS on 1 July 1997 has the following NRE and paid the following gross premiums.

	NRE	17½% of NRE	Gross premiums
	£	£	£
1997/98	35,000	6,125	5,800
1998/99	33,000	5,775	5,700
1999/00	38,000	6,650	6,850
2000/01	43,000	7,525	8,000

Show the relief available for premiums paid.

Part A: Income tax

6.34 Any contributions in excess of the amount eligible for relief must be repaid to the taxpayer.

Tax treatment of contributions

6.35 **All contributions to a personal pension scheme are treated as amounts paid net of basic rate tax.** The Inland Revenue then pays the basic rate tax to the pension provider.

6.36 Further tax relief is given if the scheme member is a higher rate taxpayer. **The relief is given by increasing the basic rate limit for the year by the gross amount of contributions for which he is entitled to relief.**

Activity 3.20: Higher rate relief

Joe has Schedule E earnings of £45,000 in 2001/02. He pays a personal pension contribution of £7,020 (net). He has no other taxable income.

Show Joe's tax liability for 2001/02.

7 INLAND REVENUE FORMS

7.1 Sample copies of the following forms are included in the appendix to this text. Please see the note regarding forms on page (x) of this text.

- A P11D
- A P60
- The supplementary pages to the income tax return form that must be completed by employed taxpayers

You should familiarise yourself with these forms now. You can practice using the forms when you try the Devolved Assessments in BPP's Unit 19 Devolved Assessment Kit.

Activity 3.21: End of chapter activity

Taker is employed at an annual salary of £35,000. He is not in a pension scheme, but receives the following benefits in 2001/02.

(a) He has the use of an 1,800 cc petrol engined motor car, which cost £20,000 in 1999. Fuel is provided for both business and private motoring, and Taker contributes £500 a year (half the cost of fuel for private motoring) for fuel. Annual business mileage is 2,400 miles.

(b) He makes occasional private calls on the mobile phone provided by his employer.

(c) He usually borrows his employer's video camera (which cost £600) at weekends, when he uses it to record weddings and parties for friends. He receives no payment for this, and he supplies blank tapes himself.

(d) He has an interest free loan of £3,000 from his employer. Take the official rate of interest to be 6.25%.

(e) His employer pays £4,000 a year to a registered childminder with whom the employer has a contract. The childminder looks after Taker's three year old son.

In 2001/02, Taker pays expenses out of his emoluments as follows.

(a) He pays subscriptions to professional bodies (relevant to his employment) of £180.

(b) He makes business telephone calls from home. The cost of business calls is £45. The cost of renting the line for the year is £100, and 40% of all Taker's calls are business calls.

3: The taxation of employment

(c) He pays a golf club subscription of £150. He does not play golf at all, but goes to the club to discuss business with potential clients. These discussions frequently lead to valuable contracts.

Task

Compute Taker's Schedule E income for 2001/02.

> **Key learning points**
>
> - The Schedule E charge has a very wide scope. For employees earning £8,500 or more a year, practically anything received by reason of their employment is taxable.
> - Deductions for expenses are extremely limited.
> - There are special rules to value many non-cash perks received by employees.
> - Contributions to pension personal pension schemes are treated as though they are paid net of basic rate tax. Additional tax relief may be given by extending the individual's basic rate band.

Quick quiz

1. On what basis are earnings taxed?
2. What accommodation does not give rise to a taxable benefit?
3. What tax exemption is available in respect of a computer made available to an employee for private use?
4. What are the conditions for expenses other than travel expenses to be deductible?
5. Give an example of a PAYE code.
6. What is the maximum pension available under an occupational pension scheme?
7. What is the limit on employee contributions to an occupational pension scheme?
8. When can a member of a personal pension plan retire?

Quick quiz answers

1. On a receipts basis.
2. Job-related accommodation.
3. The first £500 of any benefit in kind is exempt.
4. They must be incurred wholly, exclusively and necessarily in the performance of the duties.
5. 453L for example.
6. $2/3^{rd}$ of the employee's remuneration at retirement.
7. 15% of earnings.
8. Retirement age under a personal pension scheme is normally between 50 and 75.

Answers to activities

Activity 3.1

(a) 31 January 2002
(b) 30 April 2002

Activity 3.2

$2 \times £2,400 = £4,800$.

Part A: Income tax

Activity 3.3

	£
Annual value	1,600
Additional benefit £(420,000 − 75,000) × 6.25%	21,563
Taxable benefit	23,163

Activity 3.4

	£
Mileage allowance paid (9,000 × 35p)	3,150
Authorised mileage rates tax free amount	
4,000 miles @ 45p	(1,800)
5,000 miles @ 25p	(1,250)
Taxable benefit	100

Activity 3.5

	£	£
Salary		28,850
Less occupational pension scheme contributions		(1,450)
Net emoluments		27,400
Accommodation benefits		
Annual value: exempt (job related)		
Ancillary services		
Electricity	550	
Gas	400	
Gardener	750	
Redecorations	1,800	
	3,500	
Restricted to 10% of £27,400	2,740	
Less employee's contribution	(600)	
		2,140
Schedule E income		29,540

Activity 3.6

In the nine months to 5.4.02, Sue travelled 16,000 business miles. This is in excess of 18,000 miles **per annum** so the benefit is 15% × £10,000 × 9/12 = £1,125

Activity 3.7

	£
Car benefit £15,000 × 25%	3,750
Fuel benefit	3,620
	7,370
Less contribution towards use of car	(270)
	7,100

If the contribution of £270 had been towards the petrol the benefit would have been £7,370.

Activity 3.8

£ Nil. No taxable benefit arises in respect of a mobile telephone.

Activity 3.9

	£
£3,800 × 20%	760
Less: exemption	(500)
Taxable benefit	260

Activity 3.10

Average method

	£
$6.25\% \times \dfrac{30,000 + 10,000}{2}$	1,250
Less interest paid	(250)
Benefit	1,000

Alternative method (strict method)

	£
$£30,000 \times \dfrac{245}{365}$ (6 April - 6 December) × 6.25%	1,259
$£10,000 \times \dfrac{120}{365}$ (7 December - 5 April) × 6.25%	205
	1,464
Less interest paid	(250)
Benefit	1,214

The Revenue might opt for the alternative method.

Activity 3.11

Interest: no benefit because loan not over £5,000.

Loan written off: £4,000 × 35% = £1,400 taxable benefit.

Activity 3.12

	£
Salary	30,000
Season ticket loan: not over £5,000	0
Loan to buy shares £54,000 × (6.25 - 3 = 3.25%)	1,755
Schedule E	31,755
Less: charge on income (£54,000 × 6.25%)	(3,375)
	28,380
Less personal allowance	(4,535)
Taxable income	23,845
Income tax	
£1,880 × 10%	188
£21,965 × 22%	4,832
Tax liability	5,020

Activity 3.13

Zoe is not entitled to tax relief for the costs incurred in travelling between Wycombe and Chiswick since these are normal commuting costs. However, relief is available for all costs that Zoe incurs when she travels from Wycombe to Wimbledon to visit her client.

Part A: Income tax

Activity 3.14

Although Philip is spending all of his time at the Morpeth branch it will not be treated as his normal work place because his period of attendance will be less than 24 months. Thus Philip can claim relief in full for the costs of travel from his home to the Morpeth branch.

Activity 3.15

	£
Personal allowance	4,535
Benefits in kind	(560)
Unpaid tax £57.50 × 100/22	(261)
Available allowances	3,714

Adrian's PAYE code is 371L

Activity 3.16

£95,400 (the earnings cap) × 15% − £3,500 = £10,810.

£10,810 is the gross amount. It will be paid net of basic rate tax.

Activity 3.17

Tax year	Age at start of yr	% of NRE	Basis year	Maximum contribution
2001/02	45	20	2001/02(N1)	£30,000 × 20% = £6,000
2002/03	46	25(N2)	2001/02	£30,000 × 25% = £7,500
2003/04	47	25	2001/02	£30,000 × 25% = £7,500
2004/05	48	25	2001/02	£30,000 × 25% = £7,500
2005/06	49	25	2001/02	£30,000 × 25% = £7,500
2006/07	50	25	2001/02	£30,000 × 25% = £7,500
2007/08	51	30	2004/05(N3)	£28,000 × 30% = £8,400
2008/09	52	30	2008/09(N4)	£34,000 × 30% = £10,200

Notes

1. The basis year for 2001/02 will apply for 2001/02 to 2006/07 (maximum).

2. The relevant percentage is determined by the age of the individual at the start of the contribution year. The basis year used is irrelevant.

3. In 2007/08, any year from 2002/03 to 2007/08 inclusive can be chosen as the basis year. 2004/05 has been chosen as it gives the highest NRE. This does not affect the contributions made in 2004/05 to 2006/7 because the basis year for those years (2001/02) has higher NRE.

4. In 2008/09, any year from 2003/04 to 2008/09 inclusive can be chosen as the basis year. 2008/09 has been chosen as it gives the highest NRE.

5. The maximum contributions are the gross amounts. These will actually be paid net of basic rate tax.

Activity 3.18

Tax year	Age at start of yr	% of NRE	Basis year	Maximum contribution
2001/02	31	17.5	1996/97 (N1)	£40,000 × 17.5% = £7,000
2002/03	32	17.5	1996/97 (N2)	£40,000 × 17.5% = £7,000
2003/04	33	17.5	1996/97 (N2)	£40,000 × 17.5% = £7,000
2004/05	34	17.5	1996/97 (N2)	£40,000 × 17.5% = £7,000
2005/06	35	17.5	1996/97 (N2)	£40,000 × 17.5% = £7,000
2006/07	36	20	1996/97 (N2)	£40,000 × 20% = £8,000
2007/08	37	20	n/a (N3)	£3,600 (contributions threshold)

Notes

1. 2001/02 is the cessation year. Sharon can make 1996/97 her basis year for 2001/02 under the normal rules.

3: The taxation of employment

2. 2002/03 is the break year. The reference years are the preceding six tax years ie 1996/97 to 2001/02. Therefore, Sharon can again chose 1996/97 as her basis years for post cessation contributions. These can be made for 2002/03 to 2006/07 inclusive.

3. No contributions can be made above the contributions threshold in 2007/08.

If Sharon goes back to work in 2003/04, the post cessation rules cease to apply for that year. Sharon can then chose a new basis year between 1998/99 and 2001/02 (she had no NRE in 2002/03 so this cannot be a basis year). She should choose 1999/00 to give a maximum contribution of £37,000 x 17.5% = £6,475.

Activity 3.19

	£
1997/98	
17½% of NRE	6,125
Less premium paid	(5,800)
Unused relief	325
1998/99	£
17½% of NRE	5,775
Less premium paid	(5,700)
Unused relief	75
1999/00	£
17½% of NRE	6,650
Unused relief 1997/98	200
	6,850
Less premium paid	(6,850)
Unused relief	0
2000/01	£
17½% of NRE	7,525
Unused relief: 1997/98 (balance)	125
1998/99	75
	7,725
Less premium paid	(8,000)
Unrelieved premium (must be repaid)	275

Activity 3.20

	Non savings Income £
Sch E/STI	45,000
Less: PA	(4,535)
Taxable income	40,465
Tax	
	£
£1,880 × 10%	188
£27,520 × 22%	6,054
£9,000 (7,020 × 100/78) × 22%	1,980
£2,065 × 40%	826
40,465	9,048

Part A: Income tax

Activity 3.21

Schedule E income

	£	£
Salary		35,000
Car £20,000 × 35%		7,000
Fuel (partial contribution gives no reduction)		2,460
Mobile telephone		0
Use of video camera £600 × 20%		120
Loan: does not exceed £5,000		0
Childminder		4,000
		48,580
Less: professional subscriptions	180	
cost of business telephone calls	45	
		(225)
Schedule E income		48,355

Chapter 4 Investments and land

Chapter topic list

1. Schedule D Case III
2. Schedule D Case VI
3. Other financial investments
4. Individual savings accounts (ISAs)
5. The enterprise investment scheme (EIS)
6. Venture capital trusts (VCTs)
7. Schedule A
8. Inland Revenue form

Learning objectives

On completion of this chapter you will be able to:

	Performance criteria	Range Statement
• explain how to treat income from various sources received gross, income from gilts, income from bank accounts and dividends	19.2.1	19.2.1
• discuss the tax treatment of various types of tax efficient invetments such as ISAs, the EIS and VCTs	19.2.1	19.2.1
• discuss how income from renting out land and buildings is taxed and the ways in which such taxable income is calculated	19.2.2	19.2.1

Part A: Income tax

1 SCHEDULE D CASE III

1.1 **Schedule D Case III taxes interest. The taxable income is the full amount arising** without any deductions, other than the first £70 on National Savings Bank (NSB) ordinary accounts, which is exempt. Some interest is received gross. Examples of interest received gross are:

- loans between individuals;
- 3½% War Loan;
- most government stocks;
- National Savings Bank accounts;
- certificates of tax deposit.

1.2 **The amount of income taxable for a tax year is the amount arising in that year.** Income arises when it is paid or credited: accrued income not yet paid or credited is ignored.

2 SCHEDULE D CASE VI

2.1 **This case deals with any income not falling under any other schedule or case.**

2.2 Examples are income or profits from:

- the sale of patent rights;
- casual commission;
- withdrawal of EIS relief (see below);
- withdrawal of VCT relief (see below).

2.3 The income arising in a tax year is taxed in that year.

3 OTHER FINANCIAL INVESTMENTS

Tax-free investments

3.1 **The proceeds of National Savings Certificates** (including index-linked issues), **children bonus bonds** and **Premium Bond winnings are tax-free.** The first £70 a year of interest from a National Savings Bank ordinary account and all income on **individual savings accounts (ISAs)** (see below) are also tax-free.

3.2 Income arising on **Tax Exempt Special Savings Accounts** (TESSAs) is tax free. Also there is no tax on income or gains arising in a **Personal Equity Plan** (PEP). It has not been possible to open new TESSAs or PEPs since 6 April 1999 but TESSAs and PEPs that existed at that date retain their tax free status.

Taxable National Savings products

3.3 **The return on some National Savings products is taxable.** These include:

- Capital bonds. A lump sum is invested, and interest is added gross once a year. The rates are fixed in advance for five years.
- Fixed rate savings bonds. 20% tax is deducted at source. Bonds are available for various fixed terms.
- Income bonds. Interest is paid gross each month. The rate of interest may vary.
- Pensioners' guaranteed income bonds. These are like income bonds except that the interest rate is fixed for a period of up to five years. The investor must be aged 60 or over.

Bank and building society interest

3.4 **Bank deposit interest and building society interest paid to individuals is paid net of 20% tax. The tax is refundable to individuals who are not liable to pay the tax.**

3.5 **Banks and building societies may pay interest gross to investors who certify themselves as non-taxpayers.** If tax turns out to be due after all, the interest is taxed under Schedule D Case III.

3.6 Banks and building societies may also pay interest gross on fixed deposits and certificates of deposit of at least £50,000 which must be repaid at the end of a specified period of five years or less.

3.7 **National Savings Bank interest is paid gross and taxed under Schedule D Case III.**

Government or gilt-edged securities

3.8 Government or gilt-edged securities ('gilts') carry a wide range of fixed interest rates. **Interest on gilts is normally paid gross,** unless gilt holders opt for their interest to be paid net.

3.9 Interest on the following gilts has always been paid gross:

   (a) 3 ½% War Loan
   (b) Gilts acquired on the National Savings Stock Register
   (c) Strippable Gilts (gilt strips) (subject to an option for net payment)

3.10 A strippable gilt (or gilt strip) is a gilt which is separated into its constituent interest and principal payments so that they can be held or traded separately. For example, a ten year bond with two interest payments a year becomes twenty separate coupon payments and one payment of principal.

Personal tax computation

3.11 Interest is included gross in the savings (excl dividend) column of the personal tax computation. It is taxed at 10% if it falls in the starting rate band, at 20% if it falls in the basic rate band and at 40% if it exceeds the higher rate threshold. Any tax suffered on the interest is deducted in computing tax payable and may be repaid.

Activity 4.1: Tax repayment

A single taxpayer's only income in 2001/02 is bank deposit interest of £9,600 net. No arrangement to receive interest gross is made. What tax repayment is due?

Dividends

3.12 Dividends on UK shares are deemed to be paid net of a 10% tax credit. This means a dividend received must be grossed up for inclusion in the tax computation by multiplying by 100/90.

3.13 The 10% tax credit cannot be repaid.

Part A: Income tax

3.14 Dividend income is taxed as the top slice of income. If it is above the basic rate threshold of £29,400 (2001/02), it is taxed at 32.5%. Otherwise it is taxed at 10%.

Activity 4.2: Dividends

Emma's only income in 2001/02 was dividend income of £12,600 (net). Emma, who is aged 40, is single. What tax is payable / repayable?

Dividends on units in unit trusts

3.15 **A unit trust allocates units to investors in return for money they pay in. The sums paid in are then invested in shares and securities. The dividends and interest arising on those shares and securities are passed on to the investors.** When an investor wishes to withdraw his investment, he sells his units back to the unit trust managers. The price of units varies with the market values of the shares and securities, so investors may make gains or losses.

3.16 The unitholders are in general in the same position as shareholders in a company: **when the unit trust pays them a dividend, they are taxed as if they were receiving a dividend on shares,** and when they sell their units, gains are computed in the same way as gains on shares.

4 INDIVIDUAL SAVINGS ACCOUNTS (ISAs)

KEY TERM

Individual savings accounts are tax efficient savings accounts. They can be made up of three components.

- Cash
- Life insurance
- Stocks and shares

4.1 There can be a single account manager or one manager for each component of the account. The investor must normally be 18 years or over. However, a cash only ISA can be held by individuals aged 16 or 17.

4.2 There are three distinct types of ISA:

(a) **Maxi-accounts** which must normally contain a stocks and shares component and may contain the other two components (either one or both), but must contain only a cash component for investors under 18 years of age.

(b) **Mini-accounts** which comprise a single component only; and

(c) **TESSA only** accounts, which consist of a cash component and can only accept subscriptions by way of transfers from matured tax exempt special savings accounts (TESSAs)

Once an account has been designated by the manager as being of a particular type it retains that designation and cannot be altered.

4.3 A 'maxi-account', must contain a stocks and shares component with or without other components. Subscribing to a maxi-account in one year precludes an investor from also subscribing to a mini-account of any type in that year. Investment in a TESSA only account

in the same year is not, however, prohibited. **There is a general annual subscription limit for maxi-accounts of £7,000 of which a maximum of £3,000 can be in cash and £1,000 in life insurance.** For a maxi-account held by an investor between 16 and 18 years of age, there is a limit of £3,000.

4.4 A **mini-account** comprises a single component only. Once a mini-account, for any component, has been subscribed to for a particular tax year the only other ISAs that may be subscribed to for that year are other mini-accounts comprising different components and a TESSA only account. **The annual subscription limits for mini-accounts are:**

(a) **Cash component accounts; £3,000**
(b) **Insurance component accounts; £1,000, and**
(c) **Stocks and shares component accounts; £3,000.**

Investors under 18 years of age can only invest in a cash mini-ISA.

4.5 A **TESSA only** ISA can accept subscriptions by way of transfers from matured TESSAs (see above) only and from no other source. TESSAs were a type of tax fee savings account that could be opened prior to 6.4.99 but it has not been possible for investors to open a new TESSA since then. However, TESSAs opened before that date continue to earn tax free interest before they mature at the end of their five year tax life. Transfers from matured TESSAs can also be made to cash ISAs already opened as a mini-ISA or as part of a maxi-ISA.

The maximum investment in a TESSA only ISA is equal to the capital deposited in the matured TESSA. This means that it could be any amount up to £9,000; the maximum permitted investment in a TESSA over its 5 year life. The subscription limit of a TESSA only ISA is free-standing, it does not interact with the limits for maxi- or mini-accounts. The transfer from a TESSA to a TESSA only ISA account must be made within six months of the TESSA maturing.

Tax treatment

4.6 **Investments within an ISA are exempt from both income and capital gains tax. In addition, up to and including 2003/04, the 10% tax credit is repayable on dividends from UK shares.**

4.7 **There is no statutory minimum period for which an ISA must be held.** A full or partial withdrawal may be made at any time without loss of the tax exemption.

5 THE ENTERPRISE INVESTMENT SCHEME (EIS)

> **KEY TERM**
>
> The **EIS** is a scheme designed to promote enterprise and investment by helping high-risk, unlisted trading companies raise finance by the issue of ordinary shares to individual investors who are unconnected with that company.

Tax treatment

5.1 Individuals who subscribe for EIS shares are entitled to both income tax and capital gains tax reliefs.

Part A: Income tax

Income tax relief

5.2 Individuals can claim a **tax reducer of the lower of**:

(a) **20% of the amount subscribed for qualifying investments** (maximum qualifying investments are £150,000 per tax year) and

(b) **The individual's tax liability for the year** after deducting VCT relief (See next section) but before deducting other tax reducers

Activity 4.3: EIS relief

Mr Matthews, a married man aged 40, has STI of £47,000 (all non-savings income) for 2001/02. He subscribes £75,000 for shares and he claims EIS relief. The shares are issued to him in December 2001. What is his 2001/02 income tax liability?

5.3 To be eligible for relief the minimum subscription of shares in any company is £500. The maximum EIS investments qualifying for income tax relief is £150,000, but individuals can invest in excess of this amount if they wish.

5.4 **If shares are issued in the first six months of the tax year (ie before 6 October), the investor may claim to have up half of the shares treated as issued in the previous tax year.** This is subject to a maximum carry back of £25,000 if £50,000 or more shares are issued in the first six months.

5.5 When carrying back relief, relief given in the previous year must not exceed overall EIS limits for that year.

5.6 **EIS relief can be claimed by an individual who subscribes wholly in cash for new ordinary shares in a qualifying company.** All the shares issued must be issued to finance a qualifying business activity.

5.7 For three years after the later of, the issue of the shares and, the commencement of trade the shares must have no right to redemption, nor preferential right to dividends or to the company's assets in a winding up. For issues prior to 6.4.00 this condition applied for five years rather than three years.

5.8 Relief must be claimed by the 31 January which is nearly six years from the end of the tax year of investment. A certificate that the investment qualifies for relief must be issued to the taxpayer by the company before the claim can be made.

Activity 4.4: EIS

In July 2001, Petra subscribes for EIS shares at a cost of £80,000, her first such investment. What is the maximum tax reduction she could obtain in 2000/01.

Qualifying individual

5.9 **The investor must not be 'connected with' the company** during the **'designated period'** starting two years prior to the share issue (or from incorporation if later) and ending three years after the share issue (or commencement of trade, if later). Broadly an investor is connected with a company if he owns more than 30% of the company or if he is a director or employee of it.

Conditions to be satisfied by the company

5.10 In outline, a qualifying company is an unquoted trading company which exists wholly to carry on a qualifying business activity for a minimum of three years.

Qualifying trades

5.11 **The company must exist wholly to carry on qualifying trades or to act as a holding or financing company for qualifying subsidiaries.** The trade must be conducted on a commercial basis with a view to making profits. Although there are certain prohibitions, most trades are qualifying trades.

5.12 Shares issued before 6 April 2000 must be held by an investor for at least five years if the income tax relief is not to be withdrawn or reduced. This minimum holding period is reduced to three years for EIS shares issued on or after this date by a company that is carrying on a qualifying trade at the time of issue. For companies which are preparing to trade at the time of issue, the minimum holding period ends when the company has been carrying on a qualifying trade for three years.

5.13 **EIS relief is withdrawn by the issue of a Schedule D Case VI assessment for the year in which relief was originally obtained.** Withdrawal of relief does not occur in respect of events occurring after death.

5.14 The main reason for the withdrawal of relief will be the sale of the shares by the investor within the five/three year period mentioned above. The consequences depend on whether the disposal is at arms length or not:

(a) If the disposal is not a bargain at arms length the full amount of relief originally obtained is withdrawn.

(b) If the disposal is a bargain at arms length there is a withdrawal of relief on the consideration received. As the relief was originally given as a tax reduction, the withdrawal of relief must be made at the same rate of tax.

Activity 4.5: Withdrawal of EIS relief

Ted Edwards, a single man, makes a £60,000 EIS investment in 2000/01. His income (all non-savings) for the year is £40,000. In 2001/02, Ted sells the shares (an arms length bargain) for £50,000. How much EIS relief is withdrawn as a result of the sale of the shares? The personal allowance in 2000/01 was £4,385. Tax at 10% was charged on the first £1,520 of income, at 22% on the next £26,880 and thereafter at 40%.

5.15 A transfer of shares between spouses does not give rise to a withdrawal of relief. The relief remains associated with the shares, and if the recipient spouse disposes of the shares outside the marriage within five/three years of issue, it is withdrawn by taxing the recipient spouse.

Capital gains reliefs

5.16 Where shares qualify for income tax relief under the EIS there are also special rules that apply to those shares for capital gains purposes:

(a) Where shares are disposed of after the five/three year period any gain is exempt from CGT. If the shares are disposed of within five/three years any gain is computed in the normal way. You will see how to compute a chargeable gain in the next part of this text.

Part A: Income tax

(b) If EIS shares are disposed of at a loss at any time, the loss is allowable but the acquisition cost of the shares is reduced by the amount of EIS relief attributable to the shares.

5.17 EIS reinvestment relief may be available to defer chargeable gains if an individual invests in EIS shares in the period commencing one year before and ending three years after the disposal of the asset. Further details of this relief are given later in this text.

6 VENTURE CAPITAL TRUSTS (VCTs)

KEY TERM

Venture capital trusts (VCTs) are listed companies which invest in unquoted trading companies and meet certain conditions.

6.1 The VCT scheme differs from EIS in that the individual investor may spread his risk over a number of higher-risk, unquoted companies. **An individual investing in a VCT obtains the following tax benefits.**

- **A tax reduction of 20% of the amount invested,** in the year of making the investment.
- **Dividends received are tax-free income.**
- **Capital gains on the sale of shares in the VCT are exempt** from CGT (and losses are not allowable).

In addition, capital gains which the VCT itself makes on its investments are not chargeable gains, and so are not subject to tax.

The tax reduction on investment in a VCT

6.2 **An individual who is at least 18 years of age and subscribes for new VCT can claim a tax reduction of up to 20% of the amount subscribed, in the tax year of issue.** This tax reducer is given in priority to all other tax reducers but it cannot exceed the individual's tax liability for the year.

6.3 The shares must be new ordinary shares, which for at least three years from issue carry no preferential rights to dividends, assets or redemption. For issues prior to 6 April 2000 this period was a five year rather than a three year period.

6.4 The investment which can qualify as a tax reducer is limited to £100,000 per individual per tax year. More can be invested in VCTs, but the excess will not be a tax reducer.

6.5 **If the shares in the VCT are disposed of within three years of issue (five years for shares issued before 6 April 2000), the following consequences ensue.**

- If the shares are not disposed of under a bargain made at arm's length, the tax reduction is withdrawn.
- If the shares are disposed of under a bargain made at arm's length, the tax reduction is withdrawn, up to the disposal proceeds × 20%.

6.6 Relief is not withdrawn on a disposal between spouses living together. The transferee is treated as having acquired the shares when the transferor did, and as having obtained the

4: Investments and land

transferor's tax reduction. On a later disposal outside the marriage within three years of the issue (or five years for issues before 6 April 2000), the tax reduction is wholly or partly withdrawn by a charge on the transferee.

6.7 **If a VCT's approval is withdrawn within three years of the issue (five years for issues before 6 April 2000), any tax reduction given is withdrawn.**

6.8 Relief is withdrawn by charging tax under Schedule D Case VI for the year in which relief was originally given. Tax is not charged when the individual to whom the shares were issued died before the event which would have led to a withdrawal.

Tax-free dividends

6.9 **Dividends on ordinary shares in VCTs are tax-free income,** and you must leave them out of the shareholder's personal tax computation.

6.10 The shareholder must be aged at least 18, and must have acquired the shares at a time when the company qualified as a VCT.

6.11 The profits in respect of which the dividend is paid must have arisen in an accounting period, at the end of which the company qualified as a VCT.

6.12 The £100,000 limit applies, but in a slightly different way from the £100,000 limit for tax reducers. We must look at the tax year in which the shareholder acquired the shares giving rise to the dividend, and find the market value at the time of acquisition of all shares he acquired in that year (by subscription, secondhand purchase or otherwise) where the companies were VCTs at the time of his acquisitions. If the total value exceeds £100,000, dividends on shares over that limit are not tax-free.

The CGT exemption

6.13 **If an individual disposes of ordinary shares in a company which was a VCT when he acquired the shares and is still a VCT at the time of disposal, there is no chargeable gain and no allowable loss.**

6.14 The shareholder must be aged at least 18 at the time of the disposal.

6.15 The £100,000 limit applies, in the same way as for tax-free dividends. That is, a share only qualifies for the CGT exemption if, at the time of the disposal, it would also meet the £100,000 test for tax-free dividends set out above.

7 SCHEDULE A

7.1 **Income from land and buildings in the UK, including caravans and houseboats which are not moved, is taxed under Schedule A.**

7.2 **A taxpayer (or a partnership) with rental income is treated as running a business, his 'Schedule A business'. All the rents and expenses for all properties are pooled, to give a single profit or loss. Profits and losses are computed on an accruals basis.**

7.3 Expenses are deductible in computing taxable net rental income if those expenses are incurred wholly and exclusively for the letting business. Expenses will often include rent payable,

Part A: Income tax

where a landlord is himself renting the land which he in turn lets to others. Interest on loans to buy or improve properties is treated as an expense (on an accruals basis).

7.4 **Capital allowances are a form of tax depreciation given on plant and machinery used in the Schedule A business and on industrial and agricultural buildings.** If you study Unit 18 preparing business tax computations you will learn how to compute capital allowances. In this Unit you would be given the relevant figure for capital allowances and just expected to deduct it as an expense from accrued rental income.

7.5 Capital allowances are not available on plant or machinery used in a dwelling, so someone who lets property furnished cannot claim capital allowances on the furniture. Instead, he can choose between the renewals basis and the 10% wear and tear allowance.

(a) Under the *renewals* basis, there is no deduction for the cost of the first furniture provided, but the cost of replacement furniture is treated as a revenue expense. However, the part of the cost attributable to improvement, as opposed to simple replacement, is not deductible.

(b) Under the *10% wear and tear* basis, the actual cost of furniture is ignored. Instead, an annual deduction is given of 10% of rents. The rents are first reduced by amounts which are paid by the landlord but are normally a tenant's burden. These amounts include any water rates and council tax paid by the landlord.

7.6 Schedule A profits are computed for tax years. Each tax year's profit is taxed in that year.

7.7 Rent for furniture supplied with premises is taxed as part of the rent for the premises, unless there is a separate trade of renting furniture.

Loss relief

7.8 **If there is a loss in a Schedule A business, it is carried forward to set against the first future Schedule A profits.** It may be carried forward until the Schedule A business ends, but it must be used as soon as possible.

Premiums on leases

7.9 **When a premium or similar consideration is received on the grant** (that is, by a landlord to a tenant) **of a short lease (50 years or less), part of the premium is treated as rent received in the year of grant.** A lease is considered to end on the date when it is most likely to terminate.

The premium taxed under Schedule A is the whole premium, less 2% of the premium for each complete year of the lease, except the first year.

This rule does not apply on the *assignment* of a lease (one tenant selling his entire interest in the property to another).

Activity 4.6: Taxable premium received

On 1 June 2001 D granted a lease to F for a period of ten years. E paid a premium of £30,000. Calculate the amount treated as rent out of the premium received by D.

Premiums for granting subleases

7.10 **A tenant may decide to sublet property and to charge a premium on the grant of a lease to the subtenant. This premium is treated as rent received in the normal way** (because this is a grant and not an assignment, the original tenant retaining an interest in the property). **Where the tenant originally paid a premium for the grant of his own head lease, this deemed rent is reduced by:**

$$\text{Rent part of premium for head lease} \times \frac{\text{duration of sub-lease}}{\text{duration of head lease}}$$

If the relief exceeds the part of the premium for the sub-lease treated as rent (including cases where there is a sub-lease with no premium), the balance of the relief is treated as rent payable by the head tenant, spread evenly over the period of the sub-lease. This rent payable is an expense, reducing the overall Schedule A profit.

Activity 4.7: Grant of a sublease

C granted a lease to D on 1 March 1991 for a period of 40 years. D paid a premium of £16,000. On 1 June 2001 D granted a sublease to E for a period of ten years. E paid a premium of £30,000. Calculate the amount treated as rent out of the premium received by D.

The rent a room scheme

7.11 **If an individual lets a room or rooms, furnished, in his or her main residence as living accommodation, then a special exemption may apply.**

7.12 **The limit on the exemption is gross rents (before any expenses or capital allowances) of £4,250 a year.** This limit is halved if any other person (including the first person's spouse) also received income from renting accommodation in the property while the property was the first person's main residence.

7.13 **If gross rents** (plus balancing charges arising because of capital allowances in earlier years) **are not more than the limit, the rents** (and balancing charges) **are wholly exempt from income tax** and expenses and capital allowances are ignored. However, the taxpayer may claim to ignore the exemption, for example to generate a loss by taking into account both rent and expenses.

7.14 If gross rents exceed the limit, the taxpayer will be taxed in the ordinary way, ignoring the rent a room scheme, unless he elects for the 'alternative basis'. If he so elects, he will be taxable on gross receipts plus balancing charges less £4,250 (or £2,125 if the limit is halved), with no deductions for expenses or capital allowances.

Activity 4.8: Rent-a-room relief

Alison rents out a furnished room in her house, receiving rent of £5,160 a year and having expenses of £930 a year. What is her minimum annual Schedule A income?

8 INLAND REVENUE FORM

8.1 A sample of the supplementary pages to the income tax return form that need to be completed by taxpayers with property income is included in the appendix to this text. Familiarise yourself with this now. Please see page (x) regarding Revenue forms.

Part A: Income tax

Activity 4.9: End of chapter activity

On 1 May 2001, Hamburg started to invest in rented properties. He bought three houses in the first three months, as follows.

House 1

Hamburg bought house 1 for £62,000 on 1 May 2001. It needed a new roof, and Hamburg paid £5,000 for the work to be done in May. He then let it unfurnished for £400 a month from 1 June to 30 November 2001. The first tenant then left, and the house was empty throughout December 2001. On 1 January 2002, a new tenant moved in. The house was again let unfurnished. The rent was £6,000 a year, payable annually in advance.

Hamburg paid water rates of £320 for the period from 1 May 2001 to 5 April 2002 and a buildings insurance premium of £480 for the period from 1 June 2001 to 31 May 2002.

House 2

Hamburg bought house 2 for £84,000 on 1 June 2001. He immediately bought furniture for £4,300, and let the house fully furnished for £5,000 a year from 1 August 2001. The rent was payable quarterly in arrears. Hamburg paid water rates of £240 for the period from 1 June 2001 to 5 April 2002. He claimed the 10% wear and tear allowance for furniture.

House 3

Hamburg bought house 3 for £45,000 on 1 July 2001. He spent £1,200 on routine redecoration and £2,300 on furniture in July, and let the house fully furnished from 1 August 2001 for £7,800 a year, payable annually in advance. Hamburg paid water rates of £360 for the period from 1 July 2001 to 5 April 2002, a buildings insurance premium of £440 for the period from 1 July 2001 to 30 June 2002 and a contents insurance premium of £180 for the period from 1 August 2001 to 31 July 2002. He claimed the 10% wear and tear allowance for furniture.

Task

Compute Hamburg's Schedule A income for 2001/02.

Key learning points

- Schedule D Case III income and Schedule D Case VI income are taxed in the year of receipt.
- There are several tax exemptions for investment income, but they are generally limited to small amounts of income.
- The enterprise investment scheme and venture capital trusts allow certain investments to qualify as tax reducers.
- Income from land is taxed under Schedule A. There are tax benefits in relation to the letting of rooms in the owner's residence.

Quick quiz

1. What income falls within Schedule D Case VI?
2. What is the tax treatment of National Savings Certificates?
3. When may banks and building societies pay interest gross?
4. What are the three possible components of an ISA?
5. What are the three distinct types of ISA?
6. How is income tax relief given for an investment under the EIS?
7. How much EIS relief is withdrawn on a non arm's length sale of shares within three years of issue?
8. Describe the renewals basis.
9. How is relief given for a Schedule A loss?

10 How much income per annum is tax free under the rent a room scheme?

Quick quiz answers

1. Schedule Case VI deals with income not falling under any other schedule or case.
2. They are tax free.
3. Banks and building societies may pay interest gross to investors who certify themselves as non-taxpayers.

   Banks and building societies may also pay interest gross on fixed deposits and certificates of deposit of at least £50,000 which must be repaid at the end of a specified period of five years or less.
4. Cash, life insurance and stocks and shares.
5. Maxi accounts, mini accounts and TESSA only accounts.
6. 20% of the investment is given as a tax reducer.
7. All of the tax reduction is withdrawn.
8. Under the renewals basis there is no deduction for the cost of the first furniture provided but the cost of replacement furniture is treated as a revenue expense.
9. It is carried forward to set against future Schedule A profits.
10. £4,250

Answers to activities

Activity 4.1

	Savings (excl. dividend) £
STI (bank deposit interest) £9,600 × 100/80	12,000
Less personal allowance	(4,535)
Taxable income	7,465

Income tax	£
£1,880 × 10%	188
£5,585 × 20%	1,117
Tax liability	1,305
Tax suffered £12,000 × 20%	(2,400)
Repayment due	(1,095)

Activity 4.2

	Dividend income £
Dividend (× 100/90)	14,000
Less: PA	(4,535)
Taxable income	9,465

	£
£9,465 × 10%	946
Less: Tax credit	(946)
Tax payable / repayable	Nil

Note: The tax credit on dividend income cannot be repaid.

Part A: Income tax

Activity 4.3

	£
STI	47,000
Less: PA	(4,535)
Taxable income	42,465

	£
£1,880 × 10%	188
£27,520 × 22%	6,054
£13,065 × 40%	5,226
	11,468
Less: EIS relief (£75,000 × 20% = £15,000, limited to £11,468)	(11,468)
Income tax liability	Nil

Activity 4.4

Maximum carry-back = lower of £80,000/2 and £25,000 = £25,000

Maximum tax reduction in 2000/01 = £25,000 × 20% = £5,000.

Activity 4.5

	£
2000/01	
STI	40,000
Less: personal allowance	(4,385)
Taxable income	35,615

	£
£1,520 × 10%	152
£26,880 × 22%	5,914
£7,215 × 40%	2,886
	8,952
Less: EIS relief: £60,000 x 20% = £12,000, restricted to	(8,952)
Income tax liability	Nil

The effective rate of EIS relief is $\frac{8,952}{60,000} \times 100 = 14.92\%$

2001/02

The sale of the shares for £50,000 as a bargain at arms length results in the withdrawal of income tax relief in 2000/01 of £7,460 (ie £50,000 x 14.92%).

Activity 4.6

	£
Premium received by D	30,000
Less £30,000 × 2% × (10-1)	(5,400)
Premium treated as rent	24,600

Activity 4.7

	£
Premium received by D	30,000
Less £30,000 × 2% × (10-1)	(5,400)
	24,600
Less allowance for premium paid (£16,000 - (£16,000 × 39 × 2%)) × 10/40	(880)
Premium treated as rent	23,720

4: Investments and land

Activity 4.8

£(5,160 − 4,250) = £910.

Activity 4.9

	£	£
Rent		
House 1: first letting £400 × 6		2,400
House 1: second letting £6,000 × 3/12		1,500
House 2 £5,000 × 8/12		3,333
House 3 £7,800 × 8/12		5,200
		12,433
Expenses		
House 1: new roof, disallowable because capital	0	
House 1: water rates	320	
House 1: buildings insurance £480 × 10/12	400	
House 2: water rates	240	
House 2: furniture £(3,333 − 240) × 10%	309	
House 3: redecoration	1,200	
House 3: water rates	360	
House 3: buildings insurance £440 × 9/12	330	
House 3: contents insurance £180 × 8/12	120	
House 3: furniture £(5,200 − 360) × 10%	484	
		(3,763)
Schedule A income		8,670

Part B
Capital gains tax

Chapter 5 An outline of capital gains tax

Chapter topic list

1 The charge to CGT
2 Allowable losses
3 Taper relief
4 Chargeable persons, disposals and assets
5 Married couples
6 Administration and Inland Revenue form

Learning objectives

On completion of this chapter you will be able to:

	Performance criteria	Range Statement
• identify when a charge to CGT will arise	19.3.2	19.3.1
• identify the types of disposal of assets subject to CGT	19.3.3	19.3.1
• discuss what to do with losses made on asset disposals	19.3.3	19.3.1
• recognise when taper relief will apply to a chargeable gain	19.3.3	19.3.1
• discuss the treatment of asset disposals beween spouses	19.3.1	19.3.1
• record a capital gain on the appropriate Inland Revenue form	19.3.6	-

Part B: Capital gains tax

1 THE CHARGE TO CGT

1.1 **An individual pays CGT on his net chargeable gains (gains minus losses) for a tax year, less unrelieved losses brought forward from previous years, taper relief and the annual exemption.** All of these items are discussed in this chapter.

Rates of CGT

1.2 **There is an annual exemption for each tax year.** For 2001/02 it is £7,500. It is the last deduction to be made in the calculation of taxable gains.

1.3 Taxable gains are chargeable to capital gains tax as if the gains were an extra slice of savings (excl dividend) income for the year of assessment concerned. This means that CGT may be due at 10%, 20% or 40%.

1.4 The rate bands are used first to cover income and then gains. If a gift aid payment is made, the basic rate can be extended, as for income tax calculations (see Chapter 1). Similarly, the payment of a personal pension contribution can extend the basic rate band.

Activity 5.1: Rates of CGT

In 2001/02, Carol, a single woman, has the following income, gains and losses. Find the CGT payable.

	£
Salary	32,230
Chargeable gains (not eligible for taper relief - see later)	25,700
Allowable capital losses	8,000

2 ALLOWABLE LOSSES

2.1 **Deduct allowable capital losses from chargeable gains in the tax year in which they arise. Any loss which cannot be set off is carried forward to set against future chargeable gains. Losses must be used as soon as possible** (subject to the following paragraph). Losses may not normally be set against income.

2.2 Allowable losses brought forward are only set off to reduce current year chargeable gains less current year allowable losses to the annual exempt amount. No set-off is made if net chargeable gains for the current year do not exceed the annual exempt amount.

2.3 EXAMPLE: THE USE OF LOSSES

(a) George has chargeable gains for 2001/02 of £10,000 and allowable losses of £6,000. As the losses are *current year losses* they must be fully relieved against the £10,000 of gains to produce net gains of £4,000, despite the fact that net gains are below the annual exemption.

(b) Bob has gains of £11,700 for 2001/02 and allowable losses brought forward of £6,000. Bob restricts his loss relief to £4,200 so as to leave net gains of £(11,700 − 4,200) = £7,500, which will be exactly covered by his annual exemption for 2001/02. The remaining £1,800 of losses will be carried forward to 2002/03.

(c) Tom has chargeable gains of £5,000 for 2001/02 and losses brought forward from 2000/01 of £4,000. He will leapfrog 2001/02 and carry forward all of his losses to 2002/03. His gains of £5,000 are covered by his annual exemption for 2001/02.

5: An outline of capital gains tax

Losses in the year of death

2.4 The only facility to carry back capital losses arises on the death of an individual. **Losses arising in the tax year in which an individual dies can be carried back to the previous three tax years, later years first, and used so as to reduce gains for each of the years to an amount covered by the appropriate annual exemption.** Only losses in excess of gains in the year of death can be carried back.

Activity 5.2: Loss in year of death

Joe dies on 1 January 2002. His chargeable gains (no taper relief available – see later) and allowable loss have been as follows.

	Gain/(loss) £	Annual exemption £
2001/02	2,000	7,500
	(12,000)	
2000/01	7,400	7,200
1999/00	4,000	7,100
1998/99	28,000	6,800

How will the loss be set off?

---

3 TAPER RELIEF

3.1 **Taper relief may be available to reduce gains realised after 5 April 1998.**

3.2 **Taper relief reduces the percentage of the gain chargeable according to how many complete years the asset had been held since acquisition or 6 April 1998, if earlier. Taper relief is more generous for business assets than for non-business assets. In unit 19 you will only be expected to deal with non-business assets.** If you study unit 18 you will learn how to calculate gains on the disposal of business assets.

3.3 The percentages of gains which remain chargeable after taper relief are set out below.

Non business assets No of complete years after 5.4.98 for which asset held	% of gain chargeable
0	100
1	100
2	100
3	95
4	90
5	85
6	80
7	75
8	70
9	65
10 or more	60

DEVOLVED ASSESSMENT ALERT

You will be given the above percentages in your assessment

Part B: Capital gains tax

3.4 Non-business assets acquired before 17 March 1998 qualify for an addition of 1 year (a 'bonus year') to the period for which they are actually held after 5 April 1998.

3.5 EXAMPLE: COMPLETE YEARS HELD FOR TAPER RELIEF

Peter buys a non business asset on 1 January 1998 and sells it on 1 July 2002. For the purposes of the taper Peter is treated as if he had held the asset for 5 complete years (four complete years after 5 April 1998 plus one additional year).

3.6 Taper relief is applied to net chargeable gains after the deduction of current year and brought forward losses. The annual exemption is then deducted from the tapered gains.

3.7 Losses brought forward are only deducted from net current gains to the extent that the gains exceed the CGT annual exemption.

Activity 5.3: Taper relief

William sold a non-business asset in December 2001 realising a chargeable gain of £12,000 before taper relief. He had purchased the asset in May 1996. In January 2002 William sold another asset realising a loss of £1,300 but he made no other disposals in 2001/02. What are William's taxable gains for 2001/02?

Activity 5.4: Brought forward losses and taper relief

Ruby sold a non-business asset in July 2001 which she had purchased in January 1990. She realised a chargeable gain (before taper relief) of £17,300. She also sold a non-business asset in 2001/02 realising a capital loss of £6,000. She has a capital loss brought forward from 1999 of £10,000. Calculate Ruby's taxable gain and any losses carried forward at 5.4.02.

3.8 Allocate losses to gains in the way that produces the lowest tax charge. Losses should therefore be deducted from the gains attracting the lowest rate of taper (ie where the highest percentage of the gain remains chargeable).

3.9 EXAMPLE: ALLOCATION OF LOSSES TO GAINS

Alastair made the following capital losses and gains in 2001/2002:

	£
Loss	10,000
Gains (before taper relief)	
Asset A (non-business asset)	25,000
Asset B (non-business asset)	18,000

Asset A was purchased in December 1997 and sold in January 2002. Taper relief reduces the gain to 90% of the original gain (4 years including additional year; non-business asset). Asset B was purchased on 5 November 1998 and sold on 17 December 2001. Taper relief reduces the gain to 95% of the original gain (3 years; non-business asset).

5: An outline of capital gains tax

The best use of the loss is to offset it against the gain on the asset B:

	£	£
Gain – Asset A	25,000	
Gain after taper relief (£25,000 × 90%)		22,500
Gain – Asset B	18,000	
Less loss	(10,000)	
Net gain before taper relief	8,000	
Gain after taper relief £8,000 × 95%		7,600
Gains after taper relief		30,100
Less annual exemption		(7,500)
Taxable gains		22,600

3.10 There is a special situation which affects the operation of taper relief: where there has been a transfer of assets between spouses (a no loss/no gain transfer; see below) the taper on a subsequent disposal will be based on the combined period of holding by the spouses.

Shares and securities

3.11 Special rules apply to shares and securities. We cover these later in this text. However, note now that quoted shares in a trading company are a non-business asset for taper relief purposes, provided:

(a) The shareholder is not an officer or employee of the company, and
(b) The shareholder does not own 5% or more of the voting rights in the company.

In addition shares in a non-trading company are a non-business asset provided the shareholder is not an officer or employee of the company or broadly, that the shareholder does not have amore than a 10% interest in the company.

4 CHARGEABLE PERSONS, DISPOSALS AND ASSETS

Chargeable persons

4.1 The following are chargeable persons.

- Individuals
- Partnerships

4.2 The following are exempt persons.

- Charities using gains for charitable purposes
- Approved superannuation funds
- Local authorities
- Registered friendly societies
- Approved scientific research associations
- Authorised unit trusts and investment trusts
- Diplomatic representatives

Chargeable disposals

4.3 The following are chargeable disposals.

- Sales of assets or parts of assets
- Gifts of assets or parts of assets
- Receipts of capital sums following the surrender of rights to assets
- The appropriation of assets as trading stock
- the loss or destruction of assets

Part B: Capital gains tax

4.4 A chargeable disposal occurs on the date of the contract (where there is one, whether written or oral), or the date of a conditional contract becoming unconditional. This may differ from the date of transfer of the asset. However, when a capital sum is received on a surrender of rights, the disposal takes place on the day the sum is received.

Where a disposal involves an acquisition by someone else, the date of acquisition is the same as the date of disposal.

4.5 The following are exempt disposals.

- Transfers of assets on death (the heirs inherit assets as if they bought them at death for their then market values, but there is no capital gain or allowable loss on death)
- Transfers of assets as security for a loan or mortgage
- Gifts to charities and national heritage bodies

4.6 Betting winnings are not subject to CGT. Cashbacks, for example on new mortgages or cars, are also not subject to CGT.

Chargeable assets

4.7 **All forms of property, wherever in the world they are situated, are chargeable assets for CGT purposes unless they are specifically designated as exempt.**

4.8 The following are exempt assets (thus gains are not taxable and losses on their disposal are not in general allowable losses: the few exceptions are explained in this text).

- Motor vehicles suitable for private use
- National savings certificates and premium bonds
- Foreign currency for private use
- Decorations for valour unless acquired by purchase
- Damages for personal or professional injury
- Life assurance policies (only exempt in the hands of the original beneficial owner)
- Works of art, scientific collections and so on given for national purposes
- Gilt-edged securities
- Qualifying corporate bonds (QCBs)
- Certain chattels
- Debts (except debts on a security)
- Pension rights and annuity rights
- Investments held in individual savings accounts (ISAs) or personal equity plans (PEPs)
- EIS and VCT shares (provided certain conditions are met)

DEVOLVED ASSESSMENT ALERT

For a capital gain to arise there needs to be three things:

- chargeable person;
- chargeable disposal; and
- chargeable asset

otherwise no charge to tax occurs.

Activity 5.5: Chargeable disposal

In 1979, Jane bought a vintage motor car as an investment. She never drove it. She sold it in 2001, making a gain of £75,000. Is the gain chargeable to CGT?

5 MARRIED COUPLES

5.1 **A husband and wife are taxed as two separate people. Each has an annual exemption, and losses of one spouse cannot be set against gains of the other.**

5.2 **Disposals between spouses who are living together give rise to no gain and no loss, whatever actual price** (if any) **was charged by the person transferring the asset** to their spouse. A couple are treated as living together unless they are separated under a court order or separation deed, or are in fact separated in circumstances which make permanent separation likely.

5.3 Where an asset is jointly owned, the beneficial interests of the spouses will determine the treatment of any gain on disposal. If, for example, there is evidence that the wife's share in an asset was 60%, then 60% of any gain or loss on disposal would be attributed to her. If there is no evidence of the relative interests, the Revenue will normally accept that the asset is held in equal shares. Where a declaration of how income from the asset is to be shared for income tax purposes has been made, there is a presumption that the same shares will apply for CGT purposes.

5.4 If a spouse who would be liable to pay tax at 40% wishes to dispose of an asset on which a gain would arise, and the other spouse would be taxed on the gain at a lower rate, the asset should first be transferred to the spouse with the lower tax rate. Similarly, assets or parts of assets should be transferred between spouses to use both CGT annual exemptions.

5.5 Where there has been a transfer of assets between spouses taper relief on a subsequent disposal is based on the combined period of holding by the spouses.

6 ADMINISTRATION AND INLAND REVENUE FORM

6.1 **CGT is charged for tax years, like income tax.** Thus any gains arising in the year from 6 April 2001 to 5 April 2002 will be taxed in 2001/02.

6.2 **CGT is payable on 31 January following the tax year.**

6.3 Where the consideration for a disposal of any asset is receivable in instalments over a period in excess of 18 months, the taxpayer may choose to pay the CGT over the shorter of:

(a) the period of instalments;
(b) eight years.

The Revenue decide on the instalments.

6.4 Tax may also be paid by ten equal annual instalments where it arises on certain gifts, if the donor elects in writing.

6.5 A sample of the supplementary pages to the income tax return form that may need to be completed by taxpayers with chargeable gains is included in the appendix to this text. Familiarise yourself with these now. Please see the note on page (x) regarding forms.

Part B: Capital gains tax

Activity 5.6: End of chapter activity

(a) David had salary of £6,500, gross bank interest of £18,000 and gains of £35,000 in 2001/02.

Task

Calculate David's tax liabilities for 2001/02.

(b) Edwina disposed of assets as follows.

    (i) On 1 January 2001 she sold her car at a loss of £10,700.

    (ii) On 28 February 2001 she sold some shares at a loss of £6,300.

    (iii) On 1 May 2001 she sold some quoted shares (acquired August 2000) and realised a gain of £7,800.

    (iv) On 1 October 2001 she sold some shares at a loss of £2,000.

    (v) On 1 December 2001 she sold a picture (acquired July 2001) to a collector for £50,000, making a gain of £3,000.

    (vi) On 1 April 2002 she sold some gilt-edged securities (acquired May 2001), making a gain of £10,000.

Task

What loss, if any, is available to be carried forward at the end of 2001/02?

Key learning points

- CGT is charged on capital gains which arise on individuals. Individuals have an annual exemption, and pay CGT at 10%, 20% or 40%.
- Losses are set against gains before taper relief of the same year or of future years.
- Taper relief may be available to reduce the gain before the annual exemption. The amount of taper relief depends on how many years after 5 April 1998 the asset has been owned for. An additional year is added to the length of the period of ownership for assets which were owned on 5.4.98.
- Spouses are treated as separate people. Transfers of assets between spouses give rise to a nil gain.
- CGT is payable by 31 January that follows the tax year end.

Quick quiz

1. At what rate or rates do individuals pay CGT?
2. Give some examples of chargeable disposals.
3. To what extent must allowable losses be set against chargeable gains?
4. To what extent may CGT be paid in instalments when consideration is received in instalments?

Quick quiz answers

1. 10%, 20% and/or 40%.

2. (a) Sales of assets or parts of assets
   (b) Gifts of assets or parts of assets
   (c) Receipts of capital sums following the surrender of rights to assets
   (d) The loss or destruction of assets
   (e) The appropriation of assets as trading stock

3. A current year losses must be set off against gains in full, even if this reduces gains below annual exemption Losses brought forward or carried back from year of death, are set off to bring down untapered gains to level of annual exemption.

4   Where the consideration for a disposal of any asset is receivable in instalments over a period in excess of 18 months, the taxpayer may choose to pay the CGT over the shorter of:

   (a)   the period of instalments;
   (b)   eight years.

   The Revenue decide on the instalments.

Answers to activities

Activity 5.1

(a) Carol's taxable income is as follows.

	£
Salary	32,230
Less personal allowance	(4,535)
Taxable income	27,695

(b) The gains to be taxed are as follows.

	£
Gains	25,700
Less losses	(8,000)
	17,700
Less annual exemption	(7,500)
Taxable gains	10,200

(c) The tax bands are allocated as follows.

	Total	Income	Gains
Lower rate	1,880	1,880	0
Basic rate	27,520	25,815	1,705
Higher rate	8,495	0	8,495
		27,695	10,200

(d) The CGT payable is as follows.

	£
£1,705 × 20%	341
£8,495 × 40%	3,398
Total CGT payable	3,739

Activity 5.2

The £10,000 net loss which arises in 2001/02 will be carried back. We must set off the loss against the 2001/02 gains first even though the gains are more than covered by the 2001/02 annual exemption.

£200 of the loss will be used in 2000/01. None of the loss will be used in 1999/00 (because the gains for that year are covered by the annual exemption), and so the remaining £9,800 will be used in 1998/99. Repayments of CGT will follow.

Activity 5.3

The current year loss must be deducted in full from the gain before taper relief is applied:

	£
Gain	12,000
Loss	(1,300)
Net gain	10,700

The asset was owned for 4 years (including the additional year) so:

	£
Gain after taper relief (90%)	9,630
Less: Annual exemption	(7,500)
Taxable gain	2,130

Part B: Capital gains tax

Activity 5.4

	£
Gain	17,300
Loss	(6,000)
Current net gains	11,300
Less: brought forward loss	(3,800)
Gains before taper relief	7,500
Gains after taper relief (4 year ownership) £7,500 × 90%	6,750
Less: annual exemption	(7,500)
Taxable gains	Nil

Note that the benefit of the taper relief is effectively wasted since the brought forward loss reduces the gain down to the annual exemption amount but the taper is then applied to that amount reducing it further.

The loss carried forward is £6,200 (£10,000 – £3,800).

Activity 5.5

No: motor cars are exempt assets.

Activity 5.6

(a) TAXABLE INCOME AND GAINS

	£
Non-savings income £(6,500 – 4,535)	1,965
Savings income	18,000
Taxable income	19,965

	£
Gains	35,000
Less annual exemption	(7,500)
Taxable gains	27,500

£1,880 of non-savings income falls within the starting rate band of 10%. The balance is taxed at 22%.

The total of savings and non-savings income falls below the basic rate threshold, so all of the savings income is taxed at 20%.

£9,435 (£29,400 – £19,965) of the gains fall within the basic rate band and are taxed at 20%. The remaining gains are taxed at 40%.

The income tax liability is as follows.

	£
Non-savings income	
£1,880 × 10%	188
£85 × 22%	19
Savings income	
£18,000 × 20%	3,600
Income tax liability	3,807

The capital gains tax liability is as follows.

	£
£9,435 × 20%	1,887
£18,065 × 40%	7,226
	9,113

(b) Motor cars are exempt assets, so the loss brought forward from 2000/01 is £6,300.

The position for 2001/02 is as follows.

5: An outline of capital gains tax

	£
Gains	
Shares (no taper relief)	7,800
Picture (no taper relief)	3,000
	10,800
Less loss on shares	(2,000)
	8,800
Less loss brought forward	(1,300)
	7,500
Less annual exemption	(7,500)
Chargeable gains	0

Gilt-edged securities are exempt assets. Losses brought forward are (unlike current year losses) only used to bring net gains down to the annual exempt amount.

The loss carried forward at the end of 2001/02 is £(6,300 – 1,300) = £5,000.

Chapter 6 The computation of gains and losses

Chapter topic list

1. The basic computation
2. The indexation allowance
3. Assets held on 31 March 1982
4. Valuing assets
5. Connected persons
6. Intraspouse transfers of assets
7. Part disposals

Learning objectives

On completion of this chapter you will be able to:

	Performance criteria	Range Statement
• calculate a gain or loss on the disposal of an asset	19.3.3	19.3.1
• value assets for CGT purposes and thus the sale proceeds used to calculate the capital gain or loss	19.3.2	19.3.1
• discuss how gains/losses are computed on part disposals	19.3.3	19.3.1

Part B: Capital gains tax

1 THE BASIC COMPUTATION

1.1 A **chargeable gain** (or an **allowable loss**) is generally calculated as follows.

	£
Disposal consideration (or market value)	45,000
Less incidental costs of disposal	(400)
Net proceeds	44,600
Less allowable costs	(21,000)
Unindexed gain	23,600
Less indexation allowance (if available)	(8,500)
Indexed gain	15,100

Taper relief may then apply. Taper relief was discussed in the previous chapter.

1.2 **Incidental costs of disposal** may include:

- valuation fees (but not the cost of an appeal against the Revenue's valuation);
- estate agency fees;
- advertising costs;
- legal costs.

These costs should be deducted separately from any other allowable costs (because they do not qualify for any indexation allowance if it was available on that disposal).

1.3 **Allowable costs** include:

- the original cost of acquisition;
- incidental costs of acquisition;
- capital expenditure incurred in enhancing the asset.

Incidental costs of acquisition may include the types of cost listed above as incidental costs of disposal, but acquisition costs do qualify for indexation allowance (from the month of acquisition) if it is available on the disposal.

1.4 **Enhancement expenditure** is capital expenditure which enhances the value of the asset and is reflected in the state or nature of the asset at the time of disposal, or expenditure incurred in establishing, preserving or defending title to, or a right over, the asset. Excluded from this category are:

- costs of repairs and maintenance;
- costs of insurance;
- any expenditure deductible for income tax purposes;
- any expenditure met by public funds (for example council grants).

Enhancement expenditure may qualify for indexation allowance from the month in which it becomes due and payable.

The consideration for a disposal

1.5 Usually the disposal consideration is the proceeds of sale of the asset, but a disposal is deemed to take place at market value:

(a) where the disposal is **not a bargain at arm's length**;
(b) where the disposal is made for a **consideration which cannot be valued**;
(c) where the disposal is by way of a **gift**.

6: The computation of gains and losses

Activity 6.1: Enhancement expenditure

Daniella buys a plot of land for £100,000, and spends £6,000 on clearing it. However, by the time she sells the land (at a large profit) it has become overgrown, and is in the same state as it would have been if the work had not been done. Is the £6,000 deductible as enhancement expenditure?

2 THE INDEXATION ALLOWANCE

2.1 Indexation was introduced in 1982. The purpose of having an indexation allowance was to remove the inflationary element of a gain from taxation.

2.2 **Individuals are entitled to an indexation allowance until April 1998, but not thereafter.**

2.3 EXAMPLE: INDEXATION ALLOWANCE

John bought a painting on 2 January 1987 and sold it on 19 November 2001.

Indexation allowance will be available for the period January 1987 to April 1998 only.

2.4 Indexation is calculated from the month of acquisition of an asset, or March 1982 if later.

> **DEVOLVED ASSESSMENT ALERT**
>
> The indexation factor is:
>
> $$\frac{\text{RPI for month of disposal (or April 1998)} - \text{RPI for month of acquisition (or March 1982)}}{\text{RPI for month of acquisition (or March 1982)}}$$
>
> The calculation is expressed as a decimal and is rounded to three decimal places.

The indexation factor is then multiplied by the cost of the asset to calculate the indexation allowance. If the RPI has fallen, the indexation allowance is zero: it is not negative.

Values of the RPI are given in the Rates and Allowances Tables in this text.

Activity 6.2: The indexation allowance

An asset is acquired by an individual on 15 February 1983 (RPI = 83.0) at a cost of £5,000. Enhancement expenditure of £2,000 is incurred on 10 April 1984 (RPI = 88.6). The asset is sold for £20,500 on 20 December 2001. Incidental costs of sale are £500. Calculate the chargeable gain before taper relief.

Indexation and losses

2.5 **The indexation allowance cannot create or increase an allowable loss.** If there is a gain before the indexation allowance, the allowance can reduce that gain to zero, but no further. If there is a loss before the indexation allowance, there is no indexation allowance.

Activity 6.3: Losses

Simon bought a picture for £97,000 in August 1987, and sold it for £24,000 in April 2001. What is the allowable loss?

3 ASSETS HELD ON 31 MARCH 1982

3.1 **On the disposal of an asset owned on 31 March 1982, we do two calculations. One uses actual cost and the other uses the market value on 31 March 1982. In *both* calculations we base the indexation allowance on the higher of the two.** The final gain or loss is then:

- if both calculations produce gains, the lower gain;
- if both calculations produce losses, the lower loss (so if one produces a loss of £1,000 and the other a loss of £2,000, the allowable loss is £1,000);
- if one calculation produces a gain and the other a loss, or if either produces a result of £nil, no gain and no loss.

3.2 In the computation based on the 31 March 1982 value, that value replaces cost plus all enhancement expenditure up to that date. However, we still use that cost and enhancement expenditure to compute the indexation allowance if they add up to more than the 31 March 1982 value.

Activity 6.4: Assets held on 31 March 1982

Mr A acquired a second house as an investment in 1977 at a cost of £28,500. He installed central heating for £1,500 in 1981. The market value of the house on 31 March 1982 had dropped to £20,000 owing to land subsidence. The property was eventually sold to a property developer in May 2001 for £150,000, the subsidence problem having been rectified at a cost of £15,000 in March 1984.

Compute the chargeable gain before taper relief.

Activity 6.5: Calculation of gain or loss

Mr B acquired a freehold farm in 1973 for £20,000. The market value of the farm on 31 March 1982 was £150,000. He sold the farm in June 2001 for £180,000. Compute the chargeable gain or allowable loss.

3.3 It is possible for taxpayers to make a once-and-for-all election that gains and losses arising on all assets held at 31 March 1982 should be computed by reference to their 31 March 1982 values only. Indexation allowance can then only be based on 31 March 1982 value and later enhancement expenditure.

3.4 Before making the election, the taxpayer should consider the net effect on all his assets owned at 31 March 1982. The effect might be to increase the gain or decrease the loss on some assets.

4 VALUING ASSETS

4.1 **Where market value is used in a CGT computation** (for example, on a disposal to a connected person; see below), **the value to be used is the price which the assets in question might reasonably be expected to fetch on a sale in the open market.**

Shares and securities

4.2 **Quoted shares and securities are valued using prices in The Stock Exchange Daily Official List,** taking the lower of:

- lower quoted price + 0.25 × (higher quoted price - lower quoted price);
- the average of the highest and lowest marked bargains (ignoring bargains marked at special prices).

Activity 6.6: Calculation of CGT value

Shares in A plc are quoted at 100-110p. The highest and lowest marked bargains were 99p and 110p. What would be the market value for CGT purposes?

4.3 Unquoted shares are much harder to value than quoted shares. The Revenue have a special office, the Shares Valuation Division, to deal with the valuation of unquoted shares.

Negligible value claims

4.4 **If a chargeable asset's value becomes negligible a claim may be made to treat the asset as though it were sold, and then immediately reacquired at its current market value.** This will probably give rise to an allowable loss.

The sale and reacquisition are treated as taking place when the claim is made, or at a specified earlier time. The earlier time can be any time up to two years before the start of the tax year in which the claim is made. The asset must have been of negligible value at the specified earlier time.

On a subsequent actual disposal, any gain is computed using the negligible value as the acquisition cost.

5 CONNECTED PERSONS

5.1 A transaction between 'connected persons' is treated as one between parties to a transaction otherwise than by way of a bargain made at arm's length. The effect of this is that the acquisition and disposal are deemed to take place for a consideration equal to the market value of the asset, rather than the actual price paid.

5.2 If a loss results on a disposal to a connected person, **it can be set only against gains arising in the same or future years on disposals to the same connected person and the loss can only be set off if he or she is still connected with the person sustaining the loss.**

KEY TERM

Connected person

An individual is connected with:

- his spouse;
- his relatives (brothers, sisters, ancestors and lineal descendants);
- the relatives of his spouse;
- the spouses of his and his spouse's relatives.

Activity 6.7: Disposals to a connected person

On 1 August 2001 Holly sold a painting to her sister, Emily for £40,000. The market value of the painting on the date of sale was £50,000. Holly bought the painting on 1 September 2000 for £60,000.

What allowable loss arises on disposal of the painting and how may this be relieved?

Part B: Capital gains tax

6 INTRASPOUSE TRANSFERS OF ASSETS

6.1 **Disposals between spouses living together do not give rise to chargeable gains or allowable losses.** (See the previous chapter.)

6.2 Special rules apply to indexation on no gain/no loss disposals. To illustrate the rules, we assume a husband (H) buys an asset and later transfers it to his wife (W) who then sells it to an outsider. The rules are exactly the same if the roles of H and W are reversed.

- If **H buys the asset before 1 April 1982** treat W as having bought it when H bought it and for the price he paid. Thus W can use the 31 March 1982 value, and can get indexation from March 1982.

- If **H buys the asset after 31 March 1982** W is deemed to have bought the asset when H transferred it to her. Her cost is H's cost plus indexation allowance up to the date of transfer (or 6 April 1998). When W sells the asset, she computes indexation allowance from the time of the transfer. If the transfer was made after 5 April 1998 there is no further indexation allowance.

Activity 6.8: No gain/no loss disposal

Sylvia bought an antique vase for £15,000 on 1 January 1981. Its value on 31 March 1982 was £18,000. On 1 January 1994 she gave it to her husband Nicholas. On 12 April 2001 he sold it for £50,000. What is his chargeable gain before taper relief?

7 PART DISPOSALS

7.1 **The disposal of part of a chargeable asset is a chargeable event for the purpose of capital gains tax. The chargeable gain (or allowable loss) is computed by deducting from the disposal value a fraction of the original cost of the whole asset.**

DEVOLVED ASSESSMENT ALERT

The fraction is:

$$\frac{A}{A+B} = \frac{\text{value of the part disposed of}}{\text{value of the part disposed of} + \text{market value of the remainder}}$$

A is the proceeds (for arm's length disposals) *before* deducting incidental costs of disposal.

7.2 The part disposal fraction should not be applied indiscriminately. Any expenditure incurred wholly in respect of a particular part of an asset should be treated as an allowable deduction in full for that part and not apportioned. An example of this is incidental selling expenses, which are wholly attributable to the part disposed of.

Activity 6.9: Part disposal (1)

Mr Heal owns a painting which originally cost him £27,000 in March 1984. He sold a quarter interest in the painting in July 2001 for £18,000. The market value of the three-quarter share remaining is estimated to be £36,000. What is the chargeable gain after taper relief?

6: The computation of gains and losses

Activity 6.10: Part disposal (2)

Androulla bought a plot of land for £150,000 in January 1989. In August 2001, she sold part of the land for £187,000, which was net of legal fees on the sale of £3,000. At that time, the value of the remaining land was £327,000. What expenditure (apart from the indexation allowance) could she deduct in computing her chargeable gain?

Small part disposals of land

7.3 Two special reliefs apply to small part disposals of land. They are only available if the land is freehold or on a lease with at least 50 years to run.

7.4 If the disposal is the result of a compulsory purchase order and the value of the consideration is 'small', the taxpayer may claim to have the consideration received deducted from the base cost of the asset retained, instead of doing a part disposal computation. **'Small' means either 5% or less of the total value of the land immediately before the part disposal or £3,000 or less.**

7.5 If, however, the relief above is not available, an alternative relief may be claimed. If the value of the consideration is 20% or less of the total value of the land immediately before the part disposed and the total consideration in that tax year from all small part disposals of land (excluding disposals under compulsory purchase orders where the consideration is small) does not exceed £20,000, then the taxpayer may claim to deduct the consideration from the base cost of his remaining land instead of doing a part disposal computation.

7.6 The time limit for claims is the 31 January which is nearly twenty two months after the end of the tax year of disposal.

7.7 When a subsequent disposal of the remaining land occurs, indexation is calculated on the initial allowable expenditure, before adjusting for the part disposal. A negative indexation allowance is then deducted from this indexation allowance: it is calculated on the sale proceeds received for the part disposal, from the date of receipt of the part disposal proceeds to the date of sale of the remaining land.

Activity 6.11: End of chapter activity

Hardup made the following disposals in 2001/02. All disposals were to unconnected persons except where otherwise stated.

(a) On 12 May 2001 he sold an antique vase for £100,000. He had bought it for £65,000 on 1 July 1988.

(b) On 18 June 2001 he sold a plot of land for £47,000. He had bought it for £2,000 on 14 January 1970, and had spent £5,000 on permanent improvements in July 1972 and £4,000 on defending his title to the land in July 1985. On 31 March 1982, the land was worth £20,000.

(c) On 25 March 2002 he exchanged contracts for the sale of a house (which he had always rented to tenants) for £173,000. Completion took place on 24 April 2002. He had bought the house for £20,000 on 16 October 1978. On 31 March 1982, the house had been worth £65,000.

(d) On 16 October 2001 he sold an antique table to his wife (with whom he was living) for £130,000, its market value. He had bought it a year earlier for £120,000.

(e) On 1 December 2001 he sold a bungalow (which he had never lived in) to his brother for £32,000, its market value. He had bought the bungalow for £35,000 on 15 December 1990.

Hardup will pay income tax at the marginal rate of 40% in 2001/02.

Task

Compute Hardup's capital gains tax liability for 2001/02.

Part B: Capital gains tax

Key learning points

- A chargeable gain is computed by taking the proceeds and deducting both the costs and the indexation allowance. Indexation allowance only runs to April 1998.
- An asset owned on 31 March 1982 needs two computations, one based on its cost and the other based on its value on that date.
- There are special rules for disposals between connected persons and disposals between spouses.
- On a part disposal, the cost must be apportioned between the part disposed of and the part retained.

Quick quiz

1. Jed buys a house. He repairs the roof, installs double glazing and builds an extension. The extension is blown down in a storm and not replaced. Which of these improvements is allowable as enhancement expenditure on a subsequent sale?
2. How is the chargeable gain/allowable loss on assets held on 31 March 1982 computed?
3. Shares in A plc are quoted at 410 – 414, with bargains at 408, 410 and 416. What is the value for CGT?
4. With whom is an individual connected?
5. 10 acres of land are sold for £15,000 out of 25 acres. Original cost in 1990 £9,000. Costs of sale £2,000. Rest of land valued at £30,000. What is the allowable expenditure?

Quick quiz answers

1. Repairs to roof – not allowable as enhancement expenditure because not capital in nature
   Double glazing – allowable as enhancement expenditure
   Extension – not allowable as not reflected in state of asset at time of disposal.

2. Two computations required – one on cost, one on 31.3.82 MV. IA always on higher of cost and 31.3.82 MV. If two gains – take lower gain. If two losses – take lower loss. If one gain, one loss – no gain/no loss.

3. Lower of:

   $410 + \frac{1}{4}(414 - 410) = 411$

   $\frac{416 + 408}{2} = 412$

   ie <u>411</u>

4. An individual is connected with:
   his spouse
   his relatives (brothers, sisters, ancestors and lineal descendants)
   the relatives of his spouse
   the spouses of his and his spouse's relatives

5. $\frac{15,000}{15,000 + 30,000} \times £9,000 = £3,000 + £2,000$ (costs of disposal) = <u>£5,000</u>

Answers to activities

Activity 6.1

No: it is not reflected in the state or nature of the asset at the time of disposal.

Activity 6.2

The indexation allowance is available until April 1998 (RPI = 162.6) and is computed as follows.

	£
$\dfrac{162.6 - 83.0}{83.0} = 0.959 \times £5,000$	4,795
$\dfrac{162.6 - 88.6}{88.6} = 0.835 \times £2,000$	1,670
	6,465

The computation of the chargeable gain is as follows.

	£
Proceeds	20,500
Less incidental costs of sale	(500)
Net proceeds	20,000
Less allowable costs £(5,000 + 2,000)	(7,000)
Unindexed gain	13,000
Less indexation allowance (see above)	(6,465)
Chargeable gain before taper relief	6,535

Activity 6.3

	£
Proceeds	24,000
Less cost	(97,000)
Allowable loss	(73,000)

Indexation cannot increase a loss.

Activity 6.4

	Cost £	31.3.82 value £
Proceeds	150,000	150,000
Less: cost 1977	(28,500)	
enhancement cost 1981	(1,500)	
31.3.82 value (includes 1981 improvement)		(20,000)
enhancement cost 1984	(15,000)	(15,000)
Unindexed gain	105,000	115,000
Less indexation allowance		
On original cost (March 1982 to April 1998):		
$\dfrac{162.6 - 79.4}{79.4} = 1.048 \times £28,500$	(29,868)	(29,868)
On enhancement cost 1981 (March 1982 to April 1998):		
$1.048 \times £1,500$	(1,572)	(1,572)
On enhancement cost 1984 (March 1984 to April 1998):		
$\dfrac{162.6 - 87.5}{87.5} = 0.858 \times £15,000$	(12,870)	(12,870)
	60,690	70,690

The chargeable gain before taper relief is £60,690.

At 31 March 1982 the cost of the house was £30,000 (£28,500 + £1,500) compared to the equivalent March 1982 market value of £20,000. Thus the indexation allowance available from March 1982 is based on the cost values in this question.

Part B: Capital gains tax

Activity 6.5

	Cost £	31.3.82 value £
Proceeds	180,000	180,000
Less: cost	(20,000)	
31.3.82 value		(150,000)
Unindexed gain	160,000	30,000
Less indexation allowance (March 1982 to April 1998)		
$\frac{162.6 - 79.4}{79.4} = 1.048 \times £150,000$	(157,200)	(30,000)
Indexed gain (indexation cannot create or increase a loss)	2,800	0

There is no chargeable gain and no allowable loss.

Activity 6.6

The value will be the lower of:

(a) $100 + 0.25 \times (110-100) = 102.5$;

(b) $\frac{110 + 99}{2} = 104.5$.

The market value for CGT purposes will therefore be 102.5p per share.

Activity 6.7

	£
Deemed disposal proceeds (connected person)	50,000
Less: Cost	(60,000)
Allowable loss	10,000

This loss will only be available to set against chargeable gains that Holly makes on other disposals to Emily.

Activity 6.8

	Cost £	31.3.82 Value £
Proceeds	50,000	50,000
Less cost/31.3.82 value	(15,000)	(18,000)
	35,000	32,000
Less indexation allowance to April 1998		
$\frac{162.6 - 79.4}{79.4} = 1.048 \times £18,000$	(18,864)	(18,864)
	16,136	13,136

Nicholas's chargeable gain before taper relief is £13,136

Activity 6.9

The amount of the original cost attributable to the part sold is

$$\frac{18,000}{18,000 + 36,000} \times £27,000 = £9,000$$

	£
Proceeds	18,000
Less cost (see above)	(9,000)
Unindexed gain	9,000
Less indexation allowance (March 1984 to April 1998)	
$\frac{162.6 - 87.5}{87.5} = 0.858 \times £9,000$	(7,722)
Gain before taper relief	1,278

Gain after taper relief (6.4.98 – 5.4.01 = 3 years plus additional year = 4 years)

90% × £1,278   £1,150

Activity 6.10

Cost: £150,000 × 190/(190 + 327) = £55,126

Incidental costs of disposal: £3,000

Total: £58,126

Activity 6.11

CAPITAL GAINS TAX COMPUTATION

	£
Vase £940 (W1) × 90%	846
Plot of land (W2)	0
House £39,880 (W3) × 90%	35,892
	36,738
Less annual exemption	(7,500)
Taxable gains	29,238

Both the house and the vase were owned for four complete years after 6.4.98 (including the additional year), so 90% of the gains are taxable.

Capital gains tax of £29,238 × 40% = £11,695

The table was disposed of between spouses living together, so there is no chargeable gain or allowable loss.

A loss arises on the sale of the bungalow (W4), but because the bungalow was sold to a connected person, the loss can only be set against gains on disposals in the same year or future years to the same connected person while he or she remains connected. A brother cannot, of course, cease to be connected, but a connection by marriage could cease.

Workings

1   The vase

	£
Proceeds	100,000
Less cost	(65,000)
	35,000
Less indexation allowance (July 1988 to April 1998)	
$\frac{162.6 - 106.7}{106.7} = 0.524 \times £65,000$	(34,060)
Chargeable gain before taper relief	940

Part B: Capital gains tax

2 The plot of land

	Cost £	31.3.82 value £
Proceeds	47,000	47,000
Less: cost in January 1970	(2,000)	
expenditure in July 1972	(5,000)	
31.3.82 value		(20,000)
expenditure in July 1985	(4,000)	(4,000)
	36,000	23,000
Less indexation allowance to April 1998		
$\dfrac{162.6 - 79.4}{79.4} = 1.048 \times £20,000$	(20,960)	(20,960)
$\dfrac{162.6 - 95.2}{95.2} = 0.708 \times £4,000$/(restricted)	(2,832)	(2,040)
	12,208	0

As one calculation produces a gain and the other a result of zero, the result is no gain and no loss.

3 The house

	Cost £	31.3.82 value £
Proceeds	173,000	173,000
Less cost/31.3.82 value	(20,000)	(65,000)
	153,000	108,000
Less indexation allowance (March 1982 to April 1998)		
$\dfrac{162.6 - 79.4}{79.4} = 1.048 \times £65,000$	(68,120)	(68,120)
	84,880	39,880

The gain before taper relief is the lower gain, which is £39,880.

Note. the disposal of the house takes place on the date of exchange of contracts not on the date of completion.

4 The bungalow

	£
Proceeds	32,000
Less cost	(35,000)
Loss	(3,000)

Chapter 7 Shares and securities

Chapter topic list

1. The matching rules for individuals
2. The FA 1985 pool
3. Bonus and rights issues
4. Gilts and qualifying corporate bonds

Learning objectives

On completion of this chapter you will be able to:

	Performance criteria	Range Statement
• match a disposal of shares to a corresponding purchase in order to match sale proceeds to cost and compute the capital gain or loss arising	19.3.3	19.3.3
• discuss what happens on the issue of bonus shares or rights shares	19.3.4	19.3.3
• identify shares and securities whose disposal is exempt from CGT	19.3.4	19.3.3

Part B: Capital gains tax

1 THE MATCHING RULES FOR INDIVIDUALS

1.1 Shares and securities and units in a unit trust present special problems when attempting to compute gains or losses on disposal. For instance, suppose that an individual buys some quoted shares in X plc as follows.

Date	Number of shares	Cost £
5 May 1988	100	150
17 January 2000	100	375

On 15 June 2001, he sells 120 of its shares for £1,450. To determine the chargeable gain, we need to be able to work out which shares out of the two original holdings were actually sold.

1.2 We therefore need **matching rules**. These **allow us to decide which shares have been sold and so work out what the allowable cost on disposal should be.**

1.3 In what follows, we will use 'shares' to refer to both shares and securities.

1.4 **Share disposals are matched with acquisitions in the following order.**

(a) Same day acquisitions.

(b) Acquisitions within the following 30 days.

(c) Previous acquisitions after 5 April 1998 identifying the most recent acquisition first (a LIFO basis).

(d) Any shares in the **FA 1985 pool** (shares acquired between 6.4.82 and 5.4.98).

1.5 The FA 1985 pool is looked at in detail below. You will not have to deal with shares acquired before 6.4.82 so they are not considered here.

1.6 EXAMPLE

Catherine acquired the following shares in X plc.

	No of shares
1.4.90	10,000
1.9.98	5,000
10.11.00	7,000
30.12.01	2,000

On 11.12.01 Catherine sold 12,000 shares. With which acquisitions is Catherine's share disposal matched?

1.7 SOLUTION

Catherine will initially match the disposal with the 2,000 shares bought on 30.12.01 (next 30 days). She will then match with the other post April 1998 acquisitions on a LIFO basis, so the 7,000 shares bought on 10.11.00 and 3,000 of the shares bought on 1.9.98 are deemed to be sold. 2,000 of the shares acquired on 1.9.98 and the FA 1985 pool shares remain.

Activity 7.1: Computing chargeable gain

June made the following purchases of ordinary shares in Read plc, a quoted company.

Date	Number	Cost £
15 May 1999	1,800	1,900
1 March 2000	1,000	1,260

On 30 September 2001 she sold 1,600 of the shares for £14,000. The shares were not a business asset for taper relief purposes.

Compute the capital gain after taper relief or allowable loss on the sale of June's shares.

DEVOLVED ASSESSMENT ALERT

Learn the 'matching rules' because a crucial first step to getting a shares question right is to correctly match the shares sold to the original shares purchased.

2 THE FA 1985 POOL

2.1 Until taper relief was introduced we used to treat shares as a 'pool' which grew as new shares were acquired and shrank as they were sold. **The FA 1985 pool** (so called because it was introduced by rules in the Finance Act 1985) **comprises the following shares of the same class in the same company.**

- **Shares held on 6 April 1985 and acquired on or after 6 April 1982.**
- **Shares acquired on or after 6 April 1985.**

2.2 The FA 1985 pool closes on 6 April 1998. This is the date from which taper relief starts.

2.3 In making computations which use the FA 1985 pool, we must keep track of:

   (a) the **number** of shares;
   (b) the **cost** of the shares ignoring indexation;
   (b) the **indexed cost** of the shares.

2.4 Each FA 1985 **pool is started by aggregating the cost and number of shares acquired between 6 April 1982 and 6 April 1985** inclusive. In order to calculate the indexed cost of these shares, an indexation allowance, computed from the relevant date of acquisition of the shares to April 1985, is added to the cost.

2.5 **EXAMPLE: THE FA 1985 POOL**

Oliver bought 1,000 shares in Judith plc for £2,750 in August 1984 and another 1,000 for £3,250 in December 1984. The FA 1985 pool at 6 April 1985 is as follows.

2.6 SOLUTION

	No of shares	Cost £	Indexed cost £
August 1984 (a)	1,000	2,750	2,750
December 1984 (b)	1,000	3,250	3,250
	2,000	6,000	6,000

Indexation allowance

$$\frac{94.8 - 89.9}{89.9} = 0.055 \times £2,750 \qquad\qquad 151$$

$$\frac{94.8 - 90.9}{90.9} = 0.043 \times £3,250 \qquad\qquad 140$$

Indexed cost of the pool at 6 April 1985   6,291

2.7 Disposals and acquisitions of shares which affect the indexed value of the FA 1985 pool are termed 'operative events'. **Prior to reflecting each such operative event within the FA 1985 share pool, a further indexation allowance (described as an indexed rise) must be computed up to the date of the operative event concerned from the date of the last such operative event** (or from April 1985 if the operative event in question is the first one).

2.8 **Indexation calculations within the FA 1985 pool** (after its April 1985 value has been calculated) **are not rounded to three decimal places.** This is because rounding errors would accumulate and have a serious effect after several operative events.

If there are several operative events before 6 April 1998 the indexation procedure described above will have to be performed several times over.

Activity 7.2: Value of FA 1985 pool

Following on from the above example, assume that Oliver acquired 2,000 more shares on 10 July 1986 at a cost of £4,000. Recalculate the value of the FA 1985 pool on 10 July 1986 following the acquisition.

2.9 In the case of a disposal, following the calculation of the indexed rise to the date of disposal, the cost and the indexed cost attributable to the shares disposed of are deducted from the amounts within the FA 1985 pool. The proportions of the cost and indexed cost to take out of the pool should be computed using the same A/(A + B) fraction that is used for any other part disposal. However, we are not usually given the value of the remaining shares (B in the fraction). We then just use numbers of shares.

2.10 For all FA 1985 pools held on 5 April 1998 **indexation allowance to April 1998 is calculated and then effectively the pool is closed.**

Activity 7.3: Pool closes on 6 April 1998

In activity 7.2 you should have calculated the value of the pool on 10 July 1986 as:

	No of shares	Cost £	Indexed cost £
10 July 1986	4,000	10,000	10,470

Continue this example and show the value of the FA 1985 pool when it closes on 6.4.98

7: Shares and securities

2.11 When FA 1985 pool shares are sold after 6.4.98, the gain is calculated using the cost and indexed cost on 6 April 1998. Taper relief may then apply if appropriate. Now let us work through a complete example with a disposal of shares after 6.4.98.

2.12 EXAMPLE: POST APRIL 1998 DISPOSALS FOR INDIVIDUALS

Ron acquired the following shares in First plc:

Date of acquisition	No of shares	Cost
9.11.90	12,000	25,000
4.8.00	3,000	11,400
15.7.01	5,000	19,000

He disposed of all the shares on 10 July 2001 for £80,000. The shares are not business assets for the purposes of taper relief. Calculate the chargeable gain arising.

2.13 SOLUTION:

Matching of shares

(a) Acquisition in 30 days after disposal:

	£
Proceeds $\frac{5,000}{20,000} \times £80,000$	20,000
Less cost	(19,000)
Gain	1,000

(b) Post 5.4.98 acquisitions

	£
Proceeds $\frac{3,000}{20,000} \times £80,000$	12,000
Less cost	(11,400)
Gain	600

Note. No taper relief is due against this gain since the period of ownership was only 11 months.

(c) FA 1985 pool

	Number of shares	Cost £	Indexed cost £
11.90 Acquisition	12,000	25,000	25,000
Index to 4.98 $\frac{162.6 - 130.0}{130.0} \times £25,000$	–	–	6,269
Pool closes at 5.4.98	12,000	25,000	31,269
7.01 sales	12,000	25,000	31,269

Gain

	£
Proceeds $\frac{12,000}{20,000} \times £80,000$	48,000
Less cost	(25,000)
	23,000
Less indexation from FA 1985 pool £(31,269 – 25,000)	(6,269)
Gain before taper relief	16,731

The period of ownership of this non-business asset is 4 years (3 years post 5.4.98 plus the additional year). The gain after taper relief is therefore £15,058 (£16,731 × 90%).

Total gains £(1,000 + 600 + 15,058)	£16,658

3 BONUS AND RIGHTS ISSUES

Bonus issues (scrip issues)

3.1 When a company issues bonus shares all that happens is that the size of the original holding is increased. **Since bonus shares are issued at no cost there is no need to adjust the original cost. Instead the numbers purchased at particular times are increased by the bonus.** The normal matching rules will then be applied.

3.2 EXAMPLE: BONUS ISSUES

The following transactions in the ordinary shares of X plc would be matched as shown below

6.4.86	Purchase of 600 shares
6.4.90	Purchase of 600 shares
6.4.00	Purchase of 1,000 shares
6.10.01	Bonus issue of one for four
6.12.01	Sale of 1,500 shares

(a) Post 6.4.98 acquisition

			No of shares
6.4.00	Purchase		1,000
6.10.01	Bonus		250
			1,250
6.12.01	Sold		(1,250)

(b) FA 1985 pool

			No of shares
6.4.86	Purchase		600
6.4.90	Purchase		600
			1,200
6.10.01	Bonus		300
			1,500
6.12.01	Sold		(250)
Number of shares remaining in FA 1985 pool			1,250

Activity 7.4: Bonus issues

On 1 May 1999 Bruce bought 10,000 shares for £42,000. On 1 December 2000 there was a bonus issue of one for five. On 1 August 2001 Bruce sold 4,000 shares for £15,000. Calculate any chargeable gain arising after taper relief. The shares are not a business asset for taper relief purposes.

Rights issues

3.3 **The difference between a bonus issue and a rights issue is that in a rights issue the new shares are paid for and this results in an adjustment to the original cost.** As with bonus issues, rights shares derived from shares in the 1985 pool go into that holding and those derived from post 5.4.98 holdings attach to those holdings. You should add the number and cost of each of right issue to each holding as appropriate.

3.4 The length of the period of ownership for taper relief purposes depends on the date of acquisition of the original holding **not** the date of acquisition of the rights shares.

7: Shares and securities

3.5 For the purposes of calculating the indexation allowance, expenditure on a rights issue is taken as being incurred on the date of the issue and not on the date of acquisition of the original holding.

3.6 In an **open offer,** shareholders have a right to subscribe for a minimum number of shares based on their existing holdings and may buy additional shares. Subscriptions up to the minimum entitlement are treated as a rights issue. Additional subscriptions are treated as new purchases of shares.

Activity 7.5: Rights issues

Simon had the following transactions in S plc.

1.10.95	Bought 10,000 shares for £15,000
11.9.98	Bought 2,000 shares for £5,000
1.2.99	Took up rights issue 1 for 2 at £2.75 per share
14.10.01	Sold 5,000 shares for £15,000

Compute the gain arising in October 2001, after taper relief (if applicable). The shares are not a business asset for taper relief purposes.

4 GILTS AND QUALIFYING CORPORATE BONDS

> **KEY TERM**
>
> For CGT purposes, **gilts** are **British Government and Government guaranteed securities** as shown on Treasury list. Gilt strips (capital or interest entitlements sold separately) are also gilts. You may assume that the list of gilts includes all issues of Treasury Loan, Treasury Stock, Exchequer Loan, Exchequer Stock and War Loan.

4.1 **Disposals of gilt edged securities (gilts) and qualifying corporate bonds by individuals are exempt from CGT.**

Activity 7.6: End of chapter activity

Frances sold her ordinary shares in The Hastings Hardening Company plc on 17 May 2001 for £24,000. She had bought ordinary shares in the company on the following dates.

	No of shares	Cost £
19 September 1985	2,000	1,700
12 December 1998	2,000	5,500
17 January 1999	2,000	6,000

Task

Calculate, before the annual exemption, the capital gain for 2001/02. The shares are a non-business asset for taper relief purposes.

Part B: Capital gains tax

> **Key learning points**
> - There are special rules for matching shares sold to shares purchased.
> - The FA 1985 pool contains shares acquired between 6.4.82 and 5.4.98.
> - Bonus and rights issues are attached to the holding to which they relate.
> - Gilts and QCBs held by individuals are exempt from CGT. You should never waste time computing gains or losses on them.

Quick quiz

1. In what order are acquisitions of shares matched with disposals by individuals?
2. What shares are included in the FA 1985 pool of an individual?
3. When is expenditure on a right issue treated as being incurred?
4. What securities are exempt from CGT for individuals?

Quick quiz answers

1. Disposals are identified with acquisitions in the following order.

   1. Same day acquisitions.
   2. Acquisitions within the following 30 days.
   3. Acquisitions after 6.4.98 on a LIFO basis
   4. Shares in the FA 1985 pool

2. The FA 1985 pool comprises the following shares of the same class in the same company.
   - Shares held on 6 April 1985 and acquired on or after 5 April 1982.
   - Shares acquired on or after 6 April 1985 but before 5 April 1998.

3. On the date of the expenditure.

4. Disposals of gilt edged securities (gilts) and qualifying corporate bonds.

Answers to activities

Activity 7.1

Match post April 1998 acquisitions on a LIFO basis

1 March 2000

	£
Disposal proceeds (£14,000 × $\frac{1,000}{1,600}$)	8,750
Less: cost	(1,260)
Gain	7,490

15 May 1999

	£
Disposal proceeds (£14,000 × $\frac{600}{1,600}$)	5,250
Less: cost (1,900 × $\frac{600}{1,800}$)	(633)
Gain	4,617

The total chargeable gain on the sale of June's shares is £12,107 (£7,490 + £4,617). No taper relief is due in respect of either of the disposals.

Activity 7.2

	No of shares	Cost £	Indexed cost £
Value at 6.4.85	2,000	6,000	6,291
Indexed rise			
$\dfrac{97.5 - 94.8}{94.8} \times £6,291$			179
	2,000	6,000	6,470
Acquisition	2,000	4,000	4,000
Value at 10.7.86	4,000	10,000	10,470

Activity 7.3

	No of shares	Cost £	Indexed cost £
10 July 1986	4,000	10,000	10,470
Index to April 1998 $\dfrac{162.6 - 97.5}{97.5} \times 10,470$			6,991
Value of pool at 6.4.98	4,000	10,000	17,461

Activity 7.4

		No of shares	Cost £
1.5.99	Purchase	10,000	42,000
1.12.00	Bonus issue	2,000	–
		12,000	42,000

	£
Disposal proceeds	15,000
Less: Cost $\dfrac{4,000}{12,000} \times 42,000$	(14,000)
Gain	1,000

No taper relief available

Activity 7.5

(a) *Post 5.4.98 holding*

	Number	Cost £
Shares acquired 11.9.98	2,000	5,000
Shares acquired 1.2.99 (rights) 1:2 @ £2.75	1,000	2,750
	3,000	7,750

Gain

	£
Proceeds $\dfrac{3,000}{5,000} \times £15,000$	9,000
Less: cost	(7,750)
Gain	1,250

Taper relief (based on ownership of original holding 11.9.98 – 10.9.01)

95% (Three years: non business asset) × £1,250   £1,188

Part B: Capital gains tax

(b) *FA 1985 pool*

	Number	Cost £	Indexed cost £
1.10.95	10,000	15,000	15,000
IA to 4.98 $\frac{162.6 - 149.8}{149.8} \times £15,000$			1,282
Pool at 5.4.98	10,000	15,000	16,282
Rights issues 1.2.99	5,000	13,750	13,750
	15,000	28,750	30,032
14.10.01 Sale	(2,000)	(3,833)	(4,004)
c/F	13,000	24,917	26,028

Gain

	£
Proceeds $\frac{2,000}{5,000} \times £15,000$	6,000
Less: cost	(3,833)
Unindexed gain	2,167
Less: indexation £(4,004 – 3,833)	(171)
Indexed gain	1,996

Taper relief (based on original holding 6.4.98 – 5.4.01)

90% (Four years: non business asset) × £1,996	£1,796

(c) Total gains (after taper relief)

£(1,188 + 1,796)	£2,984

Activity 7.6

Post 6.4.98 acquisitions: match on a LIFO basis.

17.1.99

	£
Proceeds $\left(\frac{2,000}{6,000} \times £24,000\right)$	8,000
Less: cost	(6,000)
Chargeable gain	2,000

No taper relief

12.12.98

	£
Proceeds $\left(\frac{2,000}{6,000} \times £24,000\right)$	8,000
Less: cost	(5,500)
Chargeable gain	2,500

No taper relief

The FA 1985 pool

	Shares	Cost £	Indexed cost £
Acquisition 19.9.85	2,000	1,700	1,700
Indexation to April 1998 (Pool closes)			
$\frac{162.6 - 95.4}{95.4} \times £1,700$			1,197
Value when pool closes (5.4.98)	2,000	1,700	2,897
Disposal 17.5.01	(2,000)	(1,700)	(2,897)
	0	0	0

Tutorial note. Indexation factors are not rounded to 3 decimal places in the FA 1985 pool.

7: Shares and securities

	£
Proceeds $\frac{2,000}{6,000} \times £24,000$	8,000
Less cost	(1,700)
	6,300
Less indexation allowance £(2,897 − 1,700)	(1,197)
Chargeable gain	5,103

Taper relief is available for this non-business asset with four complete years of ownership (including the additional year) post 5 April 1998. Gain after taper relief £4,593

The total gains are £(2,000 + 2,500 + 4,593) = £9,093.

Chapter 8 Chattels, wasting assets, leases and private residences

---

Chapter topic list

1 Chattels
2 Wasting assets
3 Leases
4 Private residences

Learning objectives

On completion of this chapter you will be able to:

	Performance criteria	Range Statement
• outline the exemptions from CGT that apply to chattels, wasting chattels and an individual's home	19.3.1	19.3.1
• compute restricted gains and losses on certain chattels, wasting assets and leases	19.3.1	19.3.1

Part B: Capital gains tax

1 CHATTELS

KEY TERMS

A **chattel** is tangible movable property.

A **wasting asset** is an asset with an estimated remaining useful life of 50 years or less.

1.1 **Plant and machinery, whose predictable useful life is always deemed to be less than 50 years, is therefore an example of a wasting chattel (unless it is immovable, in which case it will be wasting but not a chattel)**. Machinery includes, in addition to its ordinary meaning, motor vehicles (unless exempt as cars), engine-powered boats and clocks.

1.2 **Wasting chattels are exempt from CGT** (so that there are no chargeable gains and no allowable losses). There is one exception to this: assets used for the purpose of a trade, profession or vocation in respect of which capital allowances have been or could have been claimed. This means that items of plant and machinery used in a trade are not exempt merely on the ground that they are wasting. (However, cars are always exempt.)

1.3 **If a chattel is not exempt under the wasting chattels rule, any gain arising on its disposal will still be exempt from CGT if the asset is sold for gross proceeds of £6,000 or less,** even if capital allowances were claimed on it.

1.4 **If sale proceeds exceed £6,000, any gain is limited** to a maximum of 5/3 × (gross proceeds − £6,000).

Activity 8.1: Gains on chattels

Adam purchased a Chippendale chair on 1 June 1998 for £1,458. On 10 October 2001 he sold the chair at auction for £6,300 (which was net of the auctioneer's 10% commission). What was the chargeable gain?

Losses

1.5 **Where a chattel, not exempt under the wasting chattels rule is sold for less than £6,000 and a loss arises, the allowable loss is restricted by assuming that the chattel was sold for £6,000.** However, this rule cannot turn a loss into a gain, only reduce the loss, perhaps to zero.

Activity 8.2: Computation of gain or loss

Eve purchased a rare first edition on 1 July 1982 for £8,000 which she sold in October 2001 at auction for £2,700 (which was net of 10% commission). Compute the gain or loss.

2 WASTING ASSETS

2.1 As we have seen, a wasting asset is one which has an estimated remaining useful life of 50 years or less and whose original value will depreciate over time. **Freehold land is never a wasting asset,** and there are special rules for leases of land, given below.

8: Chattels, wasting assets, leases and private residences

2.2 **Wasting chattels are exempt except for those on which capital allowances have been** (or could have been) **claimed**. Where capital allowances were available (on any asset, not just a chattel) and a loss would arise, the base cost is reduced by the net capital allowances obtained: the result is no gain and no loss. Gains on such assets may still be exempted or restricted under the chattels rules based on £6,000 as long as the assets are not fixed. Items of fixed plant and machinery are not movable and so are not chattels.

2.3 EXAMPLE: WASTING CHATTEL

X Ltd bought a computer for £17,000 in January 1992. The computer was sold for £8,000 in December 2001. Capital allowances were claimed on the computer which will have equalled £9,000 in total over the life of the computer.

	£	£
Sale proceeds		8,000
Cost	17,000	
Less net capital allowances claimed	(9,000)	
		(8,000)
Gain on disposal		NIL

Wasting assets other than chattels

2.4 The cost is written down on a straight line basis before calculating the indexation allowance. Thus, if a taxpayer acquires such an asset with a remaining life of 40 years and disposes of it after 15 years (with 25 years remaining) only 25/40 of the cost is deducted from the disposal consideration. Indexation allowance (if relevant) is computed on the written down cost rather than the full original cost.

2.5 Examples of such assets are copyrights (with 50 years or less to run) and registered designs.

2.6 Where the asset has an estimated residual value at the end of its predictable life, it is the cost less residual value which is written off on a straight line basis over the asset's life. Where additional expenditure is incurred on a wasting asset the additional cost is written off over the life remaining when it was incurred.

Activity 8.3: Wasting asset

Jeremy bought a copyright on 1 April 1991, when it had 40 years to run. He paid £7,000 for it, and sold it for £23,000 on 1 July 2001. What was the chargeable gain? The copyright was a non-business asset.

---

3 LEASES

Types of disposal

3.1 The gain that arises on the disposal of a lease will be chargeable according to the terms of the lease disposed of. We must consider:

- the assignment of a lease or sub-lease with 50 years or more to run;
- the assignment of a lease or sub-lease with less than 50 years to run.

3.2 **There is an assignment when a lessee sells the whole of his interest. There is a grant when a new lease or sub-lease is created out of a freehold or existing leasehold, the**

Part B: Capital gains tax

grantor retaining an interest. The Unit 19 assessor has stated that the rules on the grant of leases will not be examined.

3.3 The duration of the lease will normally be determined by the contract terms. The expiry date, however, will be taken as the first date on which the landlord has an option to terminate the lease or the date beyond which the lease is unlikely to continue because of, for example, the likelihood that the rent will be substantially increased at that date.

The assignment of a lease with 50 years or more to run

3.4 An **ordinary disposal computation** is made and the whole of any gain on disposal will be chargeable to CGT (subject to any private residence exemption, see below).

The assignment of a lease with less than 50 years less to run

3.5 **In calculating the gain on the disposal of a lease with less than 50 years to run only a certain proportion of the original expenditure counts as an allowable deduction from the disposal proceeds.** This is because a lease is losing value anyway as its life runs out: only the cost related to the tail end of the lease being sold is deductible. The proportion is determined by a table of percentages, which is reproduced in the Rates and Allowances Tables in this text.

3.6 **The allowable cost is given by original cost × X/Y, where X is the percentage for the number of years left for the lease to run at the date of the assignment, and Y is the percentage for the number of years the lease had to run when first acquired by the seller.**

3.7 The table only provides percentages for exact numbers of years. Where the duration is not an exact number of years the relevant percentage should be found by adding 1/12 of the difference between the two years on either side of the actual duration for each extra month. Fourteen or more odd days count as a month.

Activity 8.4: The assignment of a short lease

Mr A acquired a 20 year lease on a block of flats which he rents out on 1 August 1995 for £15,000. He assigned it on 1 August 2001 for £19,000. Compute the chargeable gain arising.

3.8 If a lease was acquired before 31 March 1982, then in the calculation based on 31 March 1982 value, 31 March 1982 is treated as the date of acquisition of the lease.

Activity 8.5: Calculation of gain arising

Mr B acquired a 30 year lease on an investment property on 1 January 1980 for £20,000. He assigned it on 1 July 2001 for £28,000. The lease was valued at £15,000 on 31 March 1982. Compute any chargeable gain arising.

4 PRIVATE RESIDENCES

4.1 A gain arising on the sale of an individual's only or main private residence (his principal private residence or PPR) is exempt from CGT.

4.2 **The exemption also normally covers grounds of up to half a hectare.** The grounds can exceed half a hectare if the house is large enough to warrant it, but if not, only the gain on the excess grounds is taxable. If the grounds do not adjoin the house (for example when a road separates the two), they *may* still qualify but they may not: each case must be argued on its merits. However, if the grounds are to qualify they must not be sold later than the house.

4.3 **The gain is wholly exempt where the owner has occupied the whole of the residence throughout his period of ownership. Where occupation has been for only part of the period, the proportion of the gain exempted is**

$$\text{Total gain} \times \frac{\text{Period of occupation}}{\text{Total period of ownership}}$$

A further proportionate restriction is made where only part of the property has been occupied as the owner's residence.

The period prior to 1 April 1982 is ignored. The **last 36 months of ownership are always** treated as **a period of occupation**, if at some time the residence has been the taxpayer's main residence, even if within those last 36 months the taxpayer also has another house which is his principal private residence.

Where a loss arises but all or a proportion of any gain would have been exempt, all or the same proportion of the loss is not allowable.

4.4 Where a taxpayer buys land and builds a house on it, or buys a house but delays moving in because he has work done on it or he is still disposing of his old house, the period from purchase to actual moving in counts as a period of residence so long as it is immediately followed by actual residence, and does not exceed one year. The one year period may be increased by up to a further year if there are good reasons.

Activity 8.6: Principal private residences

Zoë purchased a house on 1 April 1990 for £100,000. She lived in the house until she sold it in December 2001 for £250,000. What gain/loss arises?

4.5 Buildings within the grounds of a main dwelling house may form part of the taxpayer's principal private residence and therefore be exempt. Again each case must be argued on its merits.

4.6 A caravan connected to mains water and electricity is a qualifying dwelling for the purposes of principal private residence relief: *Makins v Elson 1977*.

Relocations

4.7 When an employee is required to move by his employer, and sells his house to the employer or to a relocation company for a guaranteed value plus a share in any profit made by the employer or relocation company when it sells the house, the profit share is exempt to the same extent as the initial gain on selling the house. Thus if only 60% of that gain was exempt, 60% of the profit share will also be exempt.

More than one residence

The election for a residence to be treated as the main residence

4.8 **Where a person has more than one residence (owned or rented), he may elect for one to be regarded as his main residence within two years of commencing occupation of the**

second residence. An election can have effect for any period beginning not more than two years prior to the date of election until it is varied by giving further notice. (The further notice may itself be backdated by up to two years.)

4.9 In order for the election to be made, the individual must actually reside in both residences.

4.10 Any period of ownership of a residence not nominated as the main residence will be a chargeable period for that residence.

4.11 Where there are two residences and the second one is being treated as a residence under the 'delay in moving in' rule (see above), the election is not needed and both may count as principal private residences simultaneously.

Job-related accommodation

4.12 **The rule limiting people to only one main residence is relaxed for individuals living in job-related accommodation.**

4.13 Such individuals will be treated as occupying any second dwelling house which they own if they intend in due course to occupy the dwelling house as their only or main residence. Thus it is not necessary to establish any actual residence in such cases. This rule extends to self-employed persons required to live in job-related accommodation (for example tenants of public houses).

> **KEY TERM**
>
> A person lives in **job-related accommodation** where:
>
> - it is necessary for the **proper performance of his duties**; or
> - it is provided for the **better performance of his duties** and his is one of the kinds of employment in which it is **customary** for employers to provide accommodation; or
> - there is a **special threat to the employee's security** and use of the accommodation is part of security arrangements.

Husbands and wives

4.14 **Where a husband and wife live together only one residence may qualify as the main residence for relief.** If each owned one property before marriage, a new two year period for electing for which is to be treated as the main residence starts on marriage.

4.15 Where a marriage has broken down and one spouse owning or having an interest in the matrimonial home has ceased to occupy the house, by concession the departing spouse will continue to be treated as resident for capital gains tax purposes provided that the other spouse has continued to reside in the home and the departing spouse has not elected that some other house should be treated as his or her main residence for this period. This only applies where one spouse disposes of his interest to the other spouse.

4.16 Where a house passes from one spouse to the other (for example on death), the new owner also inherits the old owner's periods of ownership and occupation for PPR relief purposes.

Lettings

4.17 The principal private residence exemption is extended to any gain accruing while the property is let, up to a certain limit. The two main circumstances in which the letting exemption applies are:

- when the owner is absent and lets the property;
- when the owner lets part of the property while still occupying the rest of it.

4.18 In both cases the letting must be for residential use. **The extra exemption is restricted to the lowest of:**

(a) the gain accruing during the letting period (the **letting part of the gain**);
(b) **£40,000**;
(c) the amount of the total **gain** which is already **exempt under the PPR provisions.**

The letting exemption cannot convert a gain into an allowable loss.

4.19 Where a lodger lives as a member of the owner's family, sharing their living accommodation and eating with them, the whole property is regarded as remaining the owner's main residence.

Activity 8.7: The letting exemption

Miss Coe purchased a house in May 1976 for £25,000. She sold it on 31 August 2001 for £340,000. In 1984 the house was redecorated and Miss Coe began to live on the top floor renting out the balance of the house (constituting 60% of the total house) to tenants between 1 January 1985 and 31 December 2000. On 2 January 2001 Miss Coe put the whole house on the market but continued to live only on the top floor until the house was sold. The market value of the property on 31 March 1982 was £90,000. What was the chargeable gain?

Business use

4.20 Where part of a residence is used exclusively for business purposes throughout the period of ownership, the gain attributable to use of that part is taxable.

4.21 If part of a house has been used for business purposes for part of the period of ownership, the gain is apportioned between chargeable and exempt parts in a just and reasonable manner.

Activity 8.8: Calculation of gain on property

Mr Smail purchased a property for £20,000 on 1 December 1981 and began operating a dental practice from that date in one quarter of the house. On 1 December 1999 he purchased a second house and submitted an election to treat this second house as his main residence with effect from the date of purchase. He closed down the dental practice on 1 December 2001, selling the old house on that date for £130,000. The value of the old house on 31 March 1982 was estimated to be £35,000.

Compute the chargeable gain, if any, arising before taper relief.

Part B: Capital gains tax

Activity 8.9: End of chapter activity

(a) In 2001/02, Mr California sold the following chattels.

Chattel	Date of purchase	Cost £	31.3.82 value £	Date of sale	Proceeds £
Manuscript	1.1.77	3,000	4,500	9.4.01	6,300
Painting	1.3.79	7,000	8,700	6.7.01	5,000
Vase	1.4.82	800		2.11.01	7,000
Sideboard	1.5.85	4,000		1.12.01	8,000

All proceeds are shown before selling expenses of 5% of the gross proceeds.

Task

Compute the chargeable gain or allowable loss on each chattel before taper relief.

Assume indexation: March 1982 - April 1998 = 1.048
April 1982 - April 1998 = 1.007
May 1985 - April 1998 = 0.708

(b) Mr Sacramento bought a copyright for £37,000 on 4 December 1993, when it had 47 years left to run. He sold it for £62,000 on 4 June 2001. Compute Sacramento's chargeable gain after taper relief if the indexation allowance available on this disposal is £5,402. Assume that the copyright is a non-business asset.

(c) On 31 August 2001, Dr Prance sold his house. He had bought it on 31 March 1982 for £120,000. The proceeds were £300,000 before estate agent's fees of £5,000 and legal fees of £1,200. Dr Prance lived in the property until 1 October 1986, when he moved into a flat he had purchased nearby. He sold the flat and moved back into the house on 1 September 1996 and lived there until it was sold. He let the house from 1.10.86 to 31.8.96.

Task

Calculate any chargeable gain before taper relief arising on the disposal of the house.

Assume indexation March 1982 - April 1998 = 1.048

Key learning points

- When a chattel is sold for up to £6,000, any gain is exempt and any loss is restricted. Gains on most wasting chattels sold for any amount are exempt, and losses on them are not allowable.
- Other wasting assets generally have their cost written down over time. For leases of land, a special table of percentages is used.
- There is an exemption for gains on principal private residences, but the exemption may be restricted because of periods of non-occupation.
- A letting exemption may be available during periods for which the property is let.

Quick quiz

1. How are gains on non-wasting chattels sold for more than £6,000 restricted?
2. How are losses on non-wasting chattels sold for less than £6,000 restricted?
3. Distinguish between the grant and the assignment of a lease
4. When a lease with less than 50 years to run is assigned, what proportion of the cost is allowable?
5. When are gains on the disposal of a principal private residence exempt?
6. Can a building separate from the main house benefit from the principal private residence exemption?
7. How is the principal private residence exemption extended for people in job-related accommodation?

8: Chattels, wasting assets, leases and private residences

8   What is the maximum letting exemption?

Quick quiz answers

1   Gain restricted to 5/3 × (gross proceeds − £6,000).

2   The allowable loss is restricted by deeming proceeds to be £6,000.

3   There is an assignment when a lessee sells the whole of his interest. There is a grant when a new lease or sub-lease is created out of a freehold or existing leasehold, the grantor retaining an interest.

4   The allowable cost is given by original cost × X/Y, where X is the percentage for the number of years left for the lease to run at the date of the assignment, and Y is the percentage for the number of years the lease had to run when first acquired by the seller.

5   Any gain is wholly exempt where the owner has occupied the whole of the residence throughout his period of ownership. Where occupation has been for only part of the period, the proportion of the gain exempted is

$$\text{Total gain} \times \frac{\text{Period of occupation}}{\text{Total period of ownership}}$$

A further proportionate restriction is made where only part of the property has been occupied as the owner's residence. The last 36 months of ownership are always treated as a period of occupation.

6   A building within the grounds of the main dwelling house may form part of the taxpayer's principal private residence or it may not. It will depend on the circumstances on the case.

7   The rule limiting people to only one main residence is relaxed for individuals living in job-related accommodation. Such individuals will be treated as occupying any second dwelling house which they own if they intend in due course to occupy the dwelling house as their only or main residence.

8   The maximum exemption is the lowest of:

   (a)   the gain accruing during the letting period (the letting part of the gain);
   (b)   £40,000;
   (c)   the amount of the total gain which is already exempt under the PPR provisions.

Answers to activities

Activity 8.1

Proceeds	7,000
Less incidental costs of sale	(700)
Net proceeds	6,300
Less cost	(1,458)
Gain before taper relief	4,842

The maximum gain is 5/3 × £(7,000 − 6,000) = £1,667

The chargeable gain before taper relief is the lower of £4,842 and £1,667, so it is £1,667.

Gain after taper relief £1,667 × 95%   £1,584

Note. Taper relief is available to reduce this gain on a non-business asset with three years post 5.4.98 ownership.

Activity 8.2

	£
Proceeds (assumed)	6,000
Less incidental costs of disposal (£2,700 × 10/90)	(300)
	5,700
Less cost	(8,000)
Allowable loss (indexation allowance cannot increase a loss)	(2,300)

Part B: Capital gains tax

Activity 8.3

	£
Proceeds	23,000
Less cost £7,000 x 29.75/40	(5,206)
	17,794
Less indexation allowance to April 1998	
$\dfrac{162.6 - 133.1}{133.1} = 0.222 \times £5,206$	(1,156)
Chargeable gain	16,638

Gain chargeable after taper relief £14,974 (£16,638 × 90%)

Activity 8.4

	£
Proceeds	19,000
Less cost £15,000 × $\dfrac{58.971}{72.770}$	(12,156)
Unindexed gain	6,844
Less indexation allowance (August 1995 to April 1998)	
$\dfrac{162.6 - 149.9}{149.9} = 0.085 \times £12,156$	(1,033)
Indexed gain	5,811

58.971 = percentage for 14 years (life from 1.8.01)
72.770 = percentage for 20 years (life from 1.8.95)

Gain after taper relief (4 years including additional year) 90% × £5,811   £5,230

Activity 8.5

	Cost £	31.3.82 value £
Proceeds	28,000	28,000
Less: cost		
£20,000 × $\dfrac{41.277}{87.330}$	(9,453)	
31.3.82 value		
£15,000 × $\dfrac{41.277}{84.744}$		(7,306)
Unindexed gain	18,547	20,694
Less indexation allowance (March 1982 to April 1998)		
$\dfrac{162.6 - 79.4}{79.4} = 1.048 \times £9,453$	(9,907)	(9,907)
	8,640	10,787

The indexed gain is £8,640.

Gain after taper relief (4 years including additional year) 90% × £8,640   £7,776

Percentages are as follows.

1.7.2001:	8½ years:	39.399 + (43.154 − 39.399) × 6/12 = 41.277
31.3.1982:	27¾ years:	83.816 + (85.053 − 83.816) × 9/12 = 84.744
1.1.1980:	30 years:	87.330

Activity 8.6

No gain/loss arises. The gain on the disposal of a principal private residence is exempt. Any loss is not allowable.

Activity 8.7

	£
Proceeds	340,000
Less 31.3.82 value (clearly gives a lower gain than cost)	(90,000)
Unindexed gain	250,000
Less indexation allowance (March 1982 to April 1998)	

$$\frac{162.6 - 79.4}{79.4} = 1.048 \times £90,000$$ (94,320)

Indexed gain 155,680
Less PPR exemption

$£155,680 \times \dfrac{33(1.4.82 - 31.12.84) + 36(1.9.98 - 31.8.01)}{233(1.4.82 - 31.8.01)}$ 46,103

$£155,680 \times \dfrac{164(1.1.85 - 31.8.98)}{233(1.4.82 - 31.8.01)} \times 40\%$ 43,831

(89,934)
65,746

Less letting exemption
Lowest of:

(a) gain attributable to letting $£155,680 \times \dfrac{164}{233} \times 60\% = £65,746$

(b) £40,000   (40,000)

(c) gain exempt under PPR rules £89,934

Gain left in charge   25,746

Gain after taper relief (4 years including additional year)

90% × £25,746   £23,171

Working

Period	Ownership months	Notes
1.4.82 - 31.12.84	33	100% of house occupied
1.1.85 - 31.8.98	164	40% of house occupied
		60% of house let
1.9.98 - 31.8.01	36	Last 36 months treated as 100% of house occupied
	233	

Note. The gain on the 40% of the house always occupied by Miss Coe is fully covered by PPR relief. The other 60% of the house has not always been occupied by Miss Coe and thus any gain on this part of the house is taxable where it relates to periods of time when Miss Coe was not actually (or deemed to be) living in it.

Activity 8.8

	£
Proceeds	130,000
Less 31.3.82 value (clearly gives a lower gain than cost)	(35,000)
Unindexed gain	95,000

Less indexation allowance (March 1982 to April 1998)

$$\frac{162.6 - 79.4}{79.4} = 1.048 \times £35,000$$ (36,680)

Indexed gain	58,320
Less PPR exemption 0.75 × £58,320	(43,740)
Chargeable gain before taper relief	14,580

Part B: Capital gains tax

Exemption is lost on one quarter throughout the period of ownership (including the last 36 months) because of the use of that fraction for business purposes. The last 36 months are exempt (for the non-business part), despite the acquisition of a second house which is treated as the principal private residence.

Activity 8.9

(a) (i) *The manuscript*

	Cost £	31.3.82 value £
Proceeds	6,300	6,300
Less selling expenses	(315)	(315)
	5,985	5,985
Less cost/31.3.82 value	(3,000)	(4,500)
	2,985	1,485
Less indexation allowance to April 1998 1.048 × £4,500 = £4,716	(2,985)	(1,485)
	0	0

The allowable loss is zero. The proceeds need not be increased, because the gross proceeds, £6,300, are already at least £6,000. Indexation cannot turn a gain into a loss.

(ii) *The painting*

There will clearly be a loss, so the gross proceeds must be deemed to be £6,000 for the purposes of computing the loss.

	Cost £	31.3.82 value £
Proceeds	6,000	6,000
Less selling expenses	(250)	(250)
	5,750	5,750
Less cost/31.3.82 value	(7,000)	(8,700)
	(1,250)	(2,950)

The allowable loss is the lower loss, £1,250.

(iii) *The vase*

	£
Proceeds	7,000
Less selling expenses	(350)
	6,650
Less cost	(800)
	5,850
Less indexation allowance to April 1998 1.007 × £800	(806)
Gain	5,044

The chargeable gain before taper relief is the lower of £5,044 and £(7,000 − 6,000) × 5/3 = £1,667, so it is £1,667.

(iv) *The sideboard*

	£
Proceeds	8,000
Less selling expenses	(400)
	7,600
Less cost	(4,000)
	3,600
Less indexation allowance to April 1998 0.708 × £4,000	(2,832)
Gain	768

The chargeable gain before taper relief is the lower of £768 and £(8,000 − 6,000) × 5/3 = £3,333, so it is £768.

(b)

	£
Proceeds	62,000
Less cost £37,000 × 39.5/47	(31,096)
	30,904
Less indexation allowance to April 1998	(5,402)
Chargeable gain before taper relief	25,502
Gain remaining after taper relief (90%).	£22,952

Note: Taper relief applies for this non-business asset with four complete years of ownership post 5 April 1998 (including the additional year).

(c)

	£	£
Proceeds		300,000
Less costs of disposal: estate agent's fees	5,000	
legal fees	1,200	
		(6,200)
Net proceeds		293,800
Less cost		(120,000)
Unindexed gain		173,800
Less indexation allowance to April 1998		
1.048 × £120,000		(125,760)
		48,040

Less principal private residence exemption

		Total (months)	Exempt (months)
1.4.82 - 30.9.86	Actual residence	54	54
1.10.86 - 31.8.96	House let	119	
1.9.96 - 31.8.01	Actual residence	60	60
		233	114

	£
£48,040 × $\frac{114}{233}$	(23,505)
Chargeable gain	24,535
Less: Letting exemption	
Lower of	
(i) £40,000	(23,505)
(ii) £23,505	
(iii) £24,535	
Chargeable gain before taper relief	1,030

Chapter 9   CGT reliefs

Chapter topic list

1   EIS and VCT reinvestment relief
2   Loans to traders
3   Compensation and insurance proceeds

Learning objectives

On completion of this chapter you will be able to:

	Performance criteria	Range Statement
• show how a gain can be deferred if a certain type of purchase of shares is made within a specific period of time by an individual	19.3.5	19.3.2
• discuss two reliefs, one for a loss made on a loan to a trader, the other on the receipt of compensation or insurance from the loss or destruction of an asset	19.3.5	19.3.2

Part B: Capital gains tax

1 EIS AND VCT REINVESTMENT RELIEF

1.1 A gain arising on the disposal of any type of asset may be deferred by an individual if he invests in Enterprise Investment Scheme (EIS) shares. This is a deferral relief because the deferred gain will become chargeable, for example when the shares are disposed of.

1.2 It is not necessary for the shares acquired to be subject to the EIS income tax relief. For example, there is no upper limit for investment into shares.

Calculation of relief

1.3 The amount of the gain (before taper relief) that can be deferred is the lower of:

(a) the amount subscribed by the investor for his shares; and

(b) the amount specified by the investor in the claim. This can take into account the availability of losses, taper relief and the annual exemption.

Taper relief is then applied to any remaining gain in the usual way.

1.4 The gain deferred is the gain before taper relief.

Activity 9.1: Deferral of gain

Robert made a gain of £196,000 (before taper relief) on the disposal of a property in 2001/02. The property qualifies for three years taper relief as a non-business asset. He subscribed for some shares in a company which qualified under the EIS rules. What will the gain to defer be if the shares cost £200,000 and Robert wants to take the maximum deferral relief possible.

Activity 9.2

In the above situation what will the gain to defer be if the shares cost £170,000 and Robert wants to take the maximum deferral relief possible.

Activity 9.3

In the above situation what will the gain to defer be if the shares cost £200,000 and Robert, who has no other chargeable assets, wishes to utilise his annual exemption.

1.5 The shares must be issued to the investor within the period of one year before and three years after the gain to be deferred accrues (or such longer period as the Board of Inland Revenue may allow). If the gain accrues after the issue of the shares, the shares must still be held by the investor at the time that the gain arises.

The claim

1.6 The claim to be made is broadly similar to that for the EIS income tax relief. The latest date for a claim to be made is 31 January nearly six years after the end of the tax year in which the gain to be deferred arose.

Gain coming back into charge

1.7 The gain deferred will come back into charge on the following events:

(a) the investor disposing of the shares except by an inter-spouse disposal;

(b) the spouse of an investor disposing of the shares, if the spouse acquired the shares from the investor;

(c) the shares ceasing to be eligible EIS shares.

1.8 The gain becomes chargeable in the year of the event, not the year when the original gain was made (if different). It will be charged on the holder of the shares at the date of the event eg. on the investor if he/she still holds the shares or the spouse if the shares have been passed to her/him.

1.9 Taper relief generally applies to the deferred gain with reference to the original asset which gave rise to the deferred gain. No further taper relief can be given to the deferred gain. However, separate taper relief will apply to the holding of the shares.

VCT reinvestment relief

1.10 There is a similar deferral relief in respect of investment into VCT shares. The main differences between the EIS relief and the VCT relief are:

(a) the shares must qualify for the VCT income tax relief. Therefore the investment relief limit for income tax also applies for the VCT reinvestment relief;

(b) the time for investment into the shares is 12 months before and 12 months after the gain to be deferred arises.

2 LOANS TO TRADERS

2.1 A debt, except a debt on a security (which is a debt represented by a marketable document) is normally an exempt asset, so losses are not allowable. **However, losses are allowable if they are incurred on loans, or guarantees in respect of loans, which are made to traders.**

2.2 **For a loan the taxpayer will be treated as if an allowable loss equal to the irrecoverable loan had arisen on the date of the claim or at a specified earlier time which is up to two years before the start of the tax year in which the claim is made. The amount claimed must have been irrecoverable at the earlier time. Relief is available only for the lost principal of the loan, not for lost interest.**

2.3 **For a guarantee the taxpayer will be treated as if an allowable loss equal to the payment under the guarantee had arisen on the date that payment was made or at a specified earlier time.** An individual can go back in time just as far as for a claim as lender. The amount claimed must have been irrecoverable at the earlier time. Interest, as well as principal, paid under a guarantee can qualify.

Recoveries of amounts claimed

2.4 Where the whole or part of the outstanding amount which has given rise to an allowable loss (under a loan or a guarantee) is at any time recovered by the claimant, the claimant is treated as having made a chargeable gain equal to the amount recovered at the date of recovery.

3 COMPENSATION AND INSURANCE PROCEEDS

Damaged assets

3.1 If an asset is damaged and compensation or insurance money is received as a result, then this will normally be treated as a part disposal. By election, however, the taxpayer can avoid a part disposal computation. **A capital sum received can be deducted from the cost of the asset rather than being treated as a part disposal if:**

(a) the amount not spent in restoring the asset is small; or
(b) the capital sum is small.

3.2 The Revenue accept a sum as 'small' if it is either less than 5% of the value of the asset or is less than £3,000.

3.3 If the amount not used in restoring the asset is not small, then the taxpayer can elect for the amount used in restoration to be deducted from the cost; the balance will continue to be treated as a part disposal.

Activity 9.4: Damaged assets

Mr J bought an office block for renting out which cost £18,000 on 15 April 2001. On 10 September 2001 it was damaged in a fire and, as a result, £27,000 insurance proceeds were received in December 2001. £20,000 was spent to restore the building in October 2001; the market value of the building immediately after restoration was £62,000. What gain arose and what will be the base cost of the building in future computations? Assume that Mr J elects for the amount used in restoration to be deducted from the base cost of the building.

Destroyed assets

3.4 If an asset is destroyed (as opposed to merely being damaged) any compensation or insurance monies received will normally be brought into an ordinary CGT disposal computation as proceeds. But if all the proceeds are applied for the replacement of the asset within 12 months, any gain can be deducted from the cost of the replacement asset. If only part of the proceeds are used, the gain immediately chargeable can be limited to the amount not used. The rest of the gain is then deducted from the cost of the replacement.

Activity 9.5: Destroyed assets

Fiona bought a non-business asset for £25,000 in June 2001. It was destroyed three years and one month later. Insurance proceeds were £34,000, and Fiona spent £32,500 on a replacement asset. Compute the chargeable gain and the base cost of the new asset.

The compulsory purchase of land

3.5 If land is sold to an authority exercising or having powers of compulsory purchase and the proceeds are applied to buy other land, the gain on the land disposed of may be deducted from the base cost of the land bought (instead of being chargeable). If only part of the proceeds are reinvested, the balance (up to the amount of the gain) is chargeable.

3.6 If the replacement land is a leasehold with a remaining life of 60 years or less, the deferred gain is not deducted from the base cost of the replacement. It is merely held over and becomes chargeable when the land is sold or 10 years after the acquisition, if earlier.

3.7 The replacement land must be acquired within the period from one year before to three years after the disposal of the land compulsorily purchased.

3.8 Relief is not available if, at any time in the six years after acquisition, the replacement land is the buyer's principal private residence for CGT purposes.

3.9 If a taxpayer expects to acquire new land, he can make a provisional claim on the tax return which includes the gain on the old land to reduce the gain accordingly.

Activity 9.6: End of chapter activity

Judith bought some freehold land as an investment asset in August 1986 for £50,000. In March 1991, it was compulsorily purchased for £120,000, and Judith immediately replaced it with other land costing £95,000, and claimed to defer the gain. She sold the second plot of land for £180,000 in October 2001.

Judith sold no other assets in 2001/02.

Task

Compute the chargeable gain arising in October 2001.

Key learning points

- EIS relief defers a gain until a later date.
- The gain made on any asset disposal can be deferred if EIS shares are acquired.
- The deferred gain becomes chargeable when the shares are sold.
- The gain which would otherwise arise on receipt of insurance proceeds may, subject to certain conditions be deferred.

Quick quiz

1 When is EIS reinvestment relief available?
2 Is a gain deferred by EIS relief chargeable in the year it arose or in the year of disposal of the EIS shares?
3 What is the relief available for loans to traders?
4 What happens when an asset is destroyed?

Quick quiz answers

1 When a gain arising on any asset is reinvested in EIS shares in the period staring one year before and ending three years after the gain arose.

2 In the year of disposal of the shares.

3 Losses on loans to traders are allowable losses.

4 If an asset is destroyed any compensation or insurance monies received will normally be brought into an ordinary CGT disposal computation as proceeds. But if all the proceeds are applied for the replacement of the asset within 12 months, any gain can be deducted from the cost of the replacement asset. If only part of the proceeds are used, the gain immediately chargeable can be limited to the amount not used. The rest of the gain is then deducted from the cost of the replacement.

Part B: Capital gains tax

Answers to activities

Activity 9.1

£196,000. The qualifying expenditure on the shares exceeds the gain, so the whole gain can be deferred.

Activity 9.2

£170,000. The gain deferred is restricted to the qualifying expenditure. The remainder of the gain of £26,000 will remain in charge (subject to relief for any further investment). If no such investment is made and there are no losses to take into account, the gain after taper relief left in charge will be £26,000 × 95% = £24,700.

Activity 9.3

A claim can be made to defer £188,105. This is calculated as follows:

	£
Gain before relief	196,000
Less EIS reinvestment relief (balancing figure)	(188,105)
Gain before taper relief	7,895
Gain after taper relief (95%)	7,500
Less annual exemption	(7,500)
Taxable	nil

Activity 9.4

The part disposal in December 2001	£	£
Capital sum not used for restoration		
£(27,000 - 20,000)		7,000
Less: part of original cost (incurred April 2001)		
£18,000 × $\frac{7,000}{7,000 + 62,000}$	1,826	
part of restoration cost (incurred October 2001)		
£20,000 × $\frac{7,000}{7,000 + 62,000}$	2,029	
		(3,855)
Gain before taper relief		3,145

No taper relief is due.

The base cost of the restored building	£	£
Original cost		18,000
Restoration expenditure		20,000
		38,000
Less: costs used in part disposal	3,855	
restoration expenditure rolled over	20,000	
		(23,855)
Base cost		14,145

The date of the part disposal is the date of receipt of the insurance monies (December 2001). Mr J purchased the asset in April 2001 and also spent £20,000 in restoring the building in October 2001.

Activity 9.5

	£
Proceeds	34,000
Less cost	(25,000)
	9,000
Gain immediately chargeable £(34,000 – 32,500)	(1,500)
Deduction from base cost	7,500

The base cost of the new asset is £(32,500 – 7,500) = £25,000.

The gain chargeable of £1,500 qualifies for taper relief (3 complete years of ownership of a non-business asset). 95% of the gain is charged to tax which equals £1,425.

Activity 9.6

We must first work out the gain deferred in March 1991.

	£
Proceeds	120,000
Less cost	(50,000)
	70,000
Less indexation allowance $\frac{131.4 - 97.8}{97.8} = 0.344 \times £50,000$	(17,200)
	52,800
Less gain chargeable in 1991 £(120,000 – 95,000)	(25,000)
Gain deferred	27,800

The chargeable gain arising in October 2001 is as follows.

	£
Proceeds	180,000
Less cost £(95,000 – 27,800)	(67,200)
	112,800
Less indexation allowance to April 1998 $\frac{162.6 - 131.4}{131.4} = 0.237 \times £67,200$	(15,926)
Indexed gain	96,874

Gain after taper relief (4 complete years of ownership after 6.4.98 including additional year)

90% × £96,874   £87,187

Part C
Relief for losses

Chapter 10 Relief for losses

Chapter topic list

1. Losses
2. Relief for losses by carry forward: s 385 ICTA 1988
3. Relief for losses against total income: s 380 ICTA 1988
4. Trade charges: s 387 ICTA 1988
5. Relief for losses in the early years of a trade: s 381 ICTA 1988

Learning objectives

On completion of this chapter you will be able to:

	Performance criteria	Range Statement
• offset a trading loss against the income of an individual to reduce the income tax bill	19.4.1	19.4.2
• offset a trading loss against the capital gains of an individual to reduce the CGT bill.	19.4.1	19.4.2
• recognise which trading losses can be utilised in which tax years and choose the best use of the loss if more than one option for utilisation is available.	19.4.1	19.4.2

Part C: Relief for losses

1 LOSSES

1.1 This chapter considers how a loss-suffering taxpayer can use a Schedule D Case I/II loss to reduce his tax liability. In this chapter we refer to Schedule D Case I (trade) losses but losses under Schedule D Case II (professions and vocations) are relieved in exactly the same way.

DEVOLVED ASSESSMENT ALERT

You will not be expected to compute losses in this unit but you may be expected to deal with relief for them.

1.2 Losses of one spouse cannot be relieved against income of the other spouse.

2 RELIEF FOR LOSSES BY CARRY FORWARD: S 385 ICTA 1988

2.1 A trading loss may be **carried forward to set against the first available profits of the same trade**. Losses may be carried forward for any number of years.

2.2 EXAMPLE: CARRYING FORWARD LOSSES

B has the following results.

Tax year	Schedule D Profit/(loss) £
1999/00	(6,000)
2000/01	5,000
2001/02	11,000

B's taxable profits, assuming that he claims loss relief only under s 385 are:

	1999/00 £		2000/01 £		2001/02 £
Schedule D Case I	0		5,000		11,000
Less s 385 relief	0	(i)	(5,000)	(ii)	(1,000)
Profits	0		0		10,000

		£
Loss memorandum		
Trading loss, 1999/00		6,000
Less: claim in 2000/01	(i)	(5,000)
claim in 2001/02 (balance of loss)	(ii)	(1,000)
		0

3 RELIEF FOR LOSSES AGAINST TOTAL INCOME: S 380 ICTA 1988

3.1 **Instead of carrying a loss forward against future trading income, it may be relieved against current income of all types.**

Relieving the loss

3.2 **Loss relief** under s 380 **is against the income of the tax year in which the loss was suffered. In addition or instead,** relief may be claimed **against the income of the preceding tax year.**

3.3 A claim for a loss must be made by the 31 January which is nearly 22 months after the end of the tax year of the loss: thus by 31 January 2004 for a loss in 2001/02.

3.4 The taxpayer cannot choose the amount of loss to relieve: thus the loss may have to be set against income, part of which would have been covered by the personal allowance. However, the taxpayer can choose whether to claim full relief in the current year and then relief in the preceding year for any remaining loss, or the other way round.

3.5 Set the loss against non-savings income then against savings (excl) dividend income then against dividend income.

3.6 Relief is available by carry forward under s 385 for any loss not relieved under s 380.

Activity 10.1: s 380 relief

Janet has a loss in 2001/02 of £25,000. Her other income is rental income of £18,000 a year, and she wishes to claim loss relief for the year of loss and then for the preceding year. Show her taxable income for each year, and comment on the effectiveness of the loss relief. Assume tax rates and allowances for 2001/02 have always applied.

Trading losses relieved against capital gains

3.7 Where relief is claimed against total income of a given year, the taxpayer may include **a further claim to set the loss against his net chargeable gains for the year.**

Net chargeable gains are gains after deducting any current or brought forward allowable capital losses but before deducting taper relief and the annual exempt amount.

3.8 **The trading loss is first set against total income of the year of the claim, and only any excess of loss is set against capital gains. The taxpayer cannot specify the amount to be set against capital gains, so the annual exempt amount may be wasted.**

Activity 10.2: Loss relief against income and gains

Sibyl had the following results for 2001/02.

	£
Loss available for relief under s 380	27,000
Income	19,500
Current year capital gains	10,000
Annual exemption for capital gains tax purposes	7,500
Capital losses brought forward	4,000

No taper relief is due on any current year gains.

Show how the loss would be relieved against income and gains.

DEVOLVED ASSESSMENT ALERT

Before recommending loss relief consider whether it will result in the waste of the personal allowance, the capital gains annual exemption and any tax reducers. Such waste is to be avoided if at all possible.

Part C: Relief for losses

Activity 10.3: loss relief

In 2001/02 Nicola has a loss of £18,000. Her statutory total income in 2001/02 is investment income totalling £14,000, and her personal allowance for that year is £4,535. She has no other source of income for any year. If she obtains loss relief as soon as possible, what loss is carried forward under s 385 ICTA 1988?

4 TRADE CHARGES: S 387 ICTA 1988

4.1 If charges paid for trade purposes exceed statutory total income the **excess trade charges can be carried forward against future profits from the same trade** in the same way as losses under s 385. Non-trade charges, however cannot be relieved in this way.

4.2 EXAMPLE: EXCESS TRADE CHARGES

A taxpayer has the following results for 2001/02.

	£
Schedule D Case I	4,000
Other income	1,000
	5,000
Less trade charge	(7,000)
STI	0

The taxpayer could then carry forward the £2,000 excess trade charges against future profits from the trade.

5 RELIEF FOR LOSSES IN THE EARLY YEARS OF A TRADE: S 381 ICTA 1988

5.1 This relief is available in respect of **trading losses incurred in the first four tax years of a trade**.

5.2 Relief is obtained by **setting the allowable loss against total income in the three years preceding the year of loss**, applying the loss to the earliest year first. Thus a loss arising in 2001/02 may be set off against income in 1998/99, 1999/00 and 2000/01 in that order.

5.3 A claim applies to all three years automatically, provided that the loss is large enough. The taxpayer cannot choose to relieve the loss against just one or two of the years, or to relieve only part of the loss.

5.4 Claims for the relief must be made by the 31 January which is nearly 22 months after the end of the tax year in which the loss is incurred.

Activity 10.4: S381 loss relief

Mr A is employed as an auditor until 1 January 2000. On that date he starts up his own business as a scrap metal merchant, making up his accounts to 30 June each year.

His taxable income as an auditor is as follows.

	£
1996/97	5,000
1997/98	6,000
1998/99	7,000
1999/00 (nine months)	6,000

Business losses available for relief from the scrap metal business are:

	Profit/(Loss)
	£
1999/00	(1,500)
2000/01	(2,250)
2001/02	(750)
2002/03	(1,200)

Assuming that loss relief is claimed as early as possible, show the final Schedule E income for each of the years 1996/97 to 1999/00 inclusive.

Activity 10.5: End of chapter activity

Morgan started to trade on 6 April 1998. His business has the following results.

Tax year		£
1998/99	Profit	12,000
1999/00	Profit	16,000
2000/01	Profit	18,000
2001/02	Profit	15,000
2002/03 (projected)	Loss	(32,000)

It is expected that the business will show healthy profits thereafter. In addition to his business Morgan has rental income of £8,000 a year.

Task

(a) Outline the ways in which Morgan could obtain relief for his loss.

(b) Prepare a statement showing how the loss would be relieved assuming that relief were to be claimed as soon as possible. Comment on whether this is likely to be the best relief

Key learning points

- Trading losses may be relieved against future profits of the same trade, against total income and against capital gains.

- In opening years, a special relief involving the carry back of losses against total income is available.

- It is important for a trader to choose the right loss relief, so as to save tax at the highest possible rate and so as to obtain relief reasonably quickly.

Quick quiz

1   Against what income may trading losses carried forward be set off?

2   Against which years' total income may a loss be relieved under s 380 ICTA 1988?

3   What is the relief available under s 381 ICTA 1988?

Quick quiz answers

1   The first available profits of the same trade.

2   The income of the tax year in which the loss was suffered and/or the income of the preceding tax year.

3   This relief is available in respect of trading losses incurred in the first four tax years of a trade.

Relief is obtained by setting the allowable loss against total income in the three years preceding the year of loss, applying the loss to the earliest year first. Thus a loss arising in 2001/02 may be set off against income in 1998/99, 1999/00 and 2000/01 in that order.

Part C: Relief for losses

Answers to activities

Activity 10.1

	2000/01	2001/02
	£	£
Income	18,000	18,000
Less s 380 relief	(7,000)	(18,000)
STI	11,000	0
Less personal allowance	(4,535)	(4,535)
Taxable income	6,465	0

In 2001/02, £4,535 of the loss has been wasted because that amount of income would have been covered by the personal allowance. If Janet claims relief under s 380 there is nothing she can do about this waste of loss relief. However, Janet might have been best advised to claim relief in 2000/01 before making a claim in 2001/02. This would have the effect of moving the income to 2001/02 and delaying the payment of the associated income tax.

Activity 10.2

	£
Income	19,500
Less loss relief	(19,500)
STI	0

	£
Capital gains	10,000
Less loss relief: lower of £(27,000 – 19,500) = £7,500 (note 1) and £(10,000 - 4,000) = £6,000 (note 2)	(6,000)
	4,000
Less annual exemption	(4,000)
	0

Notes:

1 This equals the loss left after the S380 claim

2 This equals the gains left after losses b/fwd but ignoring the annual exemption.

A trading loss of £(7,500 – 6,000) = £1,500 is carried forward. Sibyl's personal allowance and £(7,500 – 4,000) = £3,500 of her capital gains tax annual exemption are wasted. Her capital losses brought forward of £4,000 are carried forward to 2002/03. Although we deducted this £4,000 in working out how much trading loss we were allowed to use in the claim, we do not actually use any of the £4,000 unless there are gains remaining after the annual exemption.

Activity 10.3

£18,000 – £14,000 (s 380 claim) = £4,000

Activity 10.4

Since reliefs are to be claimed as early as possible, s 381 ICTA 1988 is applied. The losses available for relief are as follows.

The revised Schedule E income is as follows.

	£	£
1996/97		
Original	5,000	
Less 1999/00 loss	(1,500)	
		3,500
1997/98		
Original	6,000	
Less 2000/01 loss	(2,250)	
		3,750
1998/99		
Original	7,000	
Less 2001/02 loss	(750)	
		6,250
1999/00		
Original	6,000	
Less 2002/03 loss	(1,200)	
		4,800

Activity 10.5

(a) Loss relief could be claimed:

  (i) under s 380 ICTA 1988, against other income of the year of loss (2002/03), the Schedule A income of £8,000;

  under s 380 ICTA 1988, against other income of the preceding year (2001/02). This would be Schedule D Case I income of £15,000 plus Schedule A income of £8,000;

  under s 385 ICTA 1988, against the first available future profits of the same trade.

(b) *The quickest claim*

  The quickest way to obtain relief would be for Morgan to use s 380 ICTA 1988 in both years. The tax computations would then be as follows.

	2001/02 £	2002/03 £
Schedule D Case I	15,000	0
Schedule A	8,000	8,000
	23,000	8,000
Less s 380 loss relief	(23,000)	(8,000)
Taxable income	0	0

  The balance of the loss, £1,000, would be carried forward and relieved under s 385.

  Although s 380 produces loss relief quickly, it has the disadvantage of wasting Morgan's personal allowance in both years. Morgan could, if he chose, delay his relief by carrying the loss forward under s 385 ICTA 1988. The loss would then be set off only against trading income, with the rental income using his personal allowance.

Appendix: Tax Forms

Appendix

INDEX TO TAX FORMS

		Page
1	Income tax return	164
2	Employment pages	172
3	P60	174
4	P11D	175
5	Land and property pages	177
6	Capital gains pages	179
7	Self employment pages	187
8	Partnership pages	191

Appendix

Income tax return

 **Tax Return** — for the year ended 5 April 2002

UTR
Tax reference
Employer reference

Date

Inland Revenue office address

Officer in Charge

Issue address

Telephone

For Reference

 Please read this page first

The green arrows and instructions will guide you through your Tax Return.

This Notice requires you by law to send me a Tax Return for the year from 6 April 2001 to 5 April 2002. Give details of all your income and capital gains using:

- this form and any supplementary Pages you need, OR
- other Inland Revenue approved forms/software, OR
- our Self Assessment (SA) by Internet Service, OR
- our Electronic Lodgement Service (ELS).

Make sure your Tax Return, and any documents I ask for, reach me by:

- 30 September 2002 if you want me to
  - calculate your tax, OR
  - collect any tax you owe (less than £2,000) through your PAYE code for 2003-2004, OR
- **31 January 2003, at the latest,** or you will be liable to an automatic penalty of £100.

Make sure your payment of any tax you owe reaches me by 31 January 2003, or you will have to pay interest and perhaps a surcharge.

Any Tax Return may be checked. Please remember that there are penalties for supplying false information.

Your Tax Return

I have sent you pages 1 to 8 of your Tax Return:
- page 2 tells you about supplementary Pages for some types of income and gains. For example, there are Pages for employment, and for self-employment income
- pages 3 and 4 are for details of other income, for example, pensions and savings
- page 5 is for claiming reliefs
- page 6 is for claiming allowances
- pages 7 and 8 are for other information.

I have included any supplementary Pages I think you need after page 8. You are responsible for making sure you have the right ones. Use page 2 to check.

Also, unless I know you have a tax adviser, I have sent you:
- a Tax Return Guide to help you fill in your Tax Return (read pages 2 to 5 of the Guide before you start), and
- a Tax Calculation Guide to help you if you are calculating your own tax.

If you do want them, call our Orderline or download them from our website; see Step 1 on page 2 for details.

If you need help:
- refer to the Tax Return Guide, OR
- ring the number above - most questions can be answered by telephone, OR
- when the office is closed, phone our Helpline on 0845 9000 444 for general advice, OR
- if you do not want to explain your question on the phone, call in at an Inland Revenue Enquiry Centre - look under 'Inland Revenue' in the phone book.

SA100

Appendix

Inland Revenue

INCOME AND CAPITAL GAINS for the year ended 5 April 2002

Step 1

Answer Questions 1 to 9 below to find out if you have the right supplementary Pages. Please read pages 6 and 7 of your Tax Return Guide if you need help. (Ask the Orderline for one if I haven't sent you one with your Tax Return). The Questions are colour coded to help you identify the supplementary Pages and their guidance notes. If you answer 'No', go to the next question. If you answer 'Yes', you must complete the relevant supplementary Pages. Turn to the back of your Tax Return to see if you have the right ones and look at the back of the Tax Return Guide to see if you have guidance notes to go with them. **Ring the Orderline on 0845 9000 404, or fax on 0845 9000 604 for any you need (closed Christmas Day, Boxing Day and New Year's Day). Or you can download from our website at http://www.inlandrevenue.gov.uk/sa**
If I have sent you any Pages you do not need, ignore them.

Check to make sure you have the right supplementary Pages and then tick the box below.

Q1 Were you an employee, or office holder, or director, or agency worker or did you receive payments or benefits from a former employer (excluding a pension) in the year ended 5 April 2002?   NO ☐ YES ☐   EMPLOYMENT YES ☐

Q2 Did you have any taxable income from share options, shares or share related benefits in the year? (This does not include
- dividends, **or**
- dividend shares ceasing to be subject to an Inland Revenue approved all-employee share plan within 3 years of acquisition

they go in Question 10.)   NO ☐ YES ☐   SHARE SCHEMES YES ☐

Q3 Were you self-employed (but not in partnership)? (You should also tick 'Yes' if you were a Name at Lloyd's.)   NO ☐ YES ☐   SELF-EMPLOYMENT YES ☐

Q4 Were you in partnership?   NO ☐ YES ☐   PARTNERSHIP YES ☐

Q5 Did you receive any rent or other income from land and property in the UK?   NO ☐ YES ☐   LAND & PROPERTY YES ☐

Q6 Did you have any taxable income from overseas pensions or benefits, or from foreign companies or savings institutions, offshore funds or trusts abroad, or from land and property abroad or gains on foreign insurance policies?   NO ☐ YES ☐

Have you or could you have received, or enjoyed directly or indirectly, or benefited in any way from, income of a foreign entity as a result of a transfer of assets made in this or earlier years?   NO ☐ YES ☐

Do you want to claim tax credit relief for foreign tax paid on foreign income or gains?   NO ☐ YES ☐   FOREIGN YES ☐

Q7 Did you receive, or are you deemed to have, income from a trust, settlement or the residue of a deceased person's estate?   NO ☐ YES ☐   TRUSTS ETC YES ☐

Q8 Capital gains - read the guidance on page 7 of the Tax Return Guide.
- If you have disposed of your only or main residence do you need the Capital Gains Pages?   NO ☐ YES ☐
- Did you dispose of other chargeable assets worth more than £15,000 in total?   NO ☐ YES ☐
- Were your total chargeable gains more than £7,500 or do you want to make a claim or election for the year?   NO ☐ YES ☐   CAPITAL GAINS YES ☐

Q9 Are you claiming that you were not resident, or not ordinarily resident, or not domiciled, in the UK, or dual resident in the UK and another country, for all or part of the year?   NO ☐ YES ☐   NON-RESIDENCE ETC YES ☐

Step 2

Please use blue or black ink to fill in your Tax Return and please do not include pence. Round down, to the nearest pound, your income and capital gains and round up your tax credits and tax deductions.
Fill in any supplementary Pages BEFORE going to Step 3.
When you have filled in your supplementary Pages tick this box. ☐

Step 3

Fill in Questions 10 to 24. If you answer 'No' to a question, go to the next one. If you answer 'Yes', fill in the relevant boxes.
Remember
- You do not have to calculate your tax - I will do it for you if you send your Tax Return to reach me by 30 September. This will save you time and effort.
- The Tax Calculation Guide will help you if you decide to calculate the tax yourself.
- You do not have to wait until 30 September 2002, or 31 January 2003, to send me your Tax Return.

Appendix

INCOME for the year ended 5 April 2002

Q10 Did you receive any income from UK savings and investments? NO ☐ YES ☐

If yes, fill in boxes 10.1 to 10.26 as appropriate. Include only your share from any joint savings and investments.

Interest

- Interest from UK banks, building societies and deposit takers

  - where **no tax** has been deducted

    Taxable amount
    10.1 £ _____

  - where **tax has** been deducted

Amount **after** tax deducted	Tax deducted	Gross amount **before** tax
10.2 £	**10.3** £	**10.4** £

- Interest distributions from UK authorised unit trusts and open-ended investment companies (dividend distributions go below)

Amount after tax deducted	Tax deducted	Gross amount before tax
10.5 £	**10.6** £	**10.7** £

- National Savings (other than FIRST Option Bonds and Fixed Rate Savings Bonds and the first £70 of interest from a National Savings Ordinary Account)

    Taxable amount
    10.8 £ _____

- National Savings FIRST Option and Fixed Rate Savings Bonds

Amount after tax deducted	Tax deducted	Gross amount before tax
10.9 £	**10.10** £	**10.11** £

- Other income from UK savings and investments (except dividends)

Amount after tax deducted	Tax deducted	Gross amount before tax
10.12 £	**10.13** £	**10.14** £

Dividends

- Dividends and other qualifying distributions from UK companies

Dividend/distribution	Tax credit	Dividend/distribution plus credit
10.15 £	**10.16** £	**10.17** £

- Dividend distributions from UK authorised unit trusts and open-ended investment companies

Dividend/distribution	Tax credit	Dividend/distribution plus credit
10.18 £	**10.19** £	**10.20** £

- Scrip dividends from UK companies

Dividend	Notional tax	Dividend plus notional tax
10.21 £	**10.22** £	**10.23** £

- Non-qualifying distributions and loans written off

	Notional tax	Taxable amount
10.24 £	**10.25** £	**10.26** £

Appendix

INCOME for the year ended 5 April 2002, continued

Q11 Did you receive a taxable UK pension, retirement annuity or Social Security benefit? NO ☐ YES ☐ *If yes, fill in boxes 11.1 to 11.13 as appropriate.*
Read the notes on pages 12 to 14 of the Tax Return Guide.

State pensions and benefits

Taxable amount for 2001-2002

- State Retirement Pension *(enter the **total** of your entitlements for the year)* — **11.1** £
- Bereavement Allowance — **11.2** £
- Widowed Parent's Allowance — **11.3** £
- Industrial Death Benefit Pension — **11.4** £
- Jobseeker's Allowance — **11.5** £
- Invalid Care Allowance — **11.6** £
- Statutory Sick Pay and Statutory Maternity Pay paid by the Department of Social Security — **11.7** £

	Tax deducted	Gross amount before tax
Taxable Incapacity Benefit	**11.8** £	**11.9** £

Other pensions and retirement annuities

	Amount after tax deducted	Tax deducted	Gross amount before tax
Pensions (other than State pensions) and retirement annuities	**11.10** £	**11.11** £	**11.12** £

- Deduction — *see the note for box 11.13 on page 14 of your Tax Return Guide*
  Amount of deduction — **11.13** £

Q12 Did you receive any gains on UK life policies or refunds of surplus funds from AVCs? NO ☐ YES ☐ *If yes, fill in boxes 12.1 to 12.12 as appropriate.*

	Number of years		Amount of gain(s)
Gains on UK annuities and friendly societies' life insurance policies where no tax is treated as paid	**12.1**		**12.2** £

	Number of years	Tax treated as paid	Amount of gain(s)
Gains on UK life insurance policies etc. on which tax is treated as paid - *read pages 14 and 15 of the Tax Return Guide*	**12.3**	**12.4** £	**12.5** £

	Number of years	Tax deducted	Amount of gain(s)
Gains on life insurance policies in ISAs that have been made void	**12.6**	**12.7** £	**12.8** £

	Amount
Corresponding deficiency relief	**12.9** £

	Amount received	Notional tax	Amount plus notional tax
Refunds of surplus funds from additional voluntary contributions	**12.10** £	**12.11** £	**12.12** £

Q13 Did you receive any other taxable income which you have not already entered elsewhere in your Tax Return? NO ☐ YES ☐ *If yes, fill in boxes 13.1 to 13.6 as appropriate.*
Make sure you fill in any supplementary Pages *before* answering Question 13.

	Amount after tax deducted	Tax deducted	Amount before tax
Other taxable income *(read page 17 of your Tax Return Guide if you made losses)*	**13.1** £	**13.2** £	**13.3** £

	Losses brought forward	Earlier years' losses used in 2001-2002
	13.4 £	**13.5** £

	2001-2002 losses carried forward
	13.6 £

Appendix

RELIEFS for the year ended 5 April 2002

Q14 Do you want to claim relief for pension contributions? NO ☐ YES ☐ *If yes, fill in boxes 14.1 to 14.17 as appropriate.*

Do not include contributions deducted from your pay by your employer to their pension scheme or associated AVC scheme, because tax relief is given automatically. But do include your contributions to personal pension schemes and Free-Standing AVC schemes.

■ Retirement annuity contracts

Qualifying payments made in 2001-2002	**14.1** £	2001-2002 payments used in an earlier year	**14.2** £	Relief claimed box 14.1 minus (boxes 14.2 and 14.3, but not 14.4)
2001-2002 payments now to be carried back	**14.3** £	Payments brought back from 2002-2003	**14.4** £	**14.5** £

■ Self-employed contributions to personal pension plans (include your gross contribution)

Qualifying payments made in 2001-2002	**14.6** £	2001-2002 payments used in an earlier year	**14.7** £	Relief claimed box 14.6 minus (boxes 14.7 but not 14.9)
		Payments brought back from 2002-2003	**14.9** £	**14.10** £

■ Employee contributions to personal pension plans (include your gross contribution - see the note on box 14.11 in your Tax Return Guide)

Qualifying payments made in 2001-2002	**14.11** £	2001-2002 payments used in an earlier year	**14.12** £	Relief claimed box 14.11 minus (boxes 14.12 but not 14.14)
		Payments brought back from 2002-2003	**14.14** £	**14.15** £

■ Contributions to other pension schemes and Free-Standing AVC schemes

- Amount of contributions to employer's schemes **not deducted** at source from pay — **14.16** £
- Gross amount of Free-Standing Additional Voluntary Contributions paid in 2001-2002 — **14.17** £

Q15 Do you want to claim any of the following reliefs? NO ☐ YES ☐ *If yes, fill in boxes 15.1 to 15.12, as appropriate.*

If you have made any Gift Aid payments or other annual payments, after basic rate tax, answer 'Yes' to Question 15 and fill in boxes 15.6 and 15.9, as appropriate.

- Payments you made to a non-UK training provider for NVQ/SVQ training undertaken outside the UK *(read the box 15.1 note on page 20 of your Tax Return Guide)* — Amount of payment **15.1** £
- Interest eligible for relief on qualifying loans — Amount of payment **15.2** £
- Maintenance or alimony payments you have made under a court order, Child Support Agency assessment or legally binding order or agreement *(see page 21 of your Tax Return Guide)* — Amount claimed up to £2,070 **15.3** £
- Subscriptions for Venture Capital Trust shares (up to £100,000) — Amount on which relief is claimed **15.4** £
- Subscriptions under the Enterprise Investment Scheme (up to £150,000) — Amount on which relief is claimed **15.5** £
- Gift Aid and payments under charitable covenants — Amount on which relief is claimed **15.6** £
- Gifts of qualifying investments to charities — Amount of relief claimed **15.7** £
- Post-cessation expenses, pre-incorporation losses brought forward and losses on relevant discounted securities, etc. *(see page 22 of your Tax Return Guide)* — Amount of payment **15.8** £
- Annuities — Amount on which relief is claimed **15.9** £
- Payments to a trade union or friendly society for death benefits — Half amount of payment **15.10** £
- Payment to your employer's compulsory widow's, widower's or orphan's benefit scheme *(available in some circumstances – first read the notes on page 23 of your Tax Return Guide)* — Relief claimed **15.11** £
- Relief claimed on a qualifying distribution on the **redemption** of bonus shares or securities. — Relief claimed **15.12** £

Appendix

ALLOWANCES for the year ended 5 April 2002

Q16 You get your personal allowance of £4,535 automatically. **If you were born before 6 April 1937, enter your date of birth in box 22.6** - you may get a higher age-related personal allowance.

Do you want to claim any of the following allowances? NO ☐ YES ☐

If yes, please read pages 23 to 25 of your Tax Return Guide and then fill in boxes 16.1 to 16.18 as appropriate.

- **Blind person's allowance**
  - 16.1 Date of registration (if first year of claim) / /
  - 16.2 Local authority (or other register)

- **Married couple's allowance** - In 2001-2002 married couple's allowance can only be claimed if either you, or your husband or wife, were born **before 6 April 1935**. So you can only claim the allowance in 2001-2002 if either of you had reached **65 years of age before 6 April 2000**. Further guidance is given beginning on page 23 of your Tax Return Guide.

If **both** you and your husband or wife were born after 5 April 1935 you cannot claim; **do not** complete boxes 16.3 to 16.13.

If you can claim fill in boxes 16.3 and 16.4 if you are a married man or if you are a married woman and you are claiming half or all of the married couple's allowance.

- Enter your date of birth (if born before 6 April 1935) — 16.3 / /
- Enter your spouse's date of birth (**if born before 6 April 1935 and** if older than you) — 16.4 / /

Then, if you are a married man fill in boxes 16.5 to 16.9. If you are a married woman fill in boxes 16.10 to 16.13.

- Wife's full name — 16.5
- Date of marriage (if after 5 April 2001) — 16.6 / /
- Tick box 16.7 if you or your wife have allocated half the allowance to her — 16.7
- Tick box 16.8 if you and your wife have allocated all the allowance to her — 16.8
- Enter in box 16.9 the date of birth of any previous wife with whom you lived at any time during 2001-2002. Read 'Special rules if you are a man who married in the year ended 5 April 2002' on page 25 before completing box 16.9. — 16.9 / /

- Tick box 16.10 if you or your husband have allocated half the allowance to you — 16.10
- Tick box 16.11 if you and your husband have allocated all the allowance to you — 16.11
- Husband's full name — 16.12
- Date of marriage (if after 5 April 2001) — 16.13 / /

- **Widow's bereavement allowance** - see page 25 of your Tax Return Guide before completing box 16.14.
  - Date of your husband's death — 16.14 / /

- **Transfer of surplus allowances** - see page 25 of your Tax Return Guide before you fill in boxes 16.15 to 16.18.
  - Tick box 16.15 if you want your spouse to have your unused allowances — 16.15
  - Tick box 16.16 if you want to have your spouse's unused allowances — 16.16

Please give details in the 'Additional information' box, box 23.6, on page 8 - see page 25 of your Tax Return Guide for what is needed.

If you want to calculate your tax, enter the amount of the surplus allowance you can have.
- Blind person's **surplus** allowance — 16.17 £
- Married couple's **surplus** allowance — 16.18 £

Q17 **Are you liable to make Student Loan Repayments for 2001-2002 on an Income Contingent Student Loan?** NO ☐ YES ☐

Read the note on page 25 of your Tax Return Guide.

If yes, and you are calculating your tax enter in box 18.2A the amount you work out is repayable in 2001-2002.

Appendix

OTHER INFORMATION for the year ended 5 April 2002

Q18 Do you want to calculate your tax and any Student Loan Repayment? **NO** / **YES**
If yes, do it now and then fill in boxes 18.1 to 18.8. Your Tax Calculation Guide will help.

- Unpaid tax for earlier years **included in your tax code for 2001-2002** — **18.1** £
- Tax due for 2001-2002 included in your tax code for a later year — **18.2** £
- Student Loan Repayment due — **18.2A** £
- Total tax, Class 4 NIC and Student Loan Repayment due for 2001-2002 **before** you made any payments on account *(put the amount in brackets if an overpayment)* — **18.3** £
- Tax due for earlier years — **18.4** £
- Tick box 18.5 if you have calculated tax overpaid for earlier years and enter the amount in the 'Additional information' box, box 23.6 on page 8. — **18.5**
- Your first payment on account for 2002-2003 *(include the pence)* — **18.6** £
  Tick box 18.7 if you are making a claim to reduce your 2002-2003 payments on account and say why in the 'Additional information' box, box 23.6, on page 8 — **18.7**
- Tick box 18.8 if you are reclaiming any 2002-2003 tax now and enter the amount in the 'Additional information' box, box 23.6 on page 8. — **18.8**

Q19 Do you want to claim a repayment if you have paid too much tax? *(If you tick 'No' or the tax you have overpaid is below £10, I will use the amount you are owed to reduce your next tax bill.)* **NO** / **YES**
If yes, fill in boxes 19.1A to 19.12 as appropriate.

Should the repayment be sent:
- direct to your bank or building society account? Tick box 19.1A and fill in boxes 19.3 to 19.7 — **19.1A**
- by cheque to you at your home address? Tick box 19.1B — **19.1B**
or
- to a nominee? *Tick box 19.2, fill in boxes 19.3 to 19.11, as appropriate, and box 19.12* — **19.2**

Fill in boxes 19.3 to 19.7 if the repayment is to be sent to your own, or your nominees' bank or building society account

- Name of bank or building society — **19.3**
- Branch sort code — **19.4** — —
- Account number — **19.5**
- Name of account holder — **19.6**
- Building society ref. — **19.7**

- If your nominee is your agent, *tick box 19.8* — **19.8**
- Agent's reference for you (if your nominee is your agent) — **19.9**
- Name of your nominee/agent
- I authorise — **19.10**
- Nominee/agent address — **19.11**
- Postcode
- to receive on my behalf the amount due
- *This authority must be signed by you. A photocopy of your signature will not do.* — **19.12** Signature

Q20 Have you already had any 2001-2002 tax refunded or set off by your Inland Revenue office or the Benefits Agency (in Northern Ireland, the Social Security Agency)? *Read the notes on page 26 of your Tax Return Guide* **NO** / **YES** *If yes, enter the amount of the refund in box 20.1.* — **20.1** £

Q21 Are your name or address on the front of the Tax Return wrong? **NO** / **YES** *If yes, please make any corrections on the front of the form.*

Q22 **Please give other personal details in boxes 22.1 to 22.7.** This information helps us to be more efficient and effective and may support claims you have made elsewhere in your Tax Return

Please give a daytime telephone number if convenient. It is often simpler to phone if we need to ask you about your Tax Return.

- Your telephone number — **22.1**
- or, if you prefer, your agent's telephone number — **22.2**
- and their name and address — **22.3** Postcode
- Enter your first two forenames — **22.4**
- Say if you are single, married, widowed, divorced or separated — **22.5**
- Enter your date of birth — **22.6** / /
- Enter your National Insurance number (if known) — **22.7**

Appendix

OTHER INFORMATION for the year ended 5 April 2002, continued

Q23 Please tick boxes 23.1 to 23.5 if they apply. Provide any additional information in box 23.6 below.

Tick box 23.1 if you expect to receive a new pension or new Social Security benefit in 2002-2003. **23.1** ☐

Tick box 23.2 if you do **not** want any tax you owe for 2001-2002 collected through your tax code. **23.2** ☐

Tick box 23.3 if this Tax Return contains figures that are provisional because you do not yet have final figures. Page 26 of your Tax Return Guide explains the circumstances in which Tax Returns containing provisional figures may be accepted and tells you what you must enter in box 23.6 below. **23.3** ☐

Tick box 23.4 if you are claiming relief now for 2002-2003 trading, or certain capital, losses. Enter in box 23.6 the amount and year. **23.4** ☐

Tick box 23.5 if you are claiming:
- to have post-cessation or other business receipts taxed as income of an earlier year. Enter in box 23.6 the amount and year
- backwards or forwards spreading of literary or artistic income. Enter in box 23.6 details of any amounts spread back to last year and, if appropriate, the year before.

23.5 ☐

23.6 Additional information

Q24 Declaration

I have filled in and am sending back to you the following pages:

	Tick		Tick		Tick
1 TO 8 OF THIS FORM	☐				
EMPLOYMENT	☐	PARTNERSHIP	☐	TRUSTS, ETC	☐
SHARE SCHEMES	☐	LAND & PROPERTY	☐	CAPITAL GAINS	☐
SELF-EMPLOYMENT	☐	FOREIGN	☐	NON-RESIDENCE, ETC	☐

Before you send your completed Tax Return back to your Inland Revenue office, you must sign the statement below. If you give false information or conceal any part of your income or chargeable gains, you may be liable to financial penalties and/or you may be prosecuted.

24.1 The information I have given in this Tax Return is correct and complete to the best of my knowledge and belief.

Signature _____ Date _____

If you are signing for someone else please read the notes on page 27 of the Tax Return Guide, and:
- state the capacity in which you are signing (for example, as executor or receiver)

24.2 _____

- give the name of the person you are signing for and **your** name and address in box 23.6 above.

Appendix

Employment pages

Inland Revenue

Income for the year ended 5 April 2002

EMPLOYMENT

Fill in these boxes first

Name

Tax reference

If you want help, look up the box numbers in the Notes

Details of employer

Employer's PAYE reference - may be shown under 'Tax Office number and reference' on your P60 or 'PAYE reference' on your P45

1.1

Employer's name

1.2

Date employment started (only if between 6 April 2001 and 5 April 2002)

1.3 / /

Employer's address

1.5

Postcode

Date finished (only if between 6 April 2001 and 5 April 2002)

1.4 / /

Tick box 1.6 if you were a director of the company

1.6

and, if so, tick box 1.7 if it was a close company

1.7

Income from employment

- **Money** - see Notes, page EN3

  Before tax

  - Payments from P60 (or P45) — **1.8** £
  - Payments not on P60 etc. - tips — **1.9** £
    - other payments (excluding expenses entered below and lump sums and compensation payments or benefits entered overleaf) — **1.10** £

  Tax deducted
  - UK tax deducted from payments in boxes 1.8 to 1.10 — **1.11** £

- **Benefits and expenses** - see Notes, pages EN3 to EN6. If any benefits connected with termination of employment were received, or enjoyed, after that termination and were from a *former* employer you need to complete Help Sheet IR204, available from the Orderline. Do not enter such benefits here.

	Amount		Amount
• Assets transferred/ payments made for you	**1.12** £	• Vans	**1.18** £
• Vouchers, credit cards and tokens	**1.13** £	• Interest-free and low-interest loans	**1.19** £
• Living accommodation	**1.14** £	box 1.20 is not used	
• Mileage allowance	**1.15** £	• Private medical or dental insurance	**1.21** £
• Company cars	**1.16** £	• Other benefits	**1.22** £
• Fuel for company cars	**1.17** £	• Expenses payments received and balancing charges	**1.23** £

SA101

Income from employment continued

■ *Lump sums and compensation payments or benefits including such payments and benefits from a former employer*
Note that 'lump sums' here includes any contributions which your employer made to an unapproved retirement benefits scheme

You must read page EN6 of the Notes **before** filling in boxes 1.24 to 1.30

Reliefs

- £30,000 exemption — **1.24** £
- Foreign service and disability — **1.25** £
- Retirement and death lump sums — **1.26** £

Taxable lump sums

- From box B of *Help Sheet IR204* — **1.27** £
- From box K of *Help Sheet IR204* — **1.28** £
- From box L of *Help Sheet IR204* — **1.29** £

Tax deducted
- Tax deducted from payments in boxes 1.27 to 1.29 — **1.30** £

■ *Foreign earnings not taxable in the UK in the year ended 5 April 2002* - see Notes, page EN6 — **1.31** £

■ *Expenses you incurred in doing your job* - see Notes, pages EN6 to EN8

- Travel and subsistence costs — **1.32** £
- Fixed deductions for expenses — **1.33** £
- Professional fees and subscriptions — **1.34** £
- Other expenses and capital allowances — **1.35** £
- Tick box 1.36 if the figure in box 1.32 includes travel between your home and a permanent workplace — **1.36**

■ *Foreign Earnings Deduction* (seafarers only) — **1.37** £

■ *Foreign tax for which tax credit relief not claimed* — **1.38** £

Student Loans

■ *Student Loans repaid by deduction by employer* - see Notes, page EN8 — **1.39** £

1.40 Additional information

*Now fill in any other supplementary Pages that apply to you.
Otherwise, go back to page 2 in your Tax Return and finish filling it in.*

Appendix

Form P60

P60 End of Year Certificate
Tax Year to 5 April 2002

To the employee:
Please keep this certificate in a safe place as you will not be able to get a duplicate. **You will need it if you have to fill in a Tax Return.** You can also use it to check that your employer is deducting the right rate of National Insurance contributions for you and using your correct National Insurance number.

By law you are required to tell the Tax Office of any income that is not fully taxed, even if you are not sent a Tax Return.
INLAND REVENUE

Employee's details
- Surname
- Forenames or initials
- National Insurance number

Pay and Income Tax details

	Pay	Tax deducted
Previous employment(s)	£	£
This employment	£	£ (if refund mark 'R')

Figures shown here should be used for your Tax Return, if you get one

Final tax code

National Insurance contributions in this employment

NIC table letter	Earnings at or above the Lower Earnings Limit, up to and including the *employee's* Earnings Threshold *whole £s only*	Earnings above the *employee's* Earnings Threshold, up to and including the *employer's* Earnings Threshold *whole £s only*	Earnings above the *employer's* Earnings Threshold, up to and including the Upper Earnings Limit *whole £s only*	Employee's contributions payable
	£	£	£	£
	£	£	£	£
	£	£	£	£
	£	£	£	£

Employee's contributions are payable on earnings above the employee's 'Earnings Threshold', up to and including the 'Upper Earnings Limit'.
Employer's contributions are payable on all earnings above the employer's 'Earnings Threshold'.

Other details

- Student Loan Deductions in this employment: £
- Tax Credits in this employment: £

Certificate by Employer/Paying Office:
This form shows your total pay for Income Tax purposes in this employment for the year. Any overtime, bonus, commission etc, statutory sick pay or statutory maternity pay is included. It also shows, for this employment, total Income Tax and National Insurance contributions deducted (less any refunds), Student Loan deductions made, and Tax Credits paid to you.

Employer's full name _____

Full address _____

Postcode _____

Employer's PAYE reference

Do not destroy

P60 (2001-02) BMSD XX/XX

Appendix

Inland Revenue
P11D EXPENSES AND BENEFITS 2001-2002

Note for employer
Complete this return for a director, or an employee who earned at a rate of £8,500 a year or more during the year 6 April 2001 to 5 April 2002. Do not include expenses and benefits covered by a dispensation or PAYE settlement agreement. Read the P11D (Guide) and booklet 480, [Chapter 24] before you complete the form. Send the completed P11D and form P11D(b) to the Tax Office by 6 July 2002. You must give a copy of this information to the employee/director by the same date.
The term employee is used to cover both directors and employees throughout the rest of this form.

Note for employee
Your employer has filled in this form. Keep it in a safe place as you may not be able to get a duplicate. You will need it for your personal records and to complete your 2001-02 Tax Return if you get one. Your tax code may need to be adjusted to take account of the information on this P11D. The box numbers on this P11D have the same numbering as the employment pages of the Tax Return, for example 1.12. Include the total figure in the corresponding box on the Tax Return, unless you think some other figure is more appropriate.

Employer's details
Employer's name

PAYE tax reference

Employee's details
Employee's name

If a director tick here ▶

Works number / Department   National insurance number

From 6 April 2000 employers pay Class 1A National Insurance contributions on more benefits. These are shown in boxes which are brown and have a **1A** indicator.

A • Assets transferred (cars, property, goods or other assets)

Description of asset   Cost/Market value £ − Amount made good or from which tax deducted £ = Cash equivalent 1.12 £   1A

B • Payments made on behalf of the employee

Description of payment   1.12 £

Tax on notional payments not borne by the employee within 30 days of receipt of each notional payment   1.12 £

C • Vouchers and credit cards

Value of vouchers and payments made using credit cards or tokens   Gross amount £ − Amount made good or from which tax deducted £ = Cash equivalent 1.13 £

D • Living accommodation

Cash equivalent of accommodation provided for the employee or his/her family/household   Cash equivalent 1.14 £   1A

E • Mileage allowance

Car and mileage allowances paid for employee's car   Gross amount £ − Amount made good or from which tax deducted £ = Taxable payment 1.15 £

F • Cars and car fuel *If more than two cars were made available, either at the same time or in succession, please give details on a separate sheet.*

	Car 1	Car 2
Make and model		
Date first registered	/ /	/ /
Dates the car was available	From / / To / /	From / / To / /
Business mileage used in calculation **Tick one box only for each car** *If the car was unavailable for part of the year the business mileage limits are reduced proportionately*	2,499 or less ☐ 2,500 to 17,999 ☐ 18,000 or more ☐	2,499 or less ☐ 2,500 to 17,999 ☐ 18,000 or more ☐
Enter engine size and tick type of fuel only if there is a car fuel scale charge	Engine size in cc _____ Petrol ☐ Diesel ☐	Engine size in cc _____ Petrol ☐ Diesel ☐
	Car 1	Car 2
List price of the car *(If there is no list price or it is a classic car, employers see booklet 480; employees see leaflet IR 133)*		
Price of optional accessories fitted when the car was first made available to the employee		
Price of accessories added after the car was first made available to the employee		
Capital contributions (maximum of £5,000) the employee made towards the cost of the car or accessories		
Amount paid by the employee for private use of the car		
Cash equivalent of each car		

Total cash equivalent of all cars available in 2001-2002   1.16   1A

Cash equivalent of fuel for each car

Total cash equivalent of fuel for all cars available in 2001-2002   1.17   1A

P11D(2001)

Appendix

G • Vans
Cash equivalent for all vans made available for private use.   1.18 £   1A

H • Interest free and low interest loans
If the total amount outstanding on all loans does not exceed £5,000 at any time in the year there is no need for details in this section.

	Loan 1	Loan 2
Number of joint borrowers *(if applicable)*		
Amount outstanding at 5 April 2001 or at date when loan was made if later		
Amount outstanding at 5 April 2002 or at date when loan was discharged if earlier		
Maximum amount outstanding at any time in the year		
Total amount of interest paid by the borrower in 2001-2002 *enter 'NIL' if none was paid*		
Date loan was made in 2001-2002 if applicable	/ /	/ /
Date loan was discharged in 2001-2002 if applicable	/ /	/ /
Cash equivalent of loan(s) after deducting interest paid by the borrower	1.19 1A	1.19 1A

I • Private medical treatment or insurance

Private medical treatment or insurance   Cost to you − Amount made good or from which tax deducted = Cash equivalent 1.21   1A

J • **Qualifying relocation expenses payments and benefits**
(Non qualifying benefits and expenses go in N and O below)
Excess over £8,000 of all qualifying relocation expenses payments and benefits for each move.   1.22   1A

K • Services supplied
Services supplied to the employee   Cost to you − Amount made good or from which tax deducted = Cash equivalent 1.22   1A

L • Assets placed at the employee's disposal   Annual value plus expense incurred − Amount made good or from which tax deducted = Cash equivalent 1.22   1A
Description of asset

M • Shares
Tick the box if during the year there have been share-related benefits for the employee ☐

N • Other items (including subscriptions and professional fees)

	Cost to you	Amount made good or from which tax deducted	Cash equivalent
Description of other items:	−	=	1.22 1A
Description of other items:	−	=	1.22

Income tax paid but not deducted from the director's remuneration   Tax paid 1.22

O • Expenses payments made to, or on behalf of, the employee

	Cost to you	Amount made good or from which tax deducted	Taxable payment
Travelling and subsistence payments	£	£	1.23
Entertainment - *(trading organisations read P11D Guide and then enter a tick or cross as appropriate here)* ☐	£	£	1.23
General expenses allowance for business travel	£	£	1.23
Payments for use of home telephone	£	£	1.23
Non-qualifying relocation expenses (those not in section J)	£	£	1.23
Description of other expenses	£	£	1.23

P11D(2001)

Appendix

Land and property pages

Income for the year ended 5 April 2002

Inland Revenue

LAND AND PROPERTY

Fill in these boxes first

Name

Tax reference

If you want help, look up the box numbers in the Notes

Are you claiming Rent a Room relief for gross rents of £4,250 or less? (Or £2,125 if the claim is shared?)
Read the Notes on page LN2 to find out
- whether you can claim Rent a Room relief; and
- how to claim relief for gross rents over £4,250

No ☐ Yes ☐

If 'Yes', and this is your only income from UK property, you have finished these Pages

Is your income from furnished holiday lettings?
If 'No', turn over and fill in Page L2 to give details of your property income

No ☐ Yes ☐

If 'Yes', fill in boxes 5.1 to 5.18 before completing Page L2

Furnished holiday lettings

- Income from furnished holiday lettings — **5.1** £

■ *Expenses* (furnished holiday lettings only)

- Rent, rates, insurance, ground rents etc. — **5.2** £
- Repairs, maintenance and renewals — **5.3** £
- Finance charges, including interest — **5.4** £
- Legal and professional costs — **5.5** £
- Costs of services provided, including wages — **5.6** £
- Other expenses — **5.7** £

total of boxes 5.2 to 5.7
5.8 £

box 5.1 *minus* box 5.8
Net profit (put figures in brackets if a loss) — **5.9** £

■ *Tax adjustments*

- Private use — **5.10** £
- Balancing charges — **5.11** £

box 5.10 + box 5.11
5.12 £

- Capital allowances — **5.13** £

boxes 5.9 + 5.12 *minus* box 5.13
Profit for the year (copy to box 5.19). If loss, enter '0' in box 5.14 and put the loss in box 5.15 — **5.14** £

boxes 5.9 + 5.12 *minus* box 5.13
Loss for the year (if you have entered '0' in box 5.14) — **5.15** £

■ *Losses*

- Loss offset against 2001-2002 total income — **5.16** £

see Notes, page LN4
- Loss carried back — **5.17** £

see Notes, page LN4
- Loss offset against other income from property (copy to box 5.38) — **5.18** £

SA105

Other property income

■ Income

- Furnished holiday lettings profits — copy from box 5.14 — **5.19** £
- Rents and other income from land and property — **5.20** £ Tax deducted **5.21** £
- Chargeable premiums — **5.22** £
- Reverse premiums — **5.22A** £

boxes 5.19 + 5.20 + 5.22 + 5.22A
5.23 £

■ Expenses (do not include figures you have already put in boxes 5.2 to 5.7 on Page L1)

- Rent, rates, insurance, ground rents etc. — **5.24** £
- Repairs, maintenance and renewals — **5.25** £
- Finance charges, including interest — **5.26** £
- Legal and professional costs — **5.27** £
- Costs of services provided, including wages — **5.28** £
- Other expenses — **5.29** £

total for boxes 5.24 to 5.29
5.30 £

Net profit (put figures in brackets if a loss)   box 5.23 *minus* box 5.30   **5.31** £

■ Tax adjustments

- Private use — **5.32** £
- Balancing charges — **5.33** £

box 5.32 + box 5.33
5.34 £

- Rent a Room exempt amount — **5.35** £
- Capital allowances — **5.36** £
- 10% wear and tear — **5.37** £
- Furnished holiday lettings losses (from box 5.18) **5.38** £

boxes 5.35 to box 5.38
5.39 £

Adjusted profit (if loss enter '0' in box 5.40 and put the loss in box 5.41)   boxes 5.31 + 5.34 *minus* box 5.39   **5.40** £

Adjusted loss (if you have entered '0' in box 5.40)   boxes 5.31 + 5.34 *minus* box 5.39   **5.41** £

- Loss brought forward from previous year   **5.42** £

Profit for the year   box 5.40 *minus* box 5.42   **5.43** £

■ Losses etc

- Loss offset against total income (read the note on page LN8)   **5.44** £
- Loss to carry forward to following year   **5.45** £
- Pooled expenses from 'one-estate election' carried forward   **5.46** £
- Tick box 5.47 if these Pages include details of property let jointly   **5.47**
- Tick box 5.48 if **all** property income ceased in the year to 5 April 2002 **and** you don't expect to receive such income again, in the year to 5 April 2003   **5.48**

Now fill in any other supplementary Pages that apply to you.
Otherwise, go back to page 2 of your Tax Return and finish filling it in.

Appendix

Inland Revenue

CAPITAL GAINS
for the year ended 5 April 2002

Name

Tax reference

Fill in these boxes first

Use this Page if **all** your transactions were in quoted shares or other securities unless taper relief is due on any of them, or any were held at 31 March 1982, or you are claiming a relief, for example, Enterprise Investment Scheme deferral relief. Otherwise you must use Pages CG2 to CG6 to work out **all** of your capital gains or allowable losses.

A Enter details of quoted shares or other securities disposed of	B Tick box if estimate or valuation used	C Enter the date of disposal	D Disposal proceeds	E Gain or loss after indexation allowance, if due (enter loss in brackets)	F Further information, including any elections made
1		/ /	£	£	
2		/ /	£	£	
3		/ /	£	£	
4		/ /	£	£	
5		/ /	£	£	
6		/ /	£	£	
7		/ /	£	£	
8		/ /	£	£	

Total gains **F1** £ — *Total your gains in column E and enter the amount in box F1*

Total losses **F2** £ — *Total your losses in column E and enter the amount in box F2*

Net gain/(loss) box F1 *minus* box F2 **F3** £ — *If your net gains exceed £7,500, carry on. If they are below £7,500 there is no liability. If you have a net loss, please fill in the losses summary on Page CG8*

minus income losses set against gains **F4** £

box F3 *minus* box F4 **F5** £ — *If your gains are now below £7,500, there is no liability. Otherwise carry on*

minus losses brought forward **F6** £ — *Enter losses brought forward up to the **smaller** of either the total losses brought forward or the figure in box F5 **minus** £7,500*

Total taxable gains box F5 *minus* box F6 **F7** £ — *Copy this figure to box 8.7 on Page CG8 (if F7 is blank because there is no liability, leave 8.7 blank).*

Note:
This Page is only for transactions in quoted shares or other securities.
See the definition on page CGN2 of the Notes on Capital Gains.

Go to **Page CG8**

TAX RETURN ■ CAPITAL GAINS: PAGE CG1

Appendix

Your 2001-2002 Capital Gains Tax liability

A Brief description of asset	AA* Type of disposal. Enter Q, U, L or O	B Tick box if estimate or valuation used	C Tick box if asset held at 31 March 1982	D Enter the later of date of acquisition and 16 March 1998	E Enter the date of disposal	F Disposal proceeds	G Enter details of any elect claimed or due and state
Gains on assets without mixed (business and non-business) use							
1				/ /	/ /	£	
2				/ /	/ /	£	
3				/ /	/ /	£	
4				/ /	/ /	£	
5				/ /	/ /	£	
6				/ /	/ /	£	
7				/ /	/ /	£	
8				/ /	/ /	£	
Gains on assets with mixed (business and non-business) use (see the notes on page CGN4)							
9				/ /	/ /	£	
10				/ /	/ /	£	

* Column AA: for transactions in
  - quoted shares or other securities, (see the definition on page CGN2 of the Notes) enter **Q**
  - other shares or securities, enter **U**
  - land and property, enter **L**
  - other assets (for example, goodwill), enter **O** ➤ *Complete Pages CG4 to CG6 for all U, L and O transactions.*

Losses

Description of asset	Type of * disposal. Enter Q, U, L or O	Tick box if estimate or valuation used	Tick box if asset held at 31 March 1982	Enter the later of date of acquisition and 16 March 1998	Enter the date of disposal	Disposal proceeds	Enter details of any elect claimed or due and state
13				/ /	/ /	£	
14				/ /	/ /	£	
15				/ /	/ /	£	
16				/ /	/ /	£	

Total losses of

Appendix

ions made, reliefs amount (£)	H Chargeable Gains after reliefs but before losses and taper	I Enter 'Bus' if business asset	J Taper rate	K Losses deducted			L Gains after losses	M Tapered gains (gains from column L x % in column J)
				K1 Allowable losses of the year	K2 Income losses of 2001-2002 set against gains	K3 Unused losses b/f from earlier years		
	£		%	£	£	£	£	£
	£		%	£	£	£	£	£
	£		%	£	£	£	£	£
	£		%	£	£	£	£	£
	£		%	£	£	£	£	£
	£		%	£	£	£	£	£
	£		%	£	£	£	£	£
	£		%	£	£	£	£	£
	£	Bus	%	£	£	£	£	£
	£		%	£	£	£	£	£
	£	Bus	%	£	£	£	£	£
	£		%	£	£	£	£	£
Total	**8.1** £ Total column H				**8.5** £ Total column K2	**8.6** £ Total column K3		**8.3** £ Total column M

ions made, reliefs amount (£)	Losses arising
	£
	£
	£
	£
year	**8.2** £

11 Attributed gains from UK resident trusts
(enter the name of the Trust on Page CG7) £

12 Attributed gains from non UK resident trusts
(enter the name of the Trust on Page CG7) £

Total of attributed gains **8.4** £

Total taxable gains (after allowable losses and taper relief)

box 8.3 + box 8.4
£

Copy to box 8.7 on Page CG8 and complete Pages CG4 to CG6 for all U, L and O transactions

Copy to box 8.10 on Page CG8 and, unless you need only complete the totals boxes (see page CGN5), complete column K1

BS 12/2000net   TAX RETURN ■ CAPITAL GAINS: PAGE CG3   *continued over*

Appendix

Other shares or securities (U) - further information

Please give details of each transaction of this type of asset in the boxes below. If you have more than two of these transactions to return, please photocopy this Page **before** completion. (Please also complete Pages CG2 and CG3.)

1st transaction

Description of shares or securities - including name of company, company registration number (if known), number, class and nominal value of shares. Also, if possible, give a history of the shares disposed of, for instance, if there has been a reorganisation or takeover (give details of the original company and shares held in that company)

Tick box if you have already submitted form CG34 ☐

State any connection between you and the person who acquired the asset (see Notes, page CGN13)

If you have used an estimate or valuation in your capital gains computation, please enter the date to which the valuation relates, the amount (£) and the reason for the estimate or valuation. Please also attach a copy of any valuation obtained

2nd transaction

Description of shares or securities - including name of company, company registration number (if known), number, class and nominal value of shares. Also, if possible, give a history of the shares disposed of, for instance, if there has been a reorganisation or takeover (give details of the original company and shares held in that company)

Tick box if you have already submitted form CG34 ☐

State any connection between you and the person who acquired the asset (see Notes, page CGN13)

If you have used an estimate or valuation in your capital gains computation, please enter the date to which the valuation relates, the amount (£) and the reason for the estimate or valuation. Please also attach a copy of any valuation obtained

BS 12/2000net   TAX RETURN ■ CAPITAL GAINS: PAGE CG4

Appendix

Land and property disposals (L) - further information

Please give details of each transaction of this type of asset in the boxes below. If you have more than two of these transactions to return, please photocopy this Page **before** completion. (Please also complete Pages CG2 and CG3.)

1st transaction

Full address of land/property affected (attach a copy of any plan if this helps identification)

Description of land/property disposed of, including details of your ownership, for example freehold/leasehold and any tenancies affecting your ownership and the date of transaction or any other date for which a valuation has been made.

Tick box if you have already submitted form CG34 ☐

State any connection between you and the person who acquired the asset (see Notes, page CGN13)

If you have used an estimate or valuation in your capital gains computation, please enter the date to which the valuation relates, the amount (£) and the reason for the estimate or valuation. Please also attach a copy of any valuation obtained.

2nd transaction

Full address of land/property affected (attach a copy of any plan if this helps identification)

Description of land/property disposed of, including details of your ownership, for example freehold/leasehold and any tenancies affecting your ownership and the date of transaction or any other date for which a valuation has been made.

Tick box if you have already submitted form CG34 ☐

State any connection between you and the person who acquired the asset (see Notes, page CGN13)

If you have used an estimate or valuation in your capital gains computation, please enter the date to which the valuation relates, the amount (£) and the reason for the estimate or valuation. Please also attach a copy of any valuation obtained.

BS 12/2000net TAX RETURN ■ CAPITAL GAINS: PAGE CG5 *continued over*

Appendix

Other assets (O) - further information

Please give details of any transaction involving any other type of asset in the boxes below. If you have more than two of these transactions to return, please photocopy this Page **before** completion. (Please also complete Pages CG2 and CG3.)

1st transaction

Full description of the asset (other than shares or land/property) affected and any other information which helps identify the asset

Tick box if you have already submitted form CG34 ☐

State any connection between you and the person who acquired the asset
(see Notes, page CGN13)

If you have used an estimate or valuation in your capital gains computation, please enter the date to which the valuation relates, the amount (£) and the reason for the estimate or valuation. Please also attach a copy of any valuation obtained.

2nd transaction

Full description of the asset (other than shares or land/property) affected and any other information which helps identify the asset

Tick box if you have already submitted form CG34 ☐

State any connection between you and the person who acquired the asset
(see Notes, page CGN13)

If you have used an estimate or valuation in your capital gains computation, please enter the date to which the valuation relates, the amount (£) and the reason for the estimate or valuation. Please also attach a copy of any valuation obtained.

BS 12/2000net   TAX RETURN ■ CAPITAL GAINS: PAGE CG6

8.22 *Additional information*

TAX RETURN ■ CAPITAL GAINS: PAGE CG7   *continued over*

Appendix

Chargeable gains and allowable losses

Once you have completed Page CG1, or Pages CG2 to CG6, fill in this Page.

Have you 'ticked' any row in Column B, 'Tick box if estimate or valuation used' on Pages CG1 or CG2? **NO** ☐ **YES** ☐

Have you given details in Column G on Pages CG2 and CG3 of any Capital Gains reliefs claimed or due? **NO** ☐ **YES** ☐

Are you claiming, and/or using, any 'clogged' losses (see Notes, page CGN10)? **NO** ☐ **YES** ☐

Enter the number of transactions from Page CG1 or column AA on Page CG2 for:

- transactions in quoted shares or other securities **box Q** ☐
- transactions in other shares or securities **box U** ☐
- transactions in land and property **box L** ☐
- other transactions **box O** ☐

Total taxable gains (from Page CG1 **or** Page CG3) **8.7** £ _____

Your taxable gains *minus* the annual exempt amount of £7,500 (leave blank if '0' or negative) *box 8.7 minus £7,500* **8.8** £ _____

Additional liability in respect of non-resident or dual resident trusts (see Notes, page CGN6) **8.9** £ _____

Capital losses

(Remember if your loss arose on a transaction with a connected person, see Notes page CGN13, you can only set that loss against gains you make on disposals to that same connected person.)

■ *This year's losses*

- Total (from box 8.2 on Page CG3 or box F2 on Page CG1) **8.10** £ _____
- Used against gains (total of column K1 on Page CG3, or the smaller of boxes F1 and F2 on Page CG1) **8.11** £ _____
- Used against earlier years' gains (generally only available to personal representatives, see Notes, page CGN11) **8.12** £ _____
- Used against income (only losses of the type described on page CGN9 can be used against income) **8.13A** £ _____ amount claimed against income of 2001-2002
  8.13B £ _____ amount claimed against income of 2000-2001 *box 8.13A + box 8.13B* **8.13** £ _____
- This year's unused losses *box 8.10 minus (boxes 8.11 + 8.12 + 8.13)* **8.14** £ _____

■ *Earlier years' losses*

- Unused losses of 1996-97 and later years **8.15** £ _____
- Used this year (losses from box 8.15 are used in priority to losses from box 8.18) (column K3 on Page CG3 or box F6 on Page CG1) **8.16** £ _____
- Remaining unused losses of 1996-97 and later years *box 8.15 minus box 8.16* **8.17** £ _____
- Unused losses of 1995-96 and earlier years **8.18** £ _____
- Used this year (losses from box 8.15 are used in priority to losses from box 8.18) (column K3 on Page CG3 or box F6 on Page CG1) *box 8.6 minus box 8.16 (or box F6 minus box 8.16)* **8.19** £ _____

■ *Total of unused losses to carry forward*

- Carried forward losses of 1996-97 and later years *box 8.14 + box 8.17* **8.20** £ _____
- Carried forward losses of 1995-96 and earlier years *box 8.18 minus box 8.19* **8.21** £ _____

BS 12/2000net   TAX RETURN ■ CAPITAL GAINS: PAGE CG8

Appendix

Self-employment pages

Inland Revenue

Income for the year ended 5 April 2002

SELF-EMPLOYMENT

Name *(Fill in these boxes first)*

Tax reference

If you want help, look up the box numbers in the Notes

Business details

Name of business 3.1

Description of business 3.2

Address of business 3.3

Postcode

Accounting period - *read the Notes, page SEN2 before filling in these boxes*

Start 3.4 / /   End 3.5 / /

- Tick box 3.6 if details in boxes 3.1 or 3.3 have changed since your last Tax Return **3.6**

- Tick box 3.10 if you entered details for all relevant accounting periods on last year's Tax Return and boxes 3.14 to 3.73 and 3.99 to 3.115 will be blank *(read Step 3 on page SEN2)* **3.10**

- Date of commencement if after 5 April 1998 **3.7** / /

- Tick box 3.11 if your accounts do not cover the period from the last accounting date (explain why in the 'Additional information' box, box 3.116) **3.11**

- Date of cessation if before 6 April 2002 **3.8** / /

- Tick box 3.12 if your accounting date has changed (only if this is a permanent change and you want it to count for tax) **3.12**

- Tick box 3.9 if the special arrangements for certain trades apply - *read the Notes, pages SEN10 and SEN11* **3.9**

- Tick box 3.13 if this is the second or further change (explain in box 3.116 on Page SE4 why you have not used the same date as last year) **3.13**

Capital allowances - summary

	Capital allowances	Balancing charges
• Cars (Separate calculations must be made for each car costing more than £12,000 and for cars used partly for private motoring.)	3.14 £	3.15 £
• Other business plant and machinery	3.16 £	3.17 £
• Agricultural or Industrial Buildings Allowance (A separate calculation must be made for each block of expenditure.)	3.18 £	3.19 £
• Other capital allowances claimed (Separate calculations must be made.)	3.20 £	3.21 £
Total capital allowances/balancing charges	*total of column above* 3.22 £	*total of column above* 3.23 £

Income and expenses - annual turnover below £15,000

*If your annual turnover is £15,000 or more, **ignore** boxes 3.24 to 3.26. Instead fill in Page SE2*

*If your annual turnover is below £15,000, **fill in boxes 3.24 to 3.26** instead of Page SE2. Read the Notes, page SEN2.*

- Turnover, other business receipts and goods etc. taken for personal use (and balancing charges from box 3.23) **3.24** £

- Expenses allowable for tax (including capital allowances from box 3.22) **3.25** £

Net profit (put figure in brackets if a loss) *box 3.24 minus box 3.25* **3.26** £

You must now fill in Page SE3

SA103

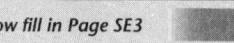

Appendix

Income and expenses - annual turnover £15,000 or more

You must fill in this Page if your annual turnover is £15,000 or more - read the Notes, page SEN2

If you were registered for VAT, do the figures in boxes 3.29 to 3.64, include VAT? **3.27** ☐ or exclude VAT? **3.28** ☐

Sales/business income (turnover)
3.29 £ _____

	Disallowable expenses included in boxes 3.46 to 3.63	Total expenses
• Cost of sales	**3.30** £	**3.46** £
• Construction industry subcontractor costs	**3.31** £	**3.47** £
• Other direct costs	**3.32** £	**3.48** £

Gross profit/(loss) **3.49** £   box 3.29 *minus* (boxes 3.46 + 3.47 + 3.48)

Other income/profits **3.50** £

• Employee costs	**3.33** £	**3.51** £
• Premises costs	**3.34** £	**3.52** £
• Repairs	**3.35** £	**3.53** £
• General administrative expenses	**3.36** £	**3.54** £
• Motor expenses	**3.37** £	**3.55** £
• Travel and subsistence	**3.38** £	**3.56** £
• Advertising, promotion and entertainment	**3.39** £	**3.57** £
• Legal and professional costs	**3.40** £	**3.58** £
• Bad debts	**3.41** £	**3.59** £
• Interest	**3.42** £	**3.60** £
• Other finance charges	**3.43** £	**3.61** £
• Depreciation and loss/(profit) on sale	**3.44** £	**3.62** £
• Other expenses	**3.45** £	**3.63** £

Put the total of boxes 3.30 to 3.45 in **box 3.66 below**

Total expenses **3.64** £   total of boxes 3.51 to 3.63

Net profit/(loss) **3.65** £   boxes 3.49 + 3.50 *minus* 3.64

Tax adjustments to net profit or loss

• Disallowable expenses   boxes 3.30 to 3.45 **3.66** £

• Goods etc. taken for personal use and other adjustments (apart from disallowable expenses) that increase profits **3.67** £

• Balancing charges (from box 3.23) **3.68** £

Total additions to net profit (deduct from net loss)   boxes 3.66 + 3.67 + 3.68 **3.69** £

• Capital allowances (from box 3.22) **3.70** £

• Deductions from net profit (add to net loss) **3.71** £   boxes 3.70 + 3.71 **3.72** £

Net business profit for tax purposes (put figure in brackets if a loss)   boxes 3.65 + 3.69 *minus* 3.72 **3.73** £

BMSD 12/2000net   TAX RETURN ■ SELF-EMPLOYMENT: PAGE SE2   *Now fill in Page SE3*

Appendix

> You **must** fill in boxes 3.74 and 3.75 and **all other boxes** that apply to you, on this Page

Adjustments to arrive at taxable profit or loss

Basis period begins **3.74** / / and ends **3.75** / /

Profit or loss of this account for tax purposes (box 3.26 or 3.73) **3.76** £

Adjustment to arrive at profit or loss for this basis period **3.77** £

- Overlap profit brought forward **3.78** £ • Deduct overlap relief used this year **3.79** £
- Overlap profit carried forward **3.80** £

Adjustment for farmers' averaging (see Notes, page SEN8, if you made a loss for 2001-2002) **3.81** £

Adjustment on change of basis **3.82** £

Net profit for 2001-2002 (if you made a loss, enter '0') **3.83** £

Allowable loss for 2001-2002 (if you made a profit, enter '0') **3.84** £

- Loss offset against other income for 2001-2002 **3.85** £
- Loss to carry back **3.86** £
- Loss to carry forward
  (that is allowable loss not claimed in any other way) **3.87** £
- Losses brought forward from earlier years **3.88** £
- Losses brought forward from earlier years used this year **3.89** £

Taxable profit after losses brought forward *box 3.83 minus box 3.89* **3.90** £

- Any other business income (for example, Business Start-up Allowance received in 2001-2002) **3.91** £

Total taxable profits from this business *box 3.90 + box 3.91* **3.92** £

- Tick box 3.93 if the figure in box 3.92 is provisional **3.93**

Class 4 National Insurance contributions

- Tick box 3.94 if exception or deferment applies **3.94**
- Adjustments to profit chargeable to Class 4 National Insurance contributions **3.95** £

Class 4 National Insurance contributions due **3.96** £

Subcontractors in the construction industry

- Deductions made by contractors on account of tax (you must send your CIS25s to us) **3.97** £

Tax deducted from trading income

- Any tax deducted (excluding deductions made by contractors on account of tax) from trading income **3.98** £

BMSD 12/2000net   TAX RETURN ■ SELF-EMPLOYMENT: PAGE SE3   *Please turn over*

189

Appendix

Summary of balance sheet

Leave these boxes blank if you do not have a balance sheet

Assets
- Plant, machinery and motor vehicles — 3.99 £
- Other fixed assets (premises, goodwill, investments etc.) — 3.100 £
- Stock and work-in-progress — 3.101 £
- Debtors/prepayments/other current assets — 3.102 £
- Bank/building society balances — 3.103 £
- Cash in hand — 3.104 £

total of boxes 3.99 to 3.104
3.105 £

Liabilities
- Trade creditors/accruals — 3.106 £
- Loans and overdrawn bank accounts — 3.107 £
- Other liabilities — 3.108 £

total of boxes 3.106 to 3.108
3.109 £

Net business assets (put the figure in brackets if you had net business liabilities)

box 3.105 *minus* 3.109
3.110 £

Represented by

Capital Account
- Balance at start of period* — 3.111 £
- Net profit/(loss)* — 3.112 £
- Capital introduced — 3.113 £
- Drawings — 3.114 £

total of boxes 3.111 to 3.113 *minus* box 3.114

- Balance at end of period* — 3.115 £

*If the Capital Account is overdrawn, or the business made a net loss, enter the figure in brackets.

3.116 *Additional information*

Now fill in any other supplementary Pages that apply to you. Otherwise, go back to Page 2 of your Tax Return and finish filling it in.

Appendix

Inland Revenue

Income for the year ended 5 April 2002

PARTNERSHIP (SHORT)

Fill in these boxes first

Name	Tax Reference

If you want help, look up the box numbers in the notes

Partnership details

Partnership reference number	Partnership trade or profession
4.1	4.2

- Date you started being a partner (if during 2001-2002) **4.3** £ / /
- Date you stopped being a partner (if during 2001-2002) **4.4** £ / /

Your share of the partnership's trading or professional income

Basis period begins **4.5** £ / / and ends **4.6** £ / /

- Your share of the profit or loss of this year's account for tax purposes — **4.7** £
- Adjustment to arrive at profit or loss for this basis period — **4.8** £
- Overlap profit brought forward **4.9** £ | Deduct overlap relief used this year **4.10** £
- Overlap profit carried forward **4.11** £
- Adjust for farmers' averaging (see notes, page PN 3 if the partnership made a loss in 2001-2002 or foreign tax deducted, if tax credit relief not claimed — **4.12** £

Adjustment on change of basis — **4.12A** £

Net profit for 2001-02 (if loss, enter '0' in box 4.13 and enter the loss in box 4.14) — **4.13** £

Allowable loss for 2001-02 — **4.14** £

- Loss offset against other income for 2001-2002 — **4.15** £
- Loss to carry back — **4.16** £
- Loss to carry forward (that is, allowable loss not claimed in any other way) — **4.17** £
- Losses brought forward from last year — **4.18** £
- Losses brought forward from last year used this year — **4.19** £

Taxable profit after losses brought forward — box 4.13 minus box 4.19 **4.20** £

- Add amounts not included in the partnership accounts that are needed to calculate your taxable profit (for example Enterprise Allowance (Business Start-up Allowance) received in 2001-2002 — **4.21** £

Total taxable profits from this business — box 4.20 + box 4.21 **4.22** £

Class 4 National Insurance Contributions

- Tick this box if exception or deferment applies — **4.23** £
- Adjustments to profit chargeable to Class 4 National Insurance Contributions — **4.24** £

Class 4 National Insurance Contributions due — **4.25** £

Your share of taxed income

- Share of taxed income (liable at 20%) — 4.70 £

Your share of Partnership Trading and Professional Profits

- Share of partnership profits (other than that liable at 20%) — from box 4.22 — 4.73 £

Your share of tax paid

- Share of income tax paid — 4.74 £
- Share of SC60/CIS25 deductions — 4.75 £
- Share of tax deducted from trading income (not SC 60/CIS25 deductions) — 4.75A £

box 4.74 + box 4.75 + box 4.75A
4.77 £

Additional information

Now fill in any other supplementary Pages that apply to you.
Otherwise, go back to page 2 in your Tax Return and finish filling it in

List of Key Terms and Index

List of key terms

Charge on income, 9
Chattel, 130
Connected person, 109

EIS, 79
Emoluments, 44

Filing due date, 30
Fiscal year, 4

Gift aid scheme, 12
Gilts, 123

Individual savings accounts, 78

Job-related accommodation, 134

Occupational pension scheme, 62

Payments on account, 33

Relevant amount, 33

Self assessment, 32
Surcharges, 35

Tax year, 4

Venture capital trusts (VCTs), 82

Wasting asset, 130

Year of assessment, 4

Index

10% wear and tear allowance, 84
3½% War Loan, 76

Additional voluntary contributions, 63
Age allowance, 11, 13
Air miles, 49
Annual exemption, 94
Annuity, 64
Assets made available for private use, 53
Assets sold to employers, 54
Assignment of a lease, 132
Authorised mileage rates, 48

Bank deposit interest, 6, 77
Beneficial loans, 55
Benefits in kind, 45, 49
Betting and gaming winnings, 7, 98
Bicycles, 48
Blind person's allowance, 12
Board of Inland Revenue, 4
Bonus issues (scrip issues), 122
Budget, 4
Building society interest, 77
Business economic notes, 4
Business expenses, 50
Business interest, 10

Capital allowances, 84
Capital contributions, 51
Capital gains tax (CGT)
  chargeable assets, 98
  chargeable disposals, 97
  chargeable persons, 97
  consideration which cannot be valued, 106
  gifts, 106
  husband and wife, 99
  instalments, 99, 101
  losses in the year of death, 95
  married couples, 99
  not a bargain at arm's length, 106
  rates of CGT, 94
  valuing assets, 108
Car fuel coupons, 49
Cars, 51, 130
Case law, 4
Cash equivalent, 45
Cash vouchers, 45
Certificates of tax deposit, 76
Charges on income, 9
Charitable donations, 62
Children's tax credit, 13

Claims, 32
Collectors of taxes, 5
Commissioners of Inland Revenue (CIR), 4
Compensation and insurance proceeds, 146
Compulsory purchase of land, 146
Computer equipment, 54
Connected persons, 109
Contributions, 65
Council tax, 47
Credit token, 45

Damaged assets, 146
Debentures and loan stocks, 6
Deduction cards, 59
Destroyed assets, 146
Determinations, 39
Directors' earnings, 44
Disabled persons tax credit (DPTC), 20
Divorce, 19
Driver, 53

Earnings cap, 63
Eligible interest, 10
Emoluments, 44, 49
Employment and self employment, 44
Enhancement expenditure, 106
Enquiries, determinations and discovery
  assessments, 36
Enterprise investment scheme, 13, 79
Entertainment, 45
Exchangeable vouchers, 45
Exempt income, 7
Expenses connected with living
  accommodation, 50
Explanatory leaflets, 4
Extra-statutory concessions, 4

FA 1985 pool, 119
Finance Acts, 4
Fiscal year, 4
Fixed deposits, 77, 87
Fixed profit car scheme, 48
Freestanding AVCs, 63
Fuel, 52

General Commissioners, 5
Gifts, 97, 100
Gilt strips, 123
Gilt-edged (Government) securities, 77, 123

Index

Husband and wife, 18, 134

Incidental costs of acquisition/disposal, 106
Incidental expenses, 50
Income taxed at source, 5, 6
Indexation allowance, 107
Individual Learning Accounts, 49
Individual savings accounts (ISAs), 78
Inspector of Taxes, 5
Insurance, 57
Interest, 35
   on loans for purchase by a partner of plant or machinery, 10
   on loans for purchase by an employee of plant or machinery, 10
   on loans for purchase of an interest in a partnership, 10
   on loans for purchase of shares in an employee-controlled company, 10
   on loans to buy or improve properties, 84
Internal guidance, 4
Investment in a co-operative, 10
Items incidental, 50

Job related, 47
Job-related accommodation, 134
Joint property, 18

Letting exemption, 135
Liabilities, 57
Living accommodation, 50
Loans to traders, 145
Long service awards, 46
Loss or destruction of assets, 100
Loss relief, 84
Loss relief (income tax), 154
Luncheon vouchers, 45

Maintenance payments, 14
Matching rules for companies, 118
MCAA: married couple's age allowance, 13
Medical services and insurance, 56
Minor children, 19
Mobile telephones, 53

National Savings Bank accounts, 76
National Savings Certificates, 7, 76, 98
Negligible value claims, 109
No gain/no loss basis, 110
Non-cash vouchers, 45

Normal Retirement Age, 64
Notification of liability to income tax and CGT, 28
Nursery, 47

Official rate, 55
Open offer, 123
Operative events, 120

P11D dispensation, 50
Parking space, 53
Part disposals, 110
Partnership return, 29
PAYE system, 59
PAYE tax liabilities, 54
Payment of income tax and capital gains tax, 33
Payroll deduction scheme, 62
Penalties for late filing, 30
Pensions, 62
Personal allowance, 11
Personal tax computation, 6
Postponement of payment of tax, 40
Premium bonds, 7, 76, 98
Premiums on leases, 84
Principal private residence, 132

Qualifying corporate bonds, 123, 124
Qualifying liability, 57
Qualifying loans, 56

Relocations, 133
Removal expenses and benefits, 47
Renewals basis, 84
Rent a room scheme, 85
Repayment of tax and repayment supplement, 36
Revenue's powers, 38

Schedular system, 6
Schedule A, 83
Schedule D Case III, 76, 77
Schedule D Case VI, 76
Schedule E, 44
Scholarship and apprenticeship schemes, 7, 49, 54
Securities, 118
Self employment, 44
Self-assessment and claims, 32
Separation, 19

Index

Shares, 118
Social security benefits, 7
Special Commissioners, 5
Special Compliance Office, 38
Statements of practice, 4
Statute, 4
Statutory total income (STI), 11
Subscriptions to professional bodies, 57
Suggestion schemes, 46
Surcharges, 35

Taper relief, 95
Tax accountant, 39
Tax Bulletin, 4
Tax law, 4
Tax management, 27
Tax reducers, 13
Tax returns, 28
Tax tables, 59
Tax year, 4
Taxes, 4
Tax-free cash, 64
Tax-free investments, 76
Taxpayer assistance offices, 5
Taxpayer district offices, 5
Taxpayer service offices, 5
Travelling expenses, 57
Treasury, 4

Unit trusts, 78

Vans, 53
Venture capital trusts (VCTs), 82
Vouchers, 45

Wasting assets, 130, 131
Wasting chattels, 130, 131
Wear and tear basis, 84
Work related benefits, 47
Work related training, 49
Working families tax credit (WFTC), 20

Year of assessment, 4
Year of death, 19
Year of marriage, 19
Year of receipt, 44

See overleaf for information on other
BPP products and how to order

AAT Order

To BPP Publishing Ltd, Aldine Place, London W12 8AW
Tel: 020 8740 2211. Fax: 020 8740 1184
E-mail: Publishing@bpp.com Web:www.bpp.com

Mr/Mrs/Ms (Full name)
Daytime delivery address
Postcode
Daytime Tel
E-mail

	5/01 Texts	6/01 Kits	Special offer	5/01 Passcards	Tapes
FOUNDATION (ALL £9.95)			All Foundation Texts and Kits (£80) ☐		
Unit 1 Recording Income and Receipts	☐	☐		£4.95 ☐	£10.00 ☐
Unit 2 Making and Recording Payments	☐	☐			
Unit 3 Ledger Balances and Initial Trial Balance	☐	☐			
Unit 4 Supplying Information for Mgmt Control	☐	☐			
Unit 20 Working with Information Technology	☐	☐			
Unit 22/23 Healthy Workplace & Personal Effectiveness	☐				
INTERMEDIATE (ALL £9.95)		8/01 Kits	All Inter'te Texts and Kits (£65) ☐		
Unit 5 Financial Records and Accounts	☐	☐		£4.95 ☐	£10.00 ☐
Unit 6 Cost Information	☐	☐		£4.95 ☐	£10.00 ☐
Unit 7 Reports and Returns	☐	☐			
Unit 21 Using Information Technology	☐	☐			
TECHNICIAN (ALL £9.95)			Set of 12 Technician Texts/Kits (Please specify titles required) (£100) ☐		
Unit 8/9 Core Managing Costs and Allocating Resources	☐	☐		£4.95 ☐	£10.00 ☐
Unit 10 Core Managing Accounting Systems	☐	☐			
Unit 11 Option Financial Statements (A/c Practice)	☐	☐		£4.95 ☐	£10.00 ☐
Unit 12 Option Financial Statements (Central Govnmt)	☐	☐			
Unit 15 Option Cash Management and Credit Control	☐	☐			
Unit 16 Option Evaluating Activities	☐	☐			
Unit 17 Option Implementing Auditing Procedures	☐	☐			
Unit 18 Option Business Tax (FA01)(8/01 Text)	☐	☐			
Unit 19 Option Personal Tax (FA 01)(8/01 Text)	☐	☐			
TECHNICIAN 2000 (ALL £9.95)					
Unit 18 Option Business Tax FA00 (8/00 Text & Kit)	☐				
Unit 19 Option Personal Tax FA00 (8/00 Text & Kit)	☐				
SUBTOTAL	£	£	£	£	£

TOTAL FOR PRODUCTS £ ▢

POSTAGE & PACKING

Texts/Kits
	First	Each extra
UK (max £10)	£2.00	£2.00
Europe*	£4.00	£2.00
Rest of world	£20.00	£10.00

Passcards/Tapes
	First	Each extra
UK	£2.00	£1.00
Europe*	£2.50	£1.00
Rest of world	£15.00	£8.00

£ ▢ £ ▢
£ ▢ £ ▢

Grand Total (Cheques to *BPP Publishing*) I enclose a cheque for (incl. Postage) £ ▢

Or charge to Access/Visa/Switch

Card Number ▢▢▢▢▢▢▢▢▢▢▢▢▢▢▢▢

Expiry date ▢▢▢▢   Start Date ▢▢▢▢

Issue Number (Switch Only) ▢▢

Signature

We aim to deliver to all UK addresses inside 5 working days; a signature will be required. Orders to all EU addresses should be delivered within 6 working days. All other orders to overseas addresses should be delivered within 8 working days. * Europe includes the Republic of Ireland and the Channel Islands.

AAT – Unit 19 Preparing personal tax computations (8/01)

REVIEW FORM & FREE PRIZE DRAW

All original review forms from the entire BPP range, completed with genuine comments, will be entered into one of two draws on 31 January 2002 and 31 July 2002. The names on the first four forms picked out on each occasion will be sent a cheque for £50.

Name: _____ Address: _____

_____

_____

How have you used this Interactive Text?
(Tick one box only)

- [ ] Home study (book only)
- [ ] On a course: college _____
- [ ] With 'correspondence' package
- [ ] Other _____

Why did you decide to purchase this Interactive Text? *(Tick one box only)*

- [ ] Have used BPP Texts in the past
- [ ] Recommendation by friend/colleague
- [ ] Recommendation by a lecturer at college
- [ ] Saw advertising
- [ ] Other _____

During the past six months do you recall seeing/receiving any of the following?
(Tick as many boxes as are relevant)

- [ ] Our advertisement in *Accounting Technician* magazine
- [ ] Our advertisement in *Pass*
- [ ] Our brochure with a letter through the post

Which (if any) aspects of our advertising do you find useful?
(Tick as many boxes as are relevant)

- [ ] Prices and publication dates of new editions
- [ ] Information on Interactive Text content
- [ ] Facility to order books off-the-page
- [ ] None of the above

Have you used the companion Assessment Kit for this subject? [ ] Yes [ ] No

Your ratings, comments and suggestions would be appreciated on the following areas

	Very useful	Useful	Not useful
Introductory section (How to use this Interactive Text etc)	[ ]	[ ]	[ ]
Chapter topic lists	[ ]	[ ]	[ ]
Chapter learning objectives	[ ]	[ ]	[ ]
Key terms	[ ]	[ ]	[ ]
Assessment alerts	[ ]	[ ]	[ ]
Examples	[ ]	[ ]	[ ]
Activities and answers	[ ]	[ ]	[ ]
Key learning points	[ ]	[ ]	[ ]
Quick quizzes and answers	[ ]	[ ]	[ ]
List of key terms and index	[ ]	[ ]	[ ]
Icons	[ ]	[ ]	[ ]

	Excellent	*Good*	*Adequate*	*Poor*
Overall opinion of this Text	[ ]	[ ]	[ ]	[ ]

Do you intend to continue using BPP Interactive Texts/Assessment Kits? [ ] Yes [ ] No

Please note any further comments and suggestions/errors on the reverse of this page.

Please return to: Nick Weller, BPP Publishing Ltd, FREEPOST, London, W12 8BR

REVIEW FORM & FREE PRIZE DRAW (continued)

Please note any further comments and suggestions/errors below

FREE PRIZE DRAW RULES

1. Closing date for 31 January 2002 draw is 31 December 2001. Closing date for 31 July 2002 draw is 30 June 2002.
2. Restricted to entries with UK and Eire addresses only. BPP employees, their families and business associates are excluded.
3. No purchase necessary. Entry forms are available upon request from BPP Publishing. No more than one entry per title, per person. Draw restricted to persons aged 16 and over.
4. Winners will be notified by post and receive their cheques not later than 6 weeks after the relevant draw date.
5. The decision of the promoter in all matters is final and binding. No correspondence will be entered into.